Living in Process

Other books by Anne Wilson Schaef

Beyond Therapy, Beyond Science

When Society Becomes an Addict

Meditations for Women Who Do Too Much

Native Wisdom for White Minds

Women's Reality

Co-dependence: Misunderstood, Mistreated

Escape from Intimacy

The Addictive Organization (coauthor)

Laugh! I Thought I'd Die (If I Didn't)

Meditations for People Who (May) Worry Too Much

Living in Process

BASIC TRUTHS FOR LIVING
THE PATH OF THE SOUL

ANNE WILSON SCHAEF

BALLANTINE WELLSPRING
THE BALLANTINE PUBLISHING GROUP
NEW YORK

A Ballantine Wellspring Book
Published by The Ballantine Publishing Group

Copyright © 1998 by Anne Wilson Schaef

All rights reserved under International and Pan-American Copyright Conventions.
Published in the United States by The Ballantine Publishing Group, a division of
Random House, Inc., New York, and simultaneously in Canada by Random
House of Canada Limited, Toronto.

Ballantine Wellspring and the accompanying design are trademarks of
The Ballantine Publishing Group, a division of Random House, Inc.

Grateful acknowledgment is made to Pamela Burch for permission to reprint
"Woman of the Corn," from *The Grandmothers' Message*, by Standing Feather.
Copyright © 1996 by Pamela Burch. Reprinted by permission of the author.

Grateful acknowledgment is also made to *HoriZons*, published by Community Aid
Abroad, and Mary Graham, for permission to reprint excerpts from "Viewpoint:
Mary Graham: A Kumbumerri Perspective" by Saskla Kouwenberg, *HoriZons*,
Summer 1993, Vol. 2, No. 3, pp. 7–8.

http://www.randomhouse.com/BB/

Library of Congress Cataloging-in-Publication Data
Schaef, Anne Wilson.
Living in process : basic truths for living the path of the soul /
Anne Wilson Schaef. — 1st ed.
p.   cm.
ISBN 0-345-39407-0 (alk. paper)
I. Conduct of life.   2. Spiritual life.   I. Title.
BF637.C5S33   1998
158—dc21   98-41128
                                                        CIP

Text design by Ann Gold

Manufactured in the United States of America

First Edition: November 1998

10 9   8   7   6   5   4   3   2   I

DEDICATION

This book is dedicated to the Creator of All That Is.

*It is dedicated to a planet longing for us to reconnect
and participate with its process.*

*It is dedicated to all those beings
wanting to become whole and to those that are.
May we learn from one another.*

CONTENTS

Contents

Contents

Contents

Contents

Contents

PREFACE

This book may be a bit more difficult to understand than my previous books since it offers a spiritual way of living and healing that is not common knowledge in our present culture. As you read, remember that the information is about operating in a completely different paradigm than the one we're used to living with on a daily basis. Often, when we're faced with something entirely new to us, we try to fit it into what we already know and feel comfortable with.

I hope you will not do that with this book. Read it with an open mind. I suggest reading through one time to get the overall picture. Then give it a second, more feeling-level reading. After that you might want to go back to specific parts that need more time to digest. The book is in the *experience* of reading it.

This is not a self-help book or do-it-yourself book. You will not be able to read it and walk away recovered from what I am calling the Techno-cratic, Materialistic, Mechanistic Personality. You won't even know how to do your deep process work, or how to live in process. All of these take time and work and only happen in context.

For example, say you want to learn Tibetan meditation. You can read all the books written. However, if you really want to know Tibetan meditation and the surrounding rich lore of living that path, you will have to seek out a teacher or teachers and spend years unfolding into it. So it is with this work.

Or, imagine that you have just laid your hands on Sigmund Freud's first publication about psychoanalysis. Do you believe that you can read the book and then lie on the couch and do your own analysis? I doubt it. One must walk a path and have experience with a practitioner to truly know it. So it is with living in process. Healing from the Technocratic, Materialistic, Mechanistic Personality is a process, not an event. Understanding deep process can only come from experiencing it. Learning to live in process is a lifelong pursuit.

Many people come to this work believing they already know about deep process because of their own experiences with one form or another of psychological or spiritual work. So far, our experience is that none have actually known it. This work is not rebirthing, breathwork, Heller work, rage reduction, core energies work, quantum release work, or Osho-Tantra. Yes, we use mats—the analogy ends there.

It's all right to not understand. That's how we learn. Yet, understanding is not knowing and this work requires knowing through experience.

Living in Process is not psychotherapy nor does it come out of that mechanistic, scientific model. It is not a religion. It is spiritual and reaches back beyond the religious for its spirituality. It is definitely not related to anything I have studied, and I have studied both psychology and theology.

I have tried to give information about Deep Process. I have introduced it, discussed it, given examples, and explored the range of it. Yet, what it truly is will probably remain hidden in the mists of the unfamiliar until you have worked with your own deep process for many years. Even then, sometimes, I feel I know less and less instead of more and more, as I do it.

Preface

Yet, our deep processes are powerful tools for healing and connecting us with the infinite.

LANGUAGE

We are limited by our use of language. I have had to use the language that I know and we all know, and it is often less than adequate. For example, the term "deep process" may feel familiar and known. In this context it is not.

When we are trying to communicate something new, we are criticized if we coin new terms and try to make up words that fit, and, on the other side of the coin, we are criticized for giving new meanings to old terms. In the face of this, I do as I please <u>and</u> do the best I can.

Some of my language needs to be noted before you read this book.

I rarely use "but." I substitute "and." I do this for two reasons. The first and easiest reason is that often everything before the but is either discounted or a lie—for example—"I really like you but . . ." The second and more important reason is that "but" sets up a dualism of either this or that. Since I am trying to encourage us to move beyond dualisms, I substitute "and." The use of "and" in such a sentence throws us into an entirely different mind-set and creates different experiences in our bodies. Try it—you might like it!

In another category, I often use "and" for emphasis. You will see it stressed at the beginning of sentences. Pay attention to these sentences.

Both of these usages expand our universes.

Another term that I use often is "wait with" or "waiting with." My copy editor kept saying waiting *for what?* There is no *for what.* That is the old paradigm, the old way of living.

Waiting with is active waiting. It is just that, alert and not expectant of what will come. Waiting with is a skill that is slowly learned and much valued.

A third term that bears notice is the use of "static" as a verb. The TMM culture tries to static the processes of the universe. There is no better way to say it.

So, there we have it. I invite you to lay aside your preconceived notions, what you think you know, your comfortable assumptions, and come with me into the adventure of learning to live in process.

ACKNOWLEDGMENTS

Much and many have participated in the evolution of this book.

Special thanks go to my "boss" whose work I do faultingly and faithfully to the best of my ability. I know in my living the help that I get from realms beyond my knowing and I give thanks for that.

I am grateful to our Mother, the Earth, who sustains all life and my life on a daily basis. I am grateful for Grandfather Sky, and the sun for that energy that sustains all our lives. I am grateful to the Great Mystery for being more than I can comprehend so I can continue to grow toward it.

I give thanks for this life and the possibility to live it.

I give special thanks for my family and the ever expanding circles of it throughout the world. Roddy, my son, is always there for me. Chuck, my husband, stands tall with support, and Pete has typed and retyped to pull the book together. Jo Potter and many of the International Living in Process network have proofread and edited and supported me at every turn. I want to particularly thank the trainees in Australia and Boulder Hot Springs for their help. Bobbi has kept the office going and all the people in Butte have lent support. And thanks to Karuna Sanctuary, an inspirational retreat center, where I was nurtured as I completed this book.

Cheryl Woodruff, as my editor and friend, has had to "work" on

Acknowledgments

this one. My first rendition of this book was "right brain," poetic, folding and refolding back on itself. She helped make it linear so those not familiar to this work could be introduced to it. Ballantine produced a lovely cover.

Support is always multidimensional and multilevel, and I want to acknowledge that my awareness and gratitude extends in all those directions and levels.

Last, but not least, I want to express my deepest gratitude to those people who agreed to read the manuscript for possible endorsements. Thank you so much for your time and energy.

Living in Process

Chapter 1

THE EMERGENCE
OF LIVING
IN PROCESS

L iving in Process is a book about living—spiritual living and living spiritually. We all have the opportunity to live completely, fully, wholly, joyfully, serenely with our spirituality expressed in every facet of our lives. Deep inside we resonate with that promise, yet may have lost our way back. This book is an invitation to journey into that deep movement of the all-encompassing spirituality that exists in each one of us and feels in tune with that life force within and beyond us all—whatever we may choose to call it or however we may choose to approach it. Each of us has the possibility to move into our spiritual wisdom and link with the oneness of the all. We only have to remember and reconnect with what we have forgotten and moved away from.

Many cultures of the world have no word for spirituality. In these cultures spirituality is in the living. It is so integrated into life that it needs no separate designation. Yet, many of us have lost that integration as we try to cope with our lives. Living in Process is the reintegration of the spiritual into all that we do and all that we are. By segmenting ourselves and our lives we have reduced the spiritual to a very small corner of our lives. Living in Process is about the relearning of living our wholeness.

3

After over four decades of working with people around the world, I have come to see that all human problems are ultimately spiritual. They result from our splitting off and compartmentalizing our spirituality or not recognizing it at all. Since we are spiritual beings, our solutions to our problems must come from our spiritual wholeness. All healing is based in our spiritual wholeness. The secret of living a whole life is accepting and being wholly who we are as full spiritual beings.

However, at the end of the twentieth century, we find ourselves estranged from our oneness in God, and ourselves. We cannot embrace the fullness of spirituality without accepting the reality of life as a process and participating in the process of our lives. We cannot be observers in our own lives and expect to know and experience our full spiritual selves. We must first acknowledge our role in the process that has created our present reality, and accept our role as active participants in all of life's process, in order to move in the direction of healing. We must see how our current worldview has contributed to where we are in our lives as a species, and in so doing be ready to move to new ways of being and living.

I am always being asked to define Living in Process in some convenient shorthand. There is no simple definition. You cannot freeze process—even in words. Can you define flowers blooming, the setting of the sun, or hold a rainbow in your hand? To try to form a definition is to make these experiences static and separate them from the dynamic qualities of growth and change that is their essence. The definition is in the experience, not in the abstract concept.

What can we really define? Something that may not seem as complex as a process, like a butterfly, even defies the kind of defining that many cultures traditionally rely on. Even an entomologist would most likely fail to define what a butterfly really is. She could pin it on a board, take serial cross sections of it, and maybe even discuss how its major systems function, and yet, would we really know what a butterfly is from all this? I doubt it.

It is my hope that reading this book will not only give you information about what Living in Process is, my fond hope is that the reading of the book itself will also provide an opening door into the experience of Living in Process. Pure information is useless without experience to ground it. Life is not an abstraction. Living must be grounded in experience.

It's not that I'm against defining things per se—although I am skeptical of destructive artificial limits we construct for ourselves. Definitions can, at times, be useful. What concerns me is that the kind of rational, reductive, systems-oriented analysis we rely on so much today also dissects us, separating our experiences from our emotions, our heads from our hearts, and our souls from our beings. Many of us have become so numb that we're accustomed to and accepting of this kind of fragmented, postmodern, disconnected thinking and being. Living was not always like this, and it does not have to be.

I want to share my own journey in coming to live my life in process as an example of learning about Living in Process.

When I was in the fifth grade, I knew that I would be doing healing work when I grew up. I had no name for it at that time. We lived in the Ozarks and were very poor. My only interactions with healers were a very occasional visit to the doctor in dire emergencies, and the "everyday" healing work that went on with my great-grandmother who was an Indian Medicine Woman. Her healing work was so integrated into our lives that I took it for granted, and only in the past year did I learn that she was, indeed, an Indian Medicine Woman.

I did not know exactly what being a healer meant, or if I would "heal" like my great-grandmother, nor did I have to know what form this work would take until I needed to know. I continued participating in my life as fully as I could in all spheres—academics, social activities, sports, creative arts, church, and family—and trusted that I would know how to follow the path that would lead me to the places I needed to be.

Just before I entered high school, I happened upon the term *psychiatrist*. I was clear that the work that I would be doing was not just physical, yet I intuitively knew that the physical would be involved, so I took the courses in high school that would prepare me for entering college as a premed student.

I was accepted at the university of my choice with a full scholarship and pursued my premed studies, working in our local hospital every summer. College was much like high school, with a full life and many adventures. I continued to enjoy dating, singing, sorority and dorm life, and athletics and became active in the YWCA and the United Student Christian Fellowship. These activities resulted in my holding national offices and being a student delegate to worldwide events. My boundaries grew and exploded as my world expanded exponentially during those years. I had many opportunities to discuss ideas and concerns with world leaders in theology and politics. I trusted what the Great Mystery wanted me to do. Not pushing for closure on my knowings has been important for me. I accepted that knowing was a process and that I would not know until I knew. The process always unfolds as it should if I will just let it. In the meantime, my responsibility was to put one foot in front of the other, participate fully in my life, and be the best person I knew how to be.

I do not want to give the impression here that life was always rosy. It was not. I struggled with boyfriends and intimate relationships. I questioned everything I had been taught in my Methodist upbringing including the existence of God. I was passed over for honors and recognitions that I clearly deserved for which I was not politically savvy. Pain was well known to me. Yet, I was not good at suffering and had a steadfast belief that I was one with God even if I was having difficulties with God definitions.

When it was time to apply to medical schools, I couldn't do it! I had some rational excuses—I did not want to become what I saw most doctors become, I did not want to focus on physical illness and physical pain and ultimately I knew that the truth was that my process was to be different. At zero hour, the dean called me in and said that she was going to recommend me for a Danforth Fellowship (nicknamed the Danny Grads), and I intuitively knew that this was my answer. I disregarded the fact that this was a very competitive fellowship and that many applied and few were chosen. I knew that this was what I should be doing, and it was! I took a year out from my academic work to be sent to another part of the country to "develop as a person, grow spiritually, and be of service to the campus." This year was just what I needed to know that medical school would not give me what I required to do my life's work. I applied and was accepted to a doctoral program in psychology.

I approached graduate school as I had grade school, high school, and college—with complete trust that I would get what I needed—and I had fun, as usual. I loved the courses and in my naïveté, a week before I discovered that "this little test" the department head had mentioned when he interviewed me was the comprehensives, I decided to go to New York City to the theater and enjoy myself as it was much too late to cram for any test. Since the comprehensives were based upon the courses we were taking and I was doing well in them, I passed with flying colors.

At the end of my first year of my doctoral work, I decided to take a year out and go to seminary in New York City. My rationale was that every educated person should know what they think theologically. My gut said, "You need to do this and you don't have to know why." I loved seminary, and I "did" New York with a trip to Europe in the middle of the second semester. My horizons continued to expand. I studied with the theological greats at Union Theological Seminary and the contemporary psychological greats at Columbia and Teacher's College Columbia. It was a great year. Let me point out that I did all these things with seemingly no money. Everything just fell into place as I trusted it would, and I always worked hard supporting myself throughout all my education and all my life.

At the end of the year, I married, went back to graduate school, and had my first child. I still seemed to be moving ahead in my life's process, and I was not sure what that was.

The next year, I did my internship at Bellevue Hospital in New

York City, mothered my child, and helped support my husband as he continued his theological studies. I continued to feel I was on my path and living my process. Then, as I look back, I believe I had a three-year detour. I took a job as a school psychologist to support my family while my husband completed seminary and did his internship. I enjoyed the work, loved being with my daughter, and enjoyed my life in a relative way, <u>and</u> my feeling was that I was somehow off my path. Little things just were not right. It never occurred to me to stop, pray, go inside, and connect with my ground of my being. I went to church every Sunday, was soloist in the choir, <u>and</u> I was not living as one with my spirituality. I was not in touch with my living process and I was not living my process. Not doing that was damaging to myself and others; I know that now.

Finally, my family and I returned to St. Louis where I completed the course work and examinations for my doctorate in psychology, my husband studied philosophy, and my daughter grew. I can see that when I let my decisions be driven by money or what I consider to be economic decisions, I always suffer. This does not mean that I do not take money into consideration; I do. I am very responsible about money, <u>and</u> it cannot be the basis of my decisions. For example, I have learned to decide what is important for me and my children and then find a way to do it. Many see what their money can afford them to do and never question what is important, therefore artificially limiting their life and their process. My living process demands that I start with what is important.

The practical should always be in the service of the important.

At the end of my doctoral work, I simply could not let myself take the final step in becoming a psychologist. This was in the 1960s and having a doctorate in psychology was not all that important. There were a lot of ABDs (all but dissertations) around with good jobs. Yet, for me, it was more than that. My intuition—there it goes again—again told me that there was something wrong with the field, and I did not know what. I was to continue to work in the field for over sixteen years before I became clear about what was wrong for me in psychology. I loved the field of psychology and hung on to it much too long, probably causing myself much more pain than I needed to experience in letting it go. Yet, I was learning all the time about my true path.

During my career as a psychotherapist, I supported people who wanted to heal old patterns developed in dysfunctional families and societies, people who wanted to heal their own confusion and estrangement from themselves. Often, I found many wanted only to be relieved of their pain; they asked for little more than mere existence. Yet, most people found that the cessation of pain did not solve their problems, even though they'd tried various means to end their suffering—medication, drugs and alcohol, frantic working, having children, trying to control their lives by always doing the right thing, endless psychotherapy, and flights into various forms of religion and New Age spirituality. Few had resonated with their wholeness or even discovered that it existed. Yet, in spite of those who sought only "the absence of," there were also those who wanted more—much more. These were the people with whom I clicked and who challenged me to continue my search and not to settle for what psychology and psychotherapy had to offer, knowing it was not enough.

In the sixties and seventies, I explored what every great teacher in the field of psychology had to offer. I did workshops, took seminars and courses. I became involved in feminist therapy and challenged the concept of therapists being more powerful than and having answers for their clients. I designed groups and workshops that were peer groups, exposing myself as a human being, rejecting the one-up stance of the psychotherapist that was becoming popular in the late seventies, and doing my own work in the groups and workshops I was doing. I was controversial, I was criticized, I was judged, and I was accused of being crazy and unethical. Yet, I was deeply committed to my search for something that fit and felt whole.

Although I was successful as a psychotherapist, I became increasingly, painfully aware of the limitations of psychotherapy. To me, it basically contented itself with adjustment to a dysfunctional society, and increasingly to a dysfunctional planet. I knew that there had to be more. Virginia Satir was one of the first to see the individual not as an isolated entity; she recognized that the individual was embedded in a family system that had its own dysfunction and exerted that dysfunction on the individual. I welcomed the broader perspective. As a feminist, I knew that we needed to accept the forces of larger and larger systems upon us in order to understand ourselves. We exist in context.

In late 1979, I could no longer tolerate the amount of stress in my life. I was a single parent, in a dysfunctional relationship, carrying a heavy load as a psychotherapist and trying to move along the path of evolving a new system for healing. My heart stopped and I had a near-death out-of-body experience. No experience is without meaning, and I came out of that experience knowing two major things in the depth of my being. First, I had to be absolutely honest about everything. Now, I was already known for my honesty. Still the level of honesty I knew I had to move to made my previous levels pale in comparison. Second, I knew that I had to clean up my life and get on with what it was really about—whatever that meant. I had to be able to see the doors in front of me when they appeared and be free to walk through them. It is not surprising then that very quickly other changes occurred in my life.

During a period of inner questioning and searching, around 1979, I met a world-famous psychic. I knew little about psychic phenomena and had only briefly scanned articles about extrasensory perception in graduate school, so I was curious. Since his visit was unique in my area, I offered my clients the opportunity to consult with him. Most accepted.

Before he left, he said to me, "Since I am a medical doctor, I have had the opportunity to interview and observe the work of psychiatrists and medical doctors throughout the country. Also, by interviewing your clients,

The Emergence of Living in Process

I have a window to see what you are doing. Your work is unique. Most practitioners start with the personality and work their way in. Your work goes right to the soul and you work your way out. The work you're doing is healing at a soul level." His words rang true. My path was unfolding and I was aware that soon I would be leaving my profession.

In early 1980, another piece of my puzzle fell into place. I had been living in a household with other women and our children, which offered support financially, emotionally, and with parenting. We had our good and bad times, and could never quite seem to get over a feeling of chaos just under the surface. Almost by accident—since many of us in the household were professionals—we discovered that one of our "family" members was an alcoholic. As a result, the rest of us plus ex-spouses, secretaries, and friends went into family treatment. There were thirteen of us in all. I was appalled by what I did not know about addictions and co-dependence. I felt resentful that my professional training had completely let me down in the area. As was always typical of me, I plunged into this new area of learning with my full being. I checked my clients for addiction, and much to my surprise found that many were dealing with a variety of addictions that they had never mentioned and I had never seen. It was still some time yet before I came to know that addictions are impervious to psychotherapy. I began to suggest that some of my clients go to meetings based on the Twelve Steps of Alcoholics Anonymous. I noticed that the clients who went seemed to improve faster than those who didn't.

I became more and more curious about the Twelve-Step meetings and started to go as an observer. However, I could not see—observe—how and why AA worked. This failure to understand why it worked catapulted me into one of the most important discoveries of my whole life and certainly one that has become one of the very baselines for Living in Process.

Quite quickly I discovered that I could not "get it" from observing. Initially, I felt confused and disoriented. After all, I was a trained observer. I earned my livelihood observing. Most of my major professional strokes came from the acuteness of my observations. And, no matter how good I was or am at observing, no matter how good a "scientist" I was, no matter how objective I was, all these skills were useless in the context of understanding the Twelve-Step program of AA. My intellect, my training, and my skills were all failing me. Trying to hold on to the security of what I knew and what I had known plunged me into an abyss of despair. Finally, I made a quantum leap. I realized that the only way I could possibly understand why AA worked, if ever, was to do it. I had to participate. I could not observe.

I now see that this shift in my universe was one of the most, if not *the* most, important shifts in my life. I had moved from observing to doing and being. I had shifted from watching life to doing life. In *The Reenchantment of the World*, Morris Berman speaks of the need to move from a nonparticipatory science to a participatory science in order to make the paradigm shift necessary at this time in history. Trying to understand the Twelve-Step program of AA forced me into participation. As I moved to a more participatory scientific worldview, doors and experiences opened to me that I could not have imagined. I was living in a different world. I reconnected with my soul and with the mystery of the oneness in a deep and profound way. Participation was the key. Quantum leaps of changes became a daily occurrence.

By this time, I had already written *Women's Reality*, and the enormous success of its publication (in 1981) established me as a recognized writer on women's issues and women's perceptions. However, with my new awarenesses about addictions and the systemic implications of addictions, I was quickly moving on to new learning and new discoveries.

As usual, my writings reflected my own personal journey, my struggles, my development, and my awarenesses. Recognizing myself as a trained co-dependent, I wrote *Co-dependence: Misunderstood, Mistreated* (1986). It was one of the first books on co-dependence, and it included a look at the larger professional and societal implications of co-dependency, as well as individual concerns. By this time, I had developed a good understanding of what I was calling the addictive process; I could see that the characteristics that defined addiction in individuals—dishonesty, self-centeredness, the illusion of control, crazy thinking, obsession, compulsion, dualistic thinking, and loss of spirituality—were endemic within our society and, indeed, were characteristics of our society. *When Society Becomes an Addict* was published in 1987.

In 1984, when I was working on the two previous books, I left the field of psychotherapy and continued to evolve what I was calling the Living in Process work. By then, I'd come to see that the healing work I was evolving with individuals and families was only a small part of the work I was here to do. Each of us has a true work, a calling that is right for us in this life. Teaching and practicing Living in Process is that work for me—my "assignment," my soul work. For me personally, it is my call to wholeness and full living. For me professionally, it is what I am here to share.

Since I was raised as a Southern Methodist, a "call" has special meaning to me. A call means hearing what God wants me to do and doing it. These calls take many forms and come from many sources, often from places and people we'd least expect, and sometimes it takes several calls before we hear them. A call does not mean that we are important or special, often quite the opposite. A call is an obligation, a responsibility, and a duty—nothing more, nothing less.

Fortunately, I have always known that inside of us all, when we are available to it, there is a wisdom that is connected to the wisdom of the All. My life has always been guided by this wisdom, and most of the pain I have experienced in life has been the result of my unwillingness to listen to that guidance, or of my indulging in my own self-will.

Living in Process has been my calling to bring to the world. Yet, I never for one moment believed that Living in Process is *my* work. It is *our* work—a work that is needed on the earth at this time. I am but one of the many messengers who are trying to open much needed paths of healing and spirituality for ourselves and the planet. I could see that now is a time for solutions. Living in Process is about global solutions. We have focused on the problems much too long.

As my writing moved in larger and larger spheres, so did my work. Working on *When Society Becomes an Addict* pushed me to look at systemic problems, as did *The Addictive Organization* (1988), which I coauthored. I was beginning to seek solutions in larger and larger spheres. I could see addiction as a systemic problem of the society. I saw addiction as a survival requirement learned in our culture that few, if any, escaped.

During these years of focusing on addiction, I wrote *Escape from Intimacy* (1989) out of my own personal interest and the request of others to write about my observations and learnings in the areas of romance, relationship, and sexual addiction, all of which I also saw as products of the culture. I also wrote a little meditation book called *Laugh! I Thought I'd Die (If I Didn't)* (1990) as a kind of fun exercise to honor the humor I had heard at Twelve-Step meetings and among recovering persons. Until this point all my books had basically been written from the perspective of participant-observer. There is no question that I was working through my own issues as I worked with others and my basic focus was still what was going on "out there," in others, in organizations, in society. I was learning a participatory system, <u>and</u> I was still caught in my old paradigm of analyzing the problem from outside.

The publication of *Meditations for Women Who Do Too Much* (1990) was a major break from my past, personally and professionally. In *Meditations for Women Who Do Too Much*, I shared the new way of living that I was developing and practicing by sharing the basic truths I had gathered thus far. This was the first time I wrote from the perspective of the Living in Process work I had been practicing and developing. This book was the beginning of putting forth my own philosophy of life. And it hit a nerve. I had shifted from women's writings to addiction, from addiction to political-social, and now, through the vehicle of a book for women, I was expressing the philosophy of life I was living in and working with, and there were literally millions of people responding from all over the world.

The Emergence of Living in Process

If I needed validation for the path I was walking, this book was it.

By this time I had discovered some of the basic truths of Living in Process. I saw the importance of noticing my feelings, intuition, discomforts, and awarenesses, the need to be in my body and to trust the information I received from it, and my absolute need for alone time in order to "hear" my process. I had developed an awareness that ultimately I had to take responsibility for myself and my life and decisions. I had always known that I had to take responsibility, as in ownership, and I could see from a new perspective the dance between owning my life and my decisions and trusting that force greater than myself. I was beginning to acknowledge the destructive role of dualism in my own and other people's lives and to see that we could, indeed, move beyond it. I had learned personally and by listening to others how destructive the illusion of control is and how much better my life progressed when I replaced this illusion with trust. And, most importantly, I had come to know that I would go to any lengths to seek and accept healing of body, mind, and spirit and the development of a global society that is healthy and respectful of all creation.

I had learned these truths from the Living in Process groups that had become the center of my work life. In these groups I did my deep-process work (see Chapter 6 on healing), continued to learn about and heal from the addictive process, and practiced Living in Process.

In 1992, I published *Beyond Therapy, Beyond Science*, in which I used the field of psychotherapy to explore and challenge the role of mechanistic science in the healing professions and the society, demonstrating how mechanistic science is antithetical to healing or wholeness and had been used to create a society that is destructive and violent from the individual to the planetary level, spawning unbridled consumerism and materialism. It was easy to make the leap from individual addictions to a technocratic society, seeing that what I had formerly delineated as the characteristics of addiction were by-products of a postmodern technocratic world and had developed what I now call the technocratic, materialistic, mechanistic personality

(TMMP). Addiction can be understood as a human response to a techno-logical world. In 1992, we were gradually becoming aware of the role and influence of mechanistic science in the destruction of all we knew from the individual to the planet, and *Beyond Therapy, Beyond Science* defined and delin-eated this destruction and violence in my little corner of the world—the "healing" professions.

In the process of writing *Beyond,* I reluctantly had to admit that psychotherapy not only was not helpful and was not healing, it was harmful. By giving psychological "fixes" and feeding the disembodied thinking process, it kept people from doing their deep-process work and therefore prevented them from moving to healing at the soul level, which was where most needed to be working.

Beyond Therapy, Beyond Science also presented the healing component of the Living in Process work. Yet, I knew that the healing component was only one aspect of the healing worldview that I was now teaching. I had left the field of psychotherapy. And I was becoming more and more concerned with spirituality and wholeness. I was becoming a teacher who could share what I had learned about Living in Process and our larger contexts.

By the time *Beyond Therapy, Beyond Science* was finished and before it came out, I was badly in need of a rest from the intensity of my own per-sonal work and the writing I had done. Intuitively, I knew that I needed to spend time with native elders and healers around the world. They say that when the pupil is ready, the teachers appear, and they certainly did! Miracu-lously, I found doors opening to be with native elders and healers wherever I went. I went only where I was invited, <u>and</u> the invitations poured in.

Initially, I believed that I was only being given these opportunities to heal myself. This happened in ways that I find difficult to describe. Then, I began to notice that what I was being taught by these native people was what I was struggling to articulate about Living in Process. In my first meet-ing with Australian Aboriginal elders, I found myself sitting and weeping uncontrollably as they talked. I realized that they already knew what I was trying to teach. They knew vastly more than I did about Living in Process and participating in the wholeness of our own spirituality and life. The relief I felt as I sat there was immense. My tears were tears of exhaustion, relief, and coming home. I had felt so alone.

Native people the world over began telling me that their myths and legends had told them that a time would come when they would have to share their wisdom and secrets to save the planet, and that time was now. Many have blessed me to carry their knowledge back with me. Their love and support has been invaluable in my own growth and healing and the evolution of the task of developing the Living in Process work to heal individuals, relationships, families, communities, organizations, societies, and the planet. I had not planned to write a book from these experiences. I had participated in them because I needed to and that was enough. However, with permission and blessings from native elders and healers, I was honored to bring *Native Wisdom for White Minds* to the world in 1995. I wrote it in the form of a meditation book, and I use it daily.

In 1996, *Meditations for People Who (May) Worry Too Much* was published as a sequel to *Meditations for Women Who Do Too Much*. We believed that two behaviors that go hand in hand are doing too much and worrying too much.

Now the time has come to openly articulate Living in Process as a philosophy, a healing force, and a way of life. This way of life was hinted at in *Meditations for Women Who Do Too Much*. The healing component was described in *Beyond Therapy, Beyond Science*. The totality of this worldview will be spelled out in *Living in Process*.

The Creator had provided me with the final piece and perspective I needed to write *Living in Process*. Through listening to native people, I had leapt to a new awareness of the planet, of the universe, and of the Great Mystery, which brought all the work I had been doing up to that point together and into perspective for me. I have spent years defining the problem. With the writing of *Living in Process*, I will be sharing the solutions that have worked so well for myself and others who know this work as it has evolved throughout the world for the last twenty years. I am sure that there will be more knowing, <u>and</u> I have what I need to see the spheres of Living in Process and articulate the possibilities for living and healing that are available to us every second of our lives.

The Living in Process approach is a solution that is both theoretical and practical. It is based on the way I live and the healing work I have done and continue to do for myself. I and others have developed the theoretical side only after we have personally participated in it. It is not possible to teach Living in Process without actively doing it. It's all about participation. I not only practice what I preach, I live it! I personally know the struggles, the ups and downs, the coming out the other side. I live this work and I love this work, and because of it my life has become both serene and joyful. My life has not always been this way, yet now I have a constant, ongoing, active relationship with the Great Mystery, and I more often than not experience the oneness of the All.

Living in Process is dynamic and ever changing. It is being evolved by all the people who participate in it. To assume that the Living in Process approach is the same as it was five years ago or even two years ago would be a grave mistake. This assumption makes static what is essentially and truly a dynamic process. The Living in Process work is not "done." I am not "done." No one who participates in it is "done." We are all "in process."

Living in Process opens up the doors to total living. This work is not for everyone, <u>and</u> it is there for those who wish for and need it. It is not a quick fix. Living in Process takes time, energy, and perseverance.

Living in Process means making a deep and ongoing spiritual commitment to oneself and to life. The process of spirituality does not take us out of our life or ask us to rise above it. Living in Process puts us more fully into life and asks us to participate, while recognizing that our primary relationship is and always will be our connection to the all-encompassing process we call God, the Creator, the Great Mystery.

At first, Living in Process may seem like the most difficult thing you've ever been asked to do. Yet, Living in Process is very simple. It is not always easy. It is not easy because we have moved so far away from the life that we were meant to live. So often, we are the ones who make our lives more difficult, and collectively, we have built societies that make life on this planet more difficult. We also hold the keys to making our lives better.

We have buried the essential in the unimportant.

Living in Process is a return to ourselves and a reconnection to all life. When viewed from outside, it may seem like too much is being asked of us. Yet, when we begin to live our lives in process, we wonder what took us so long to give up painful, death-producing patterns we called reality and move into the fullness of living.

One does not have to be active in a Twelve-Step program to learn to Live in Process. And, these programs are excellent ways for us to confront and heal from the characteristics of the technocratic, materialistic, mechanistic personality and behaviors that we have learned from our society. It's only when we've begun to move away from this dysfunction that we become ready to open and walk through the doors of Living in Process.

Some may ask, "Do I have to believe in a Higher Power to do Living in Process work?"

No, Living in Process is a path that allows each of us to enter into our own knowing. It helps us to move into our connectedness with the All That Is. No one form of spirituality is necessary to do that. And, at some point, all of us must recognize that we are spiritual beings. All spirituality moves us toward wholeness. Now for a word of caution. Our society has taught us to seek knowledge outside ourselves. Sadly, some of us no longer trust that our inner compass will give us accurate information. Worse still, many of us no longer know how to read or even access this valuable guide. Yet it has never left us. We need to relearn the importance of testing out everything with our inner knowing.

Living in Process

The best way to begin is always to ask ourselves if what we read and hear feels right to us. We need to learn to distinguish between feelings and emotions. Emotions are feelings plus confused thinking and adrenaline. Emotions are feelings run amok. We need to learn how to get back to the purity of our real feelings. We need to learn to wait. We need to make peace with our confusion and lack of clarity and not to leap into anything based on our thinking. The time has come for us to relearn the skills of discernment, feeling, and intuition. As we wait with our awareness, we give ourselves needed time to do our inner work, to check out what is right for us, and to follow it with a full heart.

When we are unclear, our perceptions tend to be muddled. As we learn to Live in Process, our perceptions become more reliable. When we take responsibility for our perceptions, we can grow, change, and clarify. Trusting our own perceptions and taking responsibility for them leads to spiritual maturity.

I encourage you to use your awareness, discernment, and intuition with this book. Take what you need and leave the rest. If my words ring true for you, trust that knowing and share it with others. If the words do not fit for you, trust that, too, and move on. There are many different paths.

If you decide now is the time and this is the place to move beyond mere adjustment and short-term fixes, this book can become your guide. It will offer you support and years of experience from many people like yourself who continue to learn and participate in the living of their lives.

This book is an invitation. It is an invitation for those who are ready to leap (or crawl!) beyond adjustment and short-term fixes. It is an invitation to those who are ready to move into the fullness of their wholeness. It is an invitation to open new doors and explore options for Living in Process.

Chapter 2

UNDERSTANDING

PROCESS

B efore we move too far into the whole idea of living life in a process way, we need to stop to make sure that we share a common understanding of what process is.

We live in a world that emphasizes and believes in the static and the instantaneous. We are taught to see ourselves, our cars, our houses as static "things." Because of this belief in stasis, we become upset and feel personally attacked when our houses or our cars—or our bodies—break down. When everything is not "perfect and perfectly perfect," we feel somehow that we have failed.

The majority of us spend our lives indoors in climate-controlled settings. This means that the processes of nature and the changing seasons have become mere abstractions for many of us. Some rarely, if ever, put their feet on the earth or feel the dirt squish between their toes and fingers. Just as asphalt and concrete mediate between our bodies and the earth, so concepts and abstractions mediate between our beings and our spirits.

We need to return to an awareness of the process of our life and to participate in it to know and experience the fullness of the dimensions of reality.

Living in Process

Returning to our knowing about process is not an easy task. Yet, this is a book about living and knowing a living spirituality. To live and experience we must know about process. I have come to know personally and professionally that the way to full living comes through my process.

I want to explore with you exactly what process is and its place and meaning in our everyday life.

> We believe that we live in "the age of information," that there has been an information "explosion," an information "revolution." While in a certain sense this is the case, in many important ways just the opposite is true. We also live at a moment of deep ignorance, when vital knowledge that human beings have always possessed about who we are and where we live seems beyond our reach: *we live in an age of missing information.* [emphasis mine]
>
> Bill McKibben
> The New Yorker
> March 9, 1992

The missing piece McKibben speaks of is our lack of knowledge of process.

When I began to understand that a working knowledge of and relationship with the concept and experience of process was not common in contemporary society and could not be assumed, I felt lost, confused, disbelieving, and bewildered. After discussing this with many people, I began to realize that my generation may have been the last one in this present technological culture to have grown up with a living awareness of process.

A static, materialistic, information-based culture has systematically filtered out an awareness of and relationship with process. This filtering-out phenomenon has removed vital experience and basic inner knowing that has far-reaching and powerful implications. This loss of understanding of and experience with process may be one of the biggest reasons for lack of understanding between generations, the ecological crisis, lack of intimacy, and increased conflict and dysfunction. Even more importantly, this vital loss has alienated us from the wisdom of our elders, nature, and ultimately ourselves.

We cannot know the meaning of being, or experience spirituality, without a knowledge of process.

As we open the doors for learning about and experiencing the concept of process, we also need to explore the implications of a world ignorant of process. Then, perhaps, learning to live in process will have more meaning and even more urgency. I want to take some time here to help you recover your knowing of what process really is.

GROWING UP IN A PROCESS WORLD

Perhaps one of the best ways for me to remind you of what your knowing about process is, is to share my own process in learning about process.

When I was a little girl, I was surrounded by nature, and much of my time was spent out in the natural world with my dogs. I remember watching spiders spin their webs and marveling at the time and patience it took to spin. I saw them build and rebuild their webs when they were knocked down or destroyed. My family wasn't afraid of bugs or spiders, and watching them and learning from them was encouraged. Spiders always seemed to know what they were doing and they never seemed frantic about doing it. The patience required to build a web never ceased to impress me. I would watch as they prepared for and then laid their eggs. Sometimes, it seemed like an eternity before they hatched, and yet there was a learning about "everything in its time . . . everything in its time." Spiders gave me an experience of process.

I can remember, at times, wishing to be a grownup. I remember my great-grandmother saying to me, "You'll have plenty of time for that. Right now you're a child. That's a special time. Enjoy it." From her, there was always an encouragement to be who, what, and where I was in my life. She gave me an implicit message that my life was a process in which I could participate, that I need not concern myself with a race to the end. She taught me to see each moment as related to and building upon the ones before it and not isolated in and of themselves. She and my mother gave me the faith to experience where I was with my life and the trust that more would come. In doing that, they gave me the gift of knowing that I was participating in a life that was itself a process, an unfolding, and that it was part of something much bigger than just myself.

I was fortunate to live in a place where there were seasons, and our lives were related to the seasons. We did not live in a climate-controlled environment, which meant there was more work and we were colder in the winter. Winter meant . . . hunkering in, and long nights with games around the fire. Winter meant a small cake whipped up for my friends late at night in the middle of a snowstorm. We all waited and withstood the smells, surviving the interminably long process of its cooking. Eagerness overcame caution as we ate it hot from the oven and flipped it from hand to hand trying not to burn ourselves.

Spring brought new life. The hills and meadows burst with the process of spring and exploded with color. The jack-in-the-pulpits sprang up the same places they had the previous year—teaching me the processes of the plants and seasons. Mayapples filled the forest, and flowers were everywhere. As I grew, I began to develop a feeling of security knowing where each flower grew. It gave me the experience of old friends recycling through my life. The land and I knew one another.

Understanding Process

My great-grandmother knew that our bodies, too, were a process and had cycles. At the first hint of spring—which is usually only felt or sensed—we were out with baskets, trowels, and hoes to dig sassafras roots to make a tea to "thin our blood." She believed that sassafras tea was a necessary spring tonic to clean out the winter stagnation from the body. Our bodies participated in the process of the seasons. Our bodies were part of the process of nature. Our bodies *were* nature. I grew up being aware of the cycles and processes of nature and knowing that I was much better off if my cycles were in tune with the larger cycles around me.

I lived the process of nature. I saw her storms as I sat on the big old porch with my mother, watching big thunderstorms sweep across the valley, trembling with excitement as the thunder rolled and the lightning crashed. Nature was respected, not feared. It was powerful and uncontrollable, yet one with us. I saw the processes that composed life. Nothing in my existence was static. I saw floods and the long process of cleaning up the aftermath. I saw the paths tornadoes left as they raged across the land. I saw the devastation, the grieving, the cleanup, and the inevitable return to full life. I was a part of that whole process.

I lived on a farm and knew the tilling, the planting, the growing, and the harvesting. I saw the cycles repeat themselves time and again. I saw birth and death and accepted them as the process for us all. I learned to see life as a process. Life was not static or something to be controlled from outside. It was a process to be lived from inside. The process of all life was not external to me. It *was* me. Nothing was static. All was in motion.

CONTENT AND PROCESS IN GROUPS

In our exploration of the meaning of process, I've found that one of the most helpful tools is learning to distinguish between content and process. My learning in this area came from looking at what happens in groups. This occurred through the campus YMCA-YWCA in my college years. The staff had all gone to Bethel, Maine, to be trained by the National Training Laboratories in group process and group dynamics. They returned to share their knowledge about groups with the students. During my freshman and sophomore years I participated in a training program offered to campus leaders in group dynamics. In my junior and senior years, I ran the training program.

I learned that there are two major aspects to any group, just as there are in life: the content and the process. The content—facts and information—is the easiest to understand. However, the process is probably the more important of the two.

I could easily see that this way of looking at what was happening in groups was an excellent model for understanding larger and more complex aspects in life as well as our own individual processes. Often, the *what* in life is not as important as the *how* or the *way* we do it.

The content is the *what*—what is the group talking about, what is the task at hand, what is the group trying to accomplish, what decisions have to be made, what is the agenda? Many of the groups we participate in have a certain task they are trying to accomplish. Often, because the task needs to be completed, the leader will try to keep the group focused on the task while paying little or no attention to the process. Sadly, this focus on content or task is frequently done at the expense of the group—its creativity, comfort, participation, and commitment levels. The focus on task can become quite tunnel-visioned, and often the agenda gets railroaded through with little concern about feelings, what is happening in the group, or any real commitment to the decisions made.

A good group facilitator will often stop a group and set the task aside in order to deal with what is going on in the group—that is, the process of the group—or the *way* the task is being accomplished. This procedure often leads to a higher functioning group and more commitment to the decisions made. The process, or dynamic, of any group is much more subtle than the content, and infinitely more important because if the process is unclear or destructive, the group's decisions will not be carried out without sabotage, regardless of how good or important they are.

The process of the group is what is actually going on among the participants and in the group itself. Are there subgroups or coalitions forming? Are there power struggles happening? What is the tone or feeling of the group? Are people in the group performing maintenance functions such as standing back and giving others a chance to speak, respecting the need for a pause, waiting respectfully while someone expresses her/his feelings, picking up on a change of feeling or tone in the group? What is actually happening in the group? Are people having fun? Are they comfortable, uncomfortable, bored, or participating? Are people isolating? The answers to all these questions-observations are one level of the process of the group.

Then there is another level operating simultaneously—the process dynamic of the group. Is the group sluggish? Is it moving from one place to another to another? Are trust and confidence building in the group? If the group has dealt with the first level of process adequately, then there can be some hope that this level of process will move in a good way. Does the group seem to be progressing, deepening, growing? Has the group taken on a life of its own, and have the members recognized this? Is the group becoming more than the individuals involved? Has the group become an entity? As an entity, is it good, bad, or indifferent?

Interestingly, there is yet another level of process operating, as well. Perhaps we can call this a metalevel of process. Is the group itself becoming a vehicle for a process to connect with a higher self, a way of opening doors for awarenesses that are larger than the individual—or the group?

There are probably an infinite number of processes and levels of process in any one aspect of our lives. These are just a few examples of the levels of process going on simultaneously in any group. This is why I feel group process concepts are an excellent vehicle for conveying the existence of process in our daily lives and its subtle complexity and nuances. The content may be the bread, and it is meaningless unless we realize that it must be chewed, swallowed, digested, separated, absorbed, and eliminated, which is the *process* of eating the bread.

An excellent facilitator moves easily between content and process, or group-dynamic issues, in a group in order to encourage a high level of creativity and participation. Both aspects of the group are important. I think of a good group facilitator or of a person who lives life well as a creative orchestra conductor. Each individual person can play the notes (the content), <u>and</u> it is the way the conductor brings them together (the process) that makes them into music.

A group cannot exist without content and process. In ultimate terms, the content may only be the vehicle that allows the process to happen. *Unfortunately, if we live in a world that knows and believes only in content—material world, static information—we have put ourselves at a severe disadvantage for the living of this life.* The facilitator may be doggedly pushing on with the agenda while the process of the group is completely dysfunctional. Many of us are that facilitator—the one who knows only about content (technology, mechanics, materialism, information)—while the processes of our lives and the myriad of processes going on at an infinite number of levels around us are buffeting us without our realizing it.

Another good example of distinguishing between process and content is in a visit to our physician.

I know a physician who specializes in allergies. He has documented all the possible allergies in his vicinity and listed the usual medications in his computer. He says the symptoms, diagnosis, and treatment are pretty cut and dried. He has the receptionist give the client a detailed questionnaire when he/she comes in, and that data is entered into the computer immediately. He then says that he needs to spend only three to four minutes with each patient for the patient to get a prescription and leave. This giving of the prescription is a very short, impersonal process (if a process at all!) and mostly is a way of dealing with a problem that is almost purely content-oriented.

The *process* of being a physician is quite different. People tend to like doctors who have a process of respect and do not treat them like machines.

A physician's content may be just what you need, and it is the physician's process that engenders trust and maybe even healing.

LEARNING AND TEACHING
AS PROCESSES

Life is an ongoing process of teaching and learning.

I remember college as a great time. I loved the learning, I loved the activities, I loved the relationships—and sometimes there was information overload. Every class seemed intent on opening up our little brains and filling them up with facts and information that we were to regurgitate on cue. Rarely did we learn *how* to do anything, or discover how what we were learning had come about. We learned facts.

Then, I ran across a class that was completely different. It was taught by a great German scholar called Vicktor Hamburger. The class was comparative anatomy and embryology. In order to learn embryology, which then led to anatomy, we had to follow the germ layers, as the different forms of embryonic tissue are called, as they developed.

For example, the eyes are part of the same primordial germ layer as the brain and the spinal cord. They all start out in the same place. The eyes push out from the brain, and the spinal cord invaginates (folds in), and then pinches off to form the spinal cord, surrounded by other germ layers that form bone and flesh and skin.

In embryology, we *saw this process happen!* True, we studied frozen (static) cross sections, <u>and</u> we studied these cross sections at various stages of development. On the slides of the cross sections we could see when the germ layer that would be the spinal cord began to invaginate. We could see when it was complete. We could see when it pinched off. *We could witness process.* Not only that (!), we could see the magic of process in this class.

Magically, the different germ layers seemed to "influence" other layers at specific stages of development in a *process* we have yet fully to understand. For example, take the external place where there will be, say, an arm. Although there is no visual or measurable difference in the tissue, at one point that germ layer can be removed and transplanted somewhere else on the embryo, where it will become whatever is normal for that site on the embryo. However, remove it a few hours later and it will become the arm it was "influenced" to be in its original location. As a process, the growth of the embryo consists of stages when germ layers are interchangeable, yet there are points in that *process* when the germ layer outcome is irreversible. In this course, we could actually almost see, feel, and touch the process we were studying.

Unfortunately, the majority of our information comes in the form of static information. Yet, the most important and difficult messages that we get about living, if we get them at all, can be adequately conveyed only through experience as we participate in the process of life. Learning is an area where content and process are easily distinguishable. The facts and the information can be easily imparted and verified by testing. Process learning is more difficult and profound. In my comparative anatomy and embryology class, I was able to see and experience the process in order to learn the facts. Over forty-five years later, that class remains one of the fullest and most memorable in my life.

Recently, I was talking with a sixth-grade teacher about her teaching. She was concerned that the school wanted to put computers in the room for every student and that the focus of their learning would be the vast array of information they could get on the computer.

"I'm willing for the computers to be an extracurricular activity," she said. "But I believe what goes on in the classroom and the interactions between the students and between the students and the teacher are just as important as anything they can get from computers."

She went on to say that she was concerned that students would become more and more isolated and withdrawn and not only would they not have any social skills, they would be devoid of the other (process!) tools they would need for living.

Clearly, her view may not be very popular. Yet, she is considered a master teacher at thirty-one years of age. The questions she is asking are important ones; the concerns she has need to be voiced. Process cannot be replaced with content in learning. Often, it is the process of the learning that is the magic that makes the content come alive.

Learning is a process. It is not an event.

Several years ago I volunteered to help an old Australian Koori (Aborigine) gentleman, Mr. Reuben Kelly, write his book. He is the last member of the Thainghetti people who speaks the language, the last initiated man, and the last priest of his tribe. He was mandated by the priests who initiated him that he should write a book and share their wisdom. I have spent many hours with him tape-recording his sharing about his life and the life of his people. Before I started spending time with this man, an Australian friend of mine of Western European descent said to me, "Don't expect too much from this old man. They don't like to give away their secrets." I was shocked! I responded that I did not care about his secrets. I just wanted to hear whatever he wanted to share with me. The experience of listening to him was what was healing to me.

Over the years, I have spent many hours with Mr. Kelly. I have listened as he told me whatever he wanted to tell me, and always loved our time together. After a while, I began to notice that he was telling some of the same stories over and over (content). Since I had already *heard* them, I would, on occasion, tune out, thinking that I already knew what he was saying (content arrogance). Often, I would suddenly be brought up short when I realized that he was *putting in something new*—a new twist, a new facet, a new emphasis, a slightly different perspective. His teaching me was a process! He was not only sharing content, the *way* he was doing it was as important as the what.

It was then that the structure of his book began to emerge. The book would have two parts. We would work on one book that would be linear and content-laden for modern-trained minds, which included the minds of his own people educated in Western ways. And then we would write a second book with some of the same information (content) and we would present it in the old way of teaching, which is a spiral, adding new information and depth as the student is ready. The latter is the way he was taught by the old women from birth. He says that his people had the equivalent of a university education by the time they were four years old because of the way they were taught.

There are no other initiated men in his tribe. In order to be initiated the men have to go through the *processes* of learning, which spiral up and down to a point where spiritually they are ready for the next steps. These *processes* take time and one cannot move to the next until the previous ones have been integrated. This is the strength and power of the wisdom he possesses. The endpoint would be too powerful to possess if the previous phases had not been integrated. It is not that the Koori are not willing to share their secrets. There is no one among his people or the white Australians, or anyone else for that matter, who is ready—who has gone through the processes—to receive the powerful information of the secrets. Sadly, he plans to take this wisdom to the grave with him.

The progressive filtering out of the process in learning and teaching may be jeopardizing the existence of human beings the same way that loss of endangered plants and animals is threatening the survival of the planet.

How much wisdom are we running the risk of losing in a world devoid of the knowledge and experience of process?

RELATIONSHIPS

When I was a young psychologist, I did a great deal of work with children and adolescents and their parents. Like most psychologists I learned all the diagnostic categories and how to fit the appropriate labels to whom, when, and where. I learned the characteristics of various "diseases" and how they clustered together to result in certain diagnoses, which in the medical model were then supposed to dictate a certain form of "treatment." I never could reconcile myself to the validity that certain people invest in the test results. From my perspective, the information gleaned from those few hours of observation was a very small sampling of the process of an unfolding life. A child was an emerging, growing, and living being, and then our tests stopped that dynamism. We thus forced the child into a diagnosis of static and fixed symptoms rather than continuing to observe the dynamic process that was her/his own life. Often, the issue was not the "illness." The issue was getting the child to *participate* again in what was the ongoing process of his or her life.

Symptoms appear when participation in the process stops.

What we perceive as symptoms are not static elements of personality. They are what erupt when one pulls back from the process of one's life, isolates, and tries to control the life process. For example, when children experience a traumatic event, they may pull back and become withdrawn in an attempt to deal with the emotional aftermath. They have shifted their consciousness in an attempt to control and halt their life process. What we can then observe is the symptom that develops when growth is halted. Even the symptoms themselves are not static; they change, although slowly because they are more static than the normal, healthy way of living for a child in process.

The child is trying to learn and participate in her or his life even when this process is not supported by the environment or life itself. There are times in the young child's life when nonparticipation and withdrawal seem the only solution. Then, learning stops. We need not see this pullback as the real person, for we need to help them participate again.

At first, I had difficulty imagining that when I said, "Relationships are a process," so many people in Western culture would have no reference point for this statement because they had no functional relationship model that allowed them to understand.

I began exploring the relationships-as-process issue with some of the people I know who come from generations younger than mine. I spoke to a friend of mine, Charlie, whom I have known for some time and had seen as a fairly enlightened person. I was shocked by his response.

"I know nothing about the process of relationships," he said. "When I see a woman, I see the package. If the package looks good, then in my mind I immediately jump to sex and what passes for a relationship. I have no idea of how to get there."

He went on to say that almost all the information that he has about relationships came from television and the movies. His parents had little or no relationship. He wanted to develop a relationship, and he simply had no experience with the *process* of relationships. Instant gratification is all that is real to him. Relationships either happen or they don't. Charlie's world is very isolated and alone. He does, however, have a very active mind and private world. It has few, if any, nuances. Without process there is no way to experience the difference between having a quick orgasm and making love.

Understanding Process

PARENTING

When content and process conflict, process always wins out.

Time and again, I have witnessed how much more powerful process is than content and how when process and content conflict, process always wins out. For example, when a parent says, *"I'm not angry!"* in a loud voice with lots of energy, the child knows the parent is angry. The child does not believe the content of that statement. The *process* of that statement—the way it is said, the communication of the energy—is much more important than what is said—the content, the information. Modern science teaches us that we can be objective, in the distorted belief that we can remove all process from the information, and that this freedom from process is a superior way of living and learning. What, in fact, all this "objectivity" does is make the information lifeless. It does not give us the important information we need for living.

Even when the child gets a mixed message from a parent, that child is interacting with a living, breathing being who is offering an *experience* of reality. The child's own process will have to get clear on what is real, what is important, and what is true and usable for maturity. This process of sorting out and working through is what life is really all about. For example, there are limitless ways the child can respond to the "I'm not angry" message used earlier. The child can say, "I must be crazy," "You must be crazy," "Obviously you are not clear and not in touch with yourself," or "This is confusing and I want no part of it." If the child focuses only on the content, there is no place to go with this comment. When the child responds to the content *and* the process, the liveliness and the learnings are limitless. The most important wisdom the child might get from this interaction is how important it is to be congruent within ourselves.

Since I left the field of psychology and psychotherapy, I have been keenly aware of how powerful television and the movies are in offering content-laden psychological interpretations as instant magic fixes that offer a subtle brainwashing, keeping the viewers hooked in the nonreality of a content-focused world.

I will discuss parenting in greater detail in Chapter 10. I mentioned it as an example here because I believe most of us can relate to the difference between content and process when we reflect on the way we were parented. We may have received conflicting messages as children. Many people discover that much of their life's work is focused around recovering from the way they were parented. If we can, in our own experience of being parented, distinguish between what was said and the process of how we were parented, we are well on our way to letting our remembered knowledge or process become meaningful for us again.

REALITY SHIFTS

We humans are an interesting bunch. For some unknown reason we glimpse a small sliver of reality, and we try to freeze it or make it static and hold on to it for dear life. We don't like to recognize that reality is going to keep on asserting its agenda (process) and its truth whether we can perceive it or not. Our desire for control is so powerful that we want to know what, where, and when, and we don't want anything to shift without first giving us a written notice. Yet, that's all illusion. Life isn't a series of little shifts or jerks. Only process, movement, and change are real.

ILLNESSES AND ACCIDENTS

Often, what breaks us through to a new level of understanding or a fuller understanding of our process reality is a crisis. Many of us experience our first major reality shift into the awareness of process through accidents or illness in ourselves or those around us. Crises often force us back into an *experience* of process even though our minds desperately try to cling to the illusion of a static world.

Often, after the crisis of a serious illness or accident, people will say something like, "I wouldn't wish this on anybody, but this has been the most significant experience of my life. It has completely changed my perspective on life." Experiences like these alter our perception of reality. They plunge us into the reality that we are spiritual beings in a spiritual universe. Those who embrace the *process* of these experiences have their lives and reality changed forever.

I had an experience with a machete that demonstrates how important learnings and reality shifts can come from accidents. My husband and I decided to spend some healing time in an isolated retreat place. We spent the first week cleaning and generally fixing everything up and settling in.

On Sunday, it was a beautiful, clear, bright, sunny day—one of those pure treasures—and we decided to take a walk. My husband, Chuck, likes tree houses, and he had found a wonderful spot to build one and wanted to check out if it was on our land. Also, there were a lot of big windfall trees down and, again, we wanted to see if they were on our land. I considered wearing my rubber boots (not good to walk in), cowboy boots (they'd get muddy), running shoes (eh?), and settled on my old faithful thongs since we were going to try to stick to roads and trails. I didn't realize how overgrown the trails had become since I had last been there and two big storms had come through. So, off we went. Chuck sharpened the machete and his hand ax in case we needed them.

I was so happy. There is nothing I would rather do than wander this land. We had walked for a little over a mile when we came to a really jammed-up spot. I wasn't quite sure where we were because of the overgrowth and downed trees. The path was blocked by fallen timbers. We sized up the situation and decided to cut through the underbrush and go around. Chuck went ahead with the machete. I was too close behind him, and just as I put my foot up to push aside some stinging nettles, he took a swing with the machete, cutting deep into the ankle of my left foot.

I keep having flashbacks of the gash and how it looked with my foot and ankle laid open. Chuck quickly grabbed my foot with both hands and said, "Oh, Anne. Oh, my God," and he prayed in those moments. I quietly thought, "Well, this has happened. Now we have to take care of it." I took off my favorite denim shirt and tied a tourniquet below my knee, then I sat down. (I had to admit I felt a little faint at that point.) I elevated my foot on a downed tree, and Chuck wrapped it tight with the rest of the shirt to stop the bleeding. We then decided that he should go for help. We could hear some building sounds, and from where I guessed we were, we had neighbors not too far away. I told him that I wasn't going anywhere, and if I fainted from shock or loss of blood, he knew where I was. He could do no good staying with me.

I felt no pain at all. I prayed, breathed, and turned my will and my life over to the Creator, calmly waiting for my rescuers. While I sat there, I wondered what I would learn from this. When Chuck and I checked in about this later, we discovered that neither of us could get into the self-centeredness of beating ourselves up about this. It was an accident. Accidents happen, just as life happens. Yet, since there are really no accidents, we must have some really important learnings that probably could not have come about in an easier, softer way.

In almost no time, the building sounds stopped and I heard shouts of "What's the shortest way? Bring the car around that way, we'll go through this way," and "Anne, can you hear me? Someone call 911 and get the ambulance." I still felt no pain, no longer felt faint, and the bleeding did not seem heavy, although it was hard to tell.

Very quickly, Chuck arrived. I could see the concern on his face. He was very pale and I felt cupped in his obvious love and caring. He said, "Are you all right?" I said, "Yes," and felt such concern for him and how bad he must feel. Immediately, another man arrived and started shouting to his son to direct him to where we were. I asked him if the Shaners (my old neighbors) were still here, and he said, "I'm Shaner." I had not seen him for some time. The Shaner boy hacked a trail to the car while Todd (the father) and Chuck tried to carry me through the forest. Chuck fell down once over a hidden log; it was rough! I feared that they both were going to have a heart attack, so I suggested hopping with my arms around them. Chuck is very tall, Todd is very short, I could see the car, and the only major obstacle was a downed tree. I crawled under it. I suspected by the way my foot was hanging that some tendons were cut.

They loaded me into the car with Todd's son driving. He was a college student now—the last time I'd seen him he was a little kid. Todd ran to check with 911 and said he would follow in the other car. On the second curve, we met the ambulance and the EMT volunteers. By this time, it seemed that everyone on my end of the island knew that

I had been injured. Still no pain! We had what was later described as an "island parade" into town: the ambulance, Todd's son in one car, Todd in another, the sheriff, my neighbor Jeff and Chuck in our car, and one or two others to see that I got to the doctor okay.

The person on call was not the most trusted MD on the island, so four EMTs—especially my neighbor Jeff—hung around to check on him and make sure I got the best care. As he cleaned up the wound, it was worse than he thought it would be, and we decided that I should be helicoptered to the nearest hospital, which had an excellent orthopedic surgeon.

Through all this, Chuck was right there, present and loving. He held my hand as the wound was cleaned out so they could see the damage. A clot had formed already, and when it was cleaned, it was clear we had a bleeder. An artery had been cut and so had some tendons. I needed an expert. Still no pain!

I had more nervousness about the twelve-minute helicopter ride than I did about the wound at that point. I prayed the whole time, no big deal. Chuck had to take the ferry over. It took him five hours. I was out of surgery and ready to leave the recovery room by the time he got there.

All in all, what a fantastic experience! I have never felt so well cared for by medical teams and rarely had such a good experience. Not one person asked me how I was going to pay. Their entire focus was on doing what I needed and attending to my wound and healing. They seemed to know what was important. From the gentle hand on my shoulder during the flight, to the anesthesiologist who listened to me and my wish not to have general anesthesia and negotiated what we would do and then gave me constant information during the hour and a half of surgery, responding to every bit of feedback from me, to the Danish nurse who sat with me throughout my recovery and suggested that I take the surgery leg pillow home with me and return it to her next week when I got my new cast—everyone was super! And still no pain (as they say in AA—we will be able to handle situations in a new way), and Chuck was right there. I later realized that I hadn't expected him to be.

I began to think about the relationship between physical pain and fear. Whenever I just stayed in the present, I was fine. When I went back to the past (what we should have done) or into the future (will my foot be normal?), I could feel the invitation to fear, but I had no need whatsoever to do that. I knew that right behind the fear was pain. I could sense it. The present was enough.

Chuck had the good sense to call for spiritual and emotional support while he waited for the ferry, and we both prayed. I prayed for him, he prayed for me, and I sent love to my foot and assured it that it would heal.

We decided not to push ourselves to catch the late ferry and stayed in a motel on the mainland that night. Then the new learnings began. I ached all over from the shock and the anesthesia. Still, almost no pain in my foot. The surgeon had had to make another incision to search for the severed main tendon, which had already started to draw up, so that leg did have a lot of trauma that day.

I assured the hospital staff that I knew how to use crutches <u>and</u> forgot that when I had broken this same leg it had been almost forty years ago! I felt more vulnerable with this gash than with the break, *and* I wasn't twenty anymore. It was a long way from the car door to the bed in the motel. I very quickly gave up the idea of going into the restaurant to eat, and let Chuck order the food and have it brought in. I also discovered that I needed help to go to the bathroom (many times) after having been on an IV. I even needed help turning this leg over in bed and keeping ice packs on it. By the next morning, I discovered that I needed help in almost everything—even getting dressed.

By the time I had showered (washing off blood, etc.), dressed myself, combed my hair, and maneuvered my way to the coffee shop and eaten breakfast, I was exhausted. Chuck was right there, but I didn't trust him to be. After I "crutched" back to the car from the coffee shop, I succumbed to my deep feelings and had a big bawl. I told him that if I needed help and needed to depend upon him *so much*, I expected him to go away.

My first husband had literally disappeared the two times I'd had surgery and needed him.

The first time was when I had a pap smear that suggested that I might have cancer. He went to do a vesper service at seminary. I had asked him not to go. I needed him to stay with me. He insisted on going and didn't get home until 2:30 A.M., even though the vesper service was at 10:00 P.M., for fifteen minutes. The second time was when I had oral surgery and the oral surgeon told him I could not be left alone for fear of hemorrhaging. He left me alone with our two-year-old for a weekend ministers' retreat. I know that these two incidents were when I began to leave the marriage.

As I write this, I'm very clear that what my first husband did is not the issue. I even feel bored as I write about it. The issue is what I carried with me from the experience and projected onto Chuck. There were other issues with my second husband. He became terrified whenever I became sick and would stand and scream at me until I got out of bed. According to him, his mother used illness to control the family, and he could not tolerate illness. This, of course, was before I learned to do deep-process work. Today, I would tell him to "hit the mats." This wasn't my issue.

All this baggage surfaced in my helplessness. I had to keep my foot elevated and immobilized. I had to wake Chuck to turn me over at night because the muscles needed for turning my leg were the ones I couldn't use. I had to be helped up, helped down, and assisted in getting in the shower and out of it. Chuck had to cook, clean, do all the chores, help me move around, change my ice packs, and generally be there. And, he was! I knew that I could ask family and friends for help, and I do, but given my earlier experience being dependent upon the man in my life, this was *terrifying*.

Eventually, of course, I had to share all this and put myself out there. Chuck basically said, "Well, can you imagine that?!" And that's how it was. No romantic drama, no crisis, no big issues, just doing what needed to be done. That's when I realized that I'd had to become almost completely immobilized to learn this one. A little flu would never have convinced me.

Chuck took care of himself, as well. We hired Sally, who is ten, to baby-sit me for a few hours a day so he could have unworried free time. And, can you believe it? We both felt even closer and had a wonderful time. We both learned a lot. Still no pain. I was even happy and sure of a complete healing.

I could see that I had unconsciously held a part of myself apart in readiness to run, in case I needed to do that. I saw that although I was very open to intimacy with Chuck, I'd held back just a little—just to be safe. My "reality" of myself in our relationship had shifted. My reality of my relationship with a man had shifted. The process of this different experience with my husband, and the process of healing, required me to shift my concept of reality.

This takes me to the second big set of learnings. Two days after the accident, it was a beautiful day and I decided to sit out in the sun and enjoy the out-of-doors. This is when I became a certified "meadow-watcher." Chuck had decided to take a rest (I can't imagine why!), and I had surrounded myself with everything I might need, including work to do, when I heard a high-pitched whistle. I looked up and saw two bald eagles circling the meadow. I cannot tell you how breathtaking it was to see the sun shining through their white tail feathers. Well, since by that time I was accustomed to waking up Chuck, I called him to come and see. He came and sat with me and watched the eagles. At one time, we counted seven eagles circling. It would take me pages to even try to tell you what this meant to me. We had just come from the Gathering of the Eagles, a large gathering of Native Americans, and the eagles seemed especially significant to us after that experience.

Chuck went back to rest, and a few minutes later, one of the eagles landed in a tree at the edge of the meadow, not more than thirty to forty feet away from where I was sitting. Again, I woke Chuck up, and he came out and we watched the bald eagle watching us. It sat there for a long time. We just sat, watching. Then, after a while, it took off and soared across the meadow very low and landed on another tree in even clearer sight and sat there for a long time. We just sat quietly sharing the meadow with this eagle. After what seemed a long time, the eagle again flew two low circles over us and left.

There I was with my leg in a cast propped up on a lounge chair, and I felt full of joy and contentment. Hardly what one would expect after an accident like this. Chuck went back inside to rest and I started reading a Native American journal a friend had sent me. In an article on an Iroquois Creation myth, I read: "Editor: What does the West Wind represent? Sadie [an Iroquois elder]: When the West Wind blows life into the daughter, he is giving her spiritual life, a gift from the natural world." Just as I read that, on an otherwise calm and clear day, a sudden gust of wind blew from the west and then stopped. I got goose pimples.

When Chuck came out, I shared this with him, and very soon thereafter the eagle came back and landed in the tree. The eagle stayed for over an hour and forty minutes, during which time Chuck had to leave to run some errands. The eagle and I continued to sit with each other. I did nothing but be with the eagle. After a while, it flew off. It was gone for five minutes, at which point I picked up the paper and wrote the first two lines of this story. Then it came back and stayed with me until a while after Chuck returned. This errand trip for Chuck was the first time I had been alone since the accident. I felt guarded. There was no doubt in my mind that the eagle was watching over me.

I was acutely aware that if I had not been confined to my chair and "meadow-watching," I might have missed most of the experience with the eagle. My accident had forced me to slow down and be present to a valuable spiritual experience.

Chuck was fixing dinner the last twenty minutes or so that the bald eagle and I had together. I spend a lot of time with nature and I heal a lot there. Perhaps this day, I needed to be completely still with nature and be available to nature. This was one of the most extraordinary days I have ever had and I actually felt grateful for my injury. It had already brought gifts beyond my imagination, and I was sure there were others yet to come as the days unfolded.

Neither Chuck nor I blamed one another for this experience. Each of us took responsibility for our part and we moved on.

As long as I was able to remain present to my situation, I felt no pain. When I connected with the greater process, I was peaceful and calm.

The *process* of the accident and the way we dealt with it were important learnings. I could not have planned such an experience to make me aware of the old baggage I was carrying from previous husbands and how I was using it as an escape from intimacy. I learned this from the accident. Likewise, I would never have known that the eagles were there for me if I had not been there for them.

We have many choices in life. When we choose in the direction of process, we are moving toward our spiritual reality.

When we make a reality shift, often the one that occurs is *a shift into an awareness and experience of process*. A serious illness or accident is not healed or dealt with in an instant. Recovery itself is a long, arduous process, as are the relearning and adjustments that need to be made to survive, live, and continue. One cannot push the process of healing and adjustment. There are various tools that can help, <u>and</u> basically, illness and accidents throw us into a process reality in which we can participate because it's not a situation we can ultimately deny or control.

Michael was a well-established and healthy contractor who experienced a major reality shift.

One day at work Michael was shot by a disgruntled employee, which resulted in his becoming a paraplegic and being confined to a wheelchair. Obviously, his life changed dramatically. Yet, the biggest change was within Michael. Suddenly, he saw how tenuous and precious life is. He moved from being a kingpin, in his own eyes, to being a vulnerable human being. He moved from being the master of his domain to a person fighting for his life.

In time, Michael emerged a much more humble man who had a clearer concept of his place in the scheme of things and an awareness of what is ultimately important. He shifted from a taker to a giver and is working for environmentally friendly and safe construction. His reality shifted from the material world as the center of his universe to a wholeness involving his spirituality. Through the *process* of his accident he learned about the sacredness of all life. He became aware of and tuned in to the process of the planet and how he could contribute to its healing instead of its depletion.

Why do people see these unfortunate experiences as so positive? Because often they are what it takes for us to *experience* the shift from a static, death-producing perception of reality to a living process *experience* of reality. The illnesses and the accidents are not fun. Yet, they can force us into an internal paradigm shift that we might not otherwise make. These experiences return us to a knowing that *all is process* and give us a powerful glimpse into the true spiritual base of our life.

That which seemed a tragedy becomes a salvation for many. Salvation through crisis often comes in many religious and spiritual forms. The key component is that it plunges us back into participating in the process of our existence.

We often are astonished by the implications and the reactions of persons who have had these serious experiences, and our mind boggles at the shifts we sense. Sometimes, we have to experience something that drastic to get us back to our true reality and our birthright. So often, we have to be catapulted into tragedy or pain in order to experience process.

Unfortunately, not everyone uses a crisis to make reality shifts. Sadly, some use it to retreat further into their illusion of control, removing themselves further and further from their spirituality.

When we try to deal with these experiences in their same old linear, static way, sadly nothing changes.

I knew a woman who was diagnosed with breast cancer. She chose not to use the illness as a chance to shift her reality into a deeper spirituality and understanding of process. When she was told of the cancer, she shifted deeper into her attempt to control.

"Cut the sucker off," she said. "I can control this. I can beat this."

Instead of moving into a greater appreciation of her spirituality and participating with her cancer to learn what she needed to learn and to heal together, she decided that she could control the illness, her life, and her world. She became increasingly bitter and angry as the process progressed. She did not see the cancer as an opportunity for an internal reality shift. When we react to crises with control, we are not able to tap in to our living process. Fear often produces the illusion of control. However, when we walk through our fear, any crisis, no matter how frightening, can result in growth and healing at many levels.

IMPLICATIONS

We are experiencing a societal crisis in the perception of reality.

Process is the very essence of existence. The implications of a generation or generations who have no concept of or no working relationship with process are far-reaching indeed. We are moving into a two-dimensional world that more and more resembles a virtual reality without depth or meaning.

When we lose the perception of process, of the unfolding ongoingness of all, we lose identity, orientation, awareness, and meaning. We lose our place in an ongoing universe. The existential emptiness and isolation that we feel is directly related to the void we have created by our absence of the awareness of process. Our estrangement from nature has caused us to see nature as a thing, as separate from us. Thus, we feel free to exploit and use up its resources in our worship of the material. This belief in the material as the only reality has required us to remove ourselves from ourselves and made the self an object to be observed. We see the self as static or fixed, as something to be analyzed, studied, and understood as separate from who we are. We no longer participate in the active unfolding of the self.

What we have done to ourselves, we have done even more to others and the world around us. Western psychology, basing itself on mechanistic science, has no real concept of the person as a process nor does it really believe that people change. In such a static universe there is no place for the ongoingness of the process of existence and being.

If we also believe that we are living in the "information age," which perpetuates a belief that all important information can be imparted as "facts," it's easy to see that we have developed a two-dimensional world devoid of a way of connecting to that most important human experience, the *process* of our lives and the process of the world around us.

In spite of the endless time and money many of us have spent in psychotherapy, unless we truly *feel* the implications of a reality devoid of process in our day-to-day living, and the decisions we make in the course of that living, we will never see the depths of our situation. I'd like to use a current community issue to illustrate the void of knowledge about process and the far-reaching implications of that void.

I live part of my year in Hawaii. For many years we have been having a major conflict over what we call the "boating issue." This issue has become the symbol for many subtle problems that face the island and is, for me, a microcosm of concerns around the planet.

We have a beautiful part of the island called the Na Pali (cliffs). There are magnificent hills, valleys, waterfalls, pristine beaches, and pure nature. The Na Pali is known to be a sacred place by all who view it. The only ways into this area are hiking (arduous and by permit only), helicopter, and boat. Mostly, the helicopters and boats are used to "view" it, not take you into it.

When I first came to this island, there were a few boat tours that went down by the Na Pali. When we took one, we could see whales and dolphins coming and going, and frequently the spinner dolphins would swim along with the boat for miles! We could view and feel some connection with a beautiful pristine land. Then, greed set in.

More and more boat companies got in on the act. Those who were making a good living started wanting to get rich. They added more and more boats to their fleet. Soon there were hundreds of trips a day going out. Most of the boats were leaving from the mouth of a river convenient to this area. There began to be a "parking problem" for the cars of all the tourists who were taking the boat trips. This was followed by a problem about where to store the boats. Something that was good was becoming bad. Few people were completely opposed to boat trips. Yet the situation had become divisive, polarized, and destructive.

This area of the island is one where there is a concentration of native Hawaiians. Along with the pristine breathtaking beauty, it is their presence and their spirit of aloha that make this part of the island so special. The Hawaiians accept and interact with Western culture, yet many do not have the financial resources that some of their "rich" neighbors who have "bought a piece of paradise" have. Although they are living on ancestral lands, gathering the money for increasingly high property taxes can almost bankrupt some of the Hawaiian families, forcing them to have to consider selling land (their 'aina) that has been in their families for generations. For many, hunting and fishing are a sheer necessity to keep food on the table and nourish their families. For all native Hawaiians, fishing and hunting signify a relationship with the process of nature, the land, and the water, and the sacredness of a lifestyle of participating with nature that they hold essential to their identity and being. They need the food to eat. And they need to care for and have a relationship with the land and the water in order to be.

It is important to remember here that although their monarchy was illegally overthrown by the United States—a fact that has been admitted by the president and the Congress of the United States—the people who are native to these islands have always welcomed intruders with "Aloha." In fact, it has been said by the Hawaiians that the reason they are on this planet is to bring aloha—the loving breath of God—to this planet. Like many native people the world over, they see everyone as "brother and sister," and part of the overall *process* of God and creation and therefore to be welcomed as one's own. With most native people, the interconnectedness of all things in the *process* of the universe is understood. Therefore, their *process* of meeting is initially to assume similarities. It has taken a long time for these local, loving people to be pushed to a point where they will "stand up and be heard."

Probably one of the greatest mistakes they have made is to believe *that Westerners are like them and know about process.* When I have discussed with some of them the issue that some people simply do not understand process, they have been incredulous with this void of knowing. This reaction was similar to their reaction when I talked with them about the void in Western culture in the knowledge of the treatment of elders. I want to detour for a moment and use this story to illustrate the depth of the chasm between a process culture and a content culture.

Every three years the international network of Living in Process has a meeting at our center at Peace Valley Hot Springs in Boulder, Montana. At the meeting in 1995, we were blessed to have native elders from throughout the world as our guests. I was appalled to see how these elders were being treated by what I considered a fairly enlightened group. People seemed "unaware" of them in the dining room, halls, and in the meeting room. They would get in front of them in the food lines, they were not alert to their needs (i.e., helping them carry things), or they rushed to get the best seats in the meeting room not holding back for the elders to choose. I could not believe my eyes.

In our group meeting, I came roaring into the group hopping mad about their behavior. I lit into them with a vengeance; being Irish and American Indian gives me an interesting combination of traits! I looked up and suddenly noticed that many people in the group were crying. I stopped in my tracks. "What's going on?" I asked, completely surprised with the reaction.

"We don't know how to treat elders," they said. "Will you please teach us?"

I was completely taken aback. We began a training period of how to treat elders. These well-educated, successful, and competent citizens of the United States, Canada, and Europe did not know how to relate to elders!

When I told my Hawaiian friends how the group had treated the elders, horror, anger, and disbelief were expressed. Then, when I shared that the group had cried and said that they didn't know how to behave and could I please teach them, my Hawaiian friends were completely incredulous. They couldn't believe it. Then *they* began to cry.

"We always thought that white people *knew* how to behave and just refused to do it," they said. "We never even thought of the possibility that they didn't know how! *We must pray for them!*" they said, with tears running down their cheeks.

The astonishment over Westerners not knowing about process has elicited an identical response from the Hawaiians.

In the boating issue, the Hawaiians began to take a stand when the fish started disappearing, the waters became polluted, and the sacred places were being desecrated.

The river mouth where the boats docked and loaded and unloaded passengers was filled with oil slicks, noise, and confusion. This river mouth was an estuary where many fish returned, spawned, and laid their eggs. The fish are gone. The boaters cried for "scientific proof."

Even the fish offshore were leaving. As one old fisherman put it, "We are making too much noise with so many boats running over their homes. They left." The boaters still wanted scientific proof and continued to increase the number of boats and trips. The boaters and businesspeople on the island seem to believe that tourism and money are the *only* legitimate issues (a materialistic orientation). They cannot understand the Hawaiian "problem." "Can't the Hawaiians see that *everyone* benefits from the expansion of business?" they ask. "They simply aren't being 'realistic.'" Their short-term bottom line was jobs and the economy.

The Hawaiians accept the need for business. They live in and have to understand the Western culture. <u>And</u>, they have a different perspective of "reality." Theirs is a process reality. They know both realities, and in knowing both realities they recognize that there is more than one perception of reality. Their perception is based upon an awareness of *process*, and they value their perception.

They recognize that tourists come to these islands because of the beauty of the Hawaiian people and their culture and the beauty of the *'aina*—the land. They also recognize that the people and the land cannot be separated. The concept of *'aina* is more than a piece of real estate to be owned and controlled. The *'aina* is a living, moving, evolving process that is interactive with the people. Both processes need one another. One cannot live fully without the other. Although many understand that the land is more complete without people than people are without the land, more importantly, together, as their processes interact in a loving positive way, both are whole. The Hawaiians cannot understand why a people would want to destroy that which gives them wholeness.

Because they come from a process orientation, the Hawaiians see that the greed for money and financial gain is a destructive process that will actually destroy that which is the source of the money. If the rivers are polluted, the fish leave, the coral reefs die, the caves and the shorelines are destroyed, then that which has been an incentive for coming here will disappear, as well as a way of life and a living land. When one has a *process* perspective, thinks in terms of life and all things being a process, and thinks of the future generations as part of their process, it is easy to see the confusion in those who do not know about processes and cannot see or understand process. The reality and the undeniability that *all is process* is so palpable and real that the Hawaiians have never even considered the possibility that there are a people who do not know about and respect process. Their shock and astonishment about this lack is even greater than their consternation and disbelief that there could be a people who do not know about how one treats elders!

A culture that believes in stasis and is based on the material puts its emphasis on the immediate and the quick fix. The material is the only thing that's important. Money and economics are the bottom line.

It is no wonder that these two cultures don't seem to be able to listen to one another or respect one another. One is willing to destroy all that is precious to the other for money and has no point of reference for the power of process. The other cannot imagine a culture that is not based in process. Is it any wonder that communication has broken down? Is it any wonder that anger is building and violence ripples just under the surface?

We are not static. The planet is not static. Life is not static. Life is an unfolding. Regardless of how we would like to think that we can even predict its course, time and again we have seen that we cannot. We can participate. That is all. We cannot predict or control.

We never know where our behavior will lead. As we participate in process, the process changes. As we participate in life, life changes, often in totally unpredictable and more creative ways than we could ever imagine. We can participate, we cannot control. The key to living life is learning to participate in the process of it.

The implications of not knowing about and honoring process are devastating, and we are seeing that devastation around the planet. The "boating issue" is a global issue. It is an issue that is asserting itself in some form or other throughout the planet. The content may be different and the actors different, and the issues are the same. There is an ignorance about process. Ultimately, the most devastating aspect of not relating to process is a loss of our spiritual connection to reality. Spirituality, in the final essence, is a process. Facts will never communicate reality of spirituality. When we try to relate to spirituality only from a content perspective, the pseudospirituality that evolves is a rigid, nonliving, controlling, and arrogant shell. Without a working concept of and relationship to process, full spirituality cannot exist. We cannot underestimate the power of God or the force of the universe, and we certainly make it difficult for these forces to connect with us, by believing we live in a static universe.

> *By insisting on a static, materialistic world, we have put ourselves on a collision course with life.*

When we do not know about or relate to process, we live in a very small, dark corner of life's possibilities. In our desire to control we only build prisons for ourselves. Every aspect of ourselves and the world around us is in process. When we participate, though, we become a part of the All. Wisdom is an awareness and knowledge of process. We can get information about facts and things electronically, <u>and</u> we have to participate to gain wisdom.

The implications of process ignorance are far-reaching indeed. We are looking at slavery of the soul and isolation of the spirit in a world viewed only from a static, materialistic perspective. So many of the attempts to make major changes in the world, though well intentioned, are failing. Those concerned about the environmental crisis will never succeed in delivering their message to a people who have no working relationship with process. Often, those who are trying to bring these changes about are themselves unaware of process, or unaware of this lack of process understanding in those they hope will change. Until the issue of ignorance of process brought about by Western mechanistic culture has been healed, little can change.

Hopefully, this exploration of what process is will open the way for you to learn about Living in Process. It is a way to welcome you back to participation in your life and reality.

Chapter 3

RETURNING TO SPIRITUAL WHOLENESS

The certainty to the Maori, is that Tane, the giver of life, has given life to all people and to all things, and following upon this gift of life, all activities performed by people will be subject to spiritual influences.

Hiwi Tauroa, Maori writer

We are spiritual beings trying to be human, not human beings trying to be spiritual.

Spirituality is that movement within ourselves that calls us to become greater than ourselves. It is our wholeness that connects us with All That Is.

Spirituality is not separate from or compartmentalized in life. It is life. All of life is spiritual.

S pirituality is so key to human existence that I want to deal with it early and up front. However, I do not in any way want to indicate that it can be separated out from any aspect of living. It can't. Yet, because it has become so isolated from our daily lives, I want to confront this issue, hopefully integrating it into all that follows.

Some time ago, I became aware of great numbers of people rushing here and rushing there trying to find spirituality. There was a flocking to Eastern religions such as Buddhism, Hinduism, and Taoism as the emptiness grew exponentially inside those in Western culture when the established Western religions no longer seemed to meet their needs. Individuals sought gurus from India and other parts of the world, and learned the lotus position, meditating for hours on end hoping to find that which seemed just out of reach. Many sought out native shamans and native ways, hoping to find a path of reconnection.

Unfortunately, with our solid indoctrination in the scientific method, we approached these various spiritual truths in a controlling mechanistic way, gained some relief, perhaps, yet rarely found the awakening we were seeking. All too often, seekers simply adopted rituals and ceremonies, hoping that the rituals themselves would transport them beyond themselves. There are many powerful rituals and ceremonies, <u>and</u> they are most meaningful when embedded in the cultural life out of which they have evolved. However, using all-day chants, pipe ceremonies, sweat lodges, or fire ceremonies in the absence of the rich cultural heritage and spiritual tradition in which these ceremonies were created is like trying to take a fifty-gram vitamin C tablet for AIDS. There may be some help, yet when the healing is not embedded in a credible context, it often loses its essence of what is most necessary for it to be effective. *We cannot heal a process problem out of control with a mechanistic cure.* More is needed, much more.

Suppose we see the present confusion as a gift to move us to a new level of spiritual living. We have needed a spirituality that comes out of this land of ours that has become the melting pot of the world. We American Indians have a profound spirituality that is at one with this land, and its roots probe down deep into the body of the Earth, our Mother, being nurtured and fed by all that is here and being one with her. All who have come here, from the early ones to those who came later, have fed this land with themselves and their ancestors. All have contributed what they had to contribute and have taken from this land. The time has come to focus on spiritual wisdom from this coming together and let our roots intertwine into new growth.

A friend of mine told me that someone asked an American Indian elder why the white people came and why they let them come—since the Indians far outnumbered the early settlers and did, indeed, welcome them; the natives here were not "conquered." The old woman answered, "Because they needed us!" Maybe the people of this land are ready to learn why what she said is true.

Perhaps as a planet, we are ready to become more holographic and one with all of creation, and this melting pot is evolving a way to the infinite that will lead us to the truths we know and beyond to new contexts of spirituality.

I remember a story that I had been told by a dear friend, Don Coyhis, a Mohican writer and consultant, who is pleased that I share it:

Long, long ago before anyone remembers, people lived in complete harmony with themselves, each other, all the animals, birds, fish, crawling creatures, all the planet, and the Great Mystery of the all. This was a time of easy blissful living, and life was happy and serene.

As time went on, the humans began to forget what they knew. They gradually became selfish and self-centered and started to believe that they were above creation and better than the rest of creation. They pulled themselves out of the oneness, and established hierarchy, not only setting themselves apart, they set themselves above.

During these times, there were elders in the tribe

who had been given the responsibility of keeping and protecting the wisdom of the tribe. Because they were so wise and were so old, they had the perspective to see what had been and what was happening, and they became greatly concerned. They called a meeting of all the elders who were responsible for the wisdom of the tribe and spent many long days and nights discussing what they should do.

"The people are becoming like children," one said. "They are selfish and self-centered. They only think of themselves and abuse what the Creator has given them."

"They abuse our Mother, the Earth, and do not recognize that everything that we have, our food, our clothing, our shelter comes from her," another added.

"They have forgotten that they are spiritual beings and all is spiritual," confided another, and they talked long days and long nights.

At last, the elders decided that the people had become so lost and their minds and hearts so distorted that they could no longer be trusted with the spiritual wisdom that had sustained the people for so long. Since they were the guardians of the wisdom, they were determined that it would not be abused, and vowed to protect it at all costs. Therefore, the elders decided to gather up all the wisdom and tie it in a big bundle and hide it.

"Where shall we hide it so that they won't find it until they are ready?" an old woman asked. "We must pray and think on this." They all agreed. Again, they devoted several days and nights fasting and praying about their next steps.

When they sat down together, the old elder asked, "Have we come upon a solution?"

"I know," said one. "There is a tall mountain far off in the forest and within that mountain there is a deep hidden cave that no one knows about. Let us take this bundle of wisdom, dig a big hole far back in the cave, and bury it deep underground. They'll never find it there."

The elders sat silent for a while and pondered this possibility.

"They are tricky, these people. They are always snooping around and looking into everything. Sooner or later they are sure to find the cave and they will start digging around and find it."

Slowly, they let this information sink in, and then sadly, they all agreed. "You're right! They do go everywhere and get into everything."

Saddened, they sat a while longer.

"I know!" said another. "I know a very, very deep lake. We do not even know the bottom. Let's wrap it up very carefully and sink it way, way down in the lake. They'll never find it there."

Initially, the elders felt hopeful with this solution as they were weary and wanted to know what to do. Yet, they also knew that this was a grave matter and they had an important responsibility. Slowly, each came to know that the lake was not an answer.

"No, they like to fish. Sooner or later someone would hook it and pull it up. We can't do that," one said.

Again, the elders sat motionless for what seemed like an eternity.

Then, very slowly, an old woman elder, the oldest among them, spoke. "I know what we must do," she said carefully, speaking with wisdom and authority.

"We will hide it inside of them. They'll never look there."
And they all knew . . . they had their answer.

Don Coyhis

And so it is. Perhaps, in this melting pot of a land, we have come together to find the ancient truths that move us beyond what we have known in our separateness and open the ways for planetary healing that encompass all that has gone before. Out of our brokenness and our dysfunctional society, truths are emerging that can build on all truth and heal us. This wisdom emerges new and timely while weaving together the threads of ancient wisdom that have been gathered here from throughout the world, and it is all inside of us waiting to be rediscovered.

For many years I have said that the Living in Process work goes back long before rituals and ceremony existed. Clearly, humans created rituals and ceremony when they began to feel separate from the Great Mystery, when they left the oneness, when they began to isolate, create hierarchies, and leave their participation with the Creator—Great Mystery—holomovement—God. Rituals and ceremonies are ways to try to recapture what we felt and know we had back in our archaic memories. Periodically they work—often enough to support our illusion that they *will* work for us and to keep us focusing for solutions (techniques, practices, rituals) outside ourselves. Perhaps they, too, are "fixes" that keep us from delving into our depths. Thus, they keep us away from the constant source of wealth that we carry inside—the knowing that is our birthright. The truth is in and through our inner beings. We have only to go there.

Spirituality is participation.

Spirituality is dealing with my life.

We need visionary leaders who are spiritually functional.

Returning to Spiritual Wholeness

SCIENCE AND LIVING IN PROCESS

To comprehend our separation from our spirituality we need to look at how mechanistic science and technology cannot meet the most basic needs of the creation of which we're a part. Even though postmodern philosophy may have changed the content of science, its processes have remained firmly embedded in the old mechanistic paradigm. For example, some more "enlightened" physicians may use herbs, visualization, or acupuncture, yet still apply it mechanistically.

We would be unwise to underestimate the strength and the power of the mechanistic paradigm on our daily living. We have come to believe that money and material objects are the only true reality as seen and measured "objectively" through the senses. We have set up a world that does not recognize internal reality, or realities that cannot be seen and measured.

What follows is a brief discussion of the role Western science plays in our perception of reality. I hope it will help us become clearer about the power of the scientific model on our day-to-day living, and how important it is for us to open ourselves to other models.

In dealing with the way things are, it's important to remember that each of us has our own sense of reality. Things happen to us, and we evaluate and interpret them according to our own mind-set. This, then, is our personal reality. It does not have to be verified by observable "facts." It can, at the same time, be true for us and not be a true, verifiable fact for others.

For example, psychology and law get themselves into trouble by believing everything a "victim" says is true. The goal then becomes punishing the supposed perpetrator. This completely takes our attention away from the individual and what that person *needs to do* to heal from the experience. For healing, the issue is not to focus upon the supposed perpetrator. The real issue is to pay attention to the felt experience, so that each person can own the experience as part of their life process, and to do their healing work. Both parties have to be responsible for their actions. When the focus is healing and bringing back balance, the victim-perpetrator dualism vanishes.

The interpretation that we put on an experience is colored by the available information. We may pull this information out of our past, out of the All That Is, out of what is present in our DNA (possible past lives, intergenerational experiences, our genetic makeup, or whatever we tap into at the time). To believe that our perceptions are based only on what can be observed, measured, and verified is unbelievably naive. When we limit ourselves to phenomena that are easily observable and see them as the "facts," we're attempting to simplify and reduce our world into a very narrow band of understanding. When we simplify in this way, we have to come up with tricks and distortions to "prove" what is "right and wrong." However, it is possible to support and validate the reality of the individual without having to make that reality an objective, operationally defined, verifiable reality.

Mechanistic science depends upon establishing an objective, empirically defined, verifiable reality. Mechanistic science demands one, true reality—a clear-cut reality on which everyone can agree and that will be true for everyone. There is no place in this scientific worldview for differing realities, clashing realities, parallel realities, or unrelated realities.

When we open ourselves to the possibility that other forces and other influences can enter our lives from different levels and different aspects of the holomovement, we realize that these influences occur and may have nothing to do with what is observable and verifiably "real."

A focus on the external means that anything and everything outside ourselves becomes more important than it might otherwise be. In fact, this worldview sets us up to blame what we feel, think, and experience on anything and everything outside ourselves. In so doing, we become disempowered.

We've come to understand that one of the major issues of dysfunction is to blame others for what happens to us in our lives. When we're not spiritually healthy, we don't want to take responsibility for our lives. We look for somebody, anybody, to blame for our feelings, or our inability to take charge of our lives or to live our lives. As long as we can focus outside ourselves, we don't have to deal with ourselves, our feelings, and our lives. As long as we focus outside ourselves, we give up our personal power and our ability to heal. To be spiritually healthy means taking responsibility for ourselves.

I think it's important to see how these two issues interrelate and feed into one another. Looking for and only believing in an external, verifiable reality, and focusing on others and trying to make them responsible for our lives continually takes us outside of ourselves. These approaches result in our getting progressively out of touch with our reality and refusing to trust it. As we lose touch with our reality, we need some reality to link up with and to trust and we start looking outside ourselves. It's an easy step after that to give up our personal power, make others responsible for our lives, and then to blame them for whatever "goes wrong." The more we do this, the more we abandon our own reality, and the further and further we get from it, ourselves, and our spirituality. This circular process feeds on itself and is fed in turn by the psychological and scientific beliefs of our time.

In modern psychology, which is based on mechanistic science, there essentially *is* no internal reality. Any internal reality that emerges is suspect and not believed. And since most psychologists do not believe in an internal reality that may not be verifiable, they tend then to try to make people's internal reality into an external reality and therefore objectively verifiable as in the previous example of focusing on and believing in the perpetrator and victim as real. This results in some psychotherapists being gullible about what their clients tell them. Since they don't know the difference between internal and external realities, they try to make internal realities objective. Internal realities cannot necessarily be objective, <u>and</u> they can still be real.

A lawyer recently told me he thinks that this issue of realities will be the demise of psychology because practitioners are going to be sued more and more often for believing that one person's internal reality is another person's internal reality. For example, if a woman says she was molested as a child by her father, that's her internal reality. However, this may not be the objective reality, so if the professional swears in court that this person was raped by her father, the professional is then at risk to be sued by the father. We have a clash of internal and external realities. There are many internal realities, and yet, we act as if there were none. No wonder we're confused about reality.

Combine this issue with a culture that teaches us that there is no internal reality and that everything in our lives should be externalized, and it's no wonder we become victims, blame others for our lives and our nonlives, and get so out of touch with our own realities that we see materialism as the only reality and therefore our salvation.

When we accept a belief system—and science is a belief system—that tells us that there is only one, true reality, we are limited and handicapped in trying to deal with a Creation that has many separate and interconnected realities operating at the same time. Mechanistic science is by definition reductionistic. In its attempt to "understand" through the senses, it has had to try to reduce complexity to oversimplification and process to stasis. This creates an illusionary world or virtual reality, and that has little or nothing to do with the complexity of the process of the reality of creation as we know, experience, and participate in it.

How much we have limited ourselves and our ability to perceive reality becomes even more obvious when we explore healing and wholeness.

If we're looking for healing and spiritual wholeness, mechanistic science cannot get us there. We can get "patched up," we can get relief—for a while—and we can adjust to a world with a high tolerance for insanity—for a while. We will not find healing and spiritual wholeness when we and all reality are conceptualized as a machine.

Living in Process is in keeping with many of the "new" discoveries of contemporary physics. And, we are discovering that all these "new" discoveries are part of the ancient lore of native people and are buried deep inside of us in our own process.

> How much we miss when we don't know the presence of the unseen.
>
> *Nani, Hawaiian Kapuna*

As my mother said to me when I was a very young girl:

> Remember, Elizabeth Anne, it isn't only what you can see that's important. Sometimes it's the unseen that makes the seen worth living.
>
> *Manilla Maude Longan*

What she told me when I was a child has more and more meaning for me.

As Ken Wilber said in *The Holographic Paradigm and Other Paradoxes,* "In the implicit frequency realm, all things and events are spacelessly, timelessly, intrinsically one and individual."

The reality about which Wilber speaks is easy to grasp experientially as we do our deep-process work and find ourselves completely present in two or more realities at the same time. We can also grasp this awareness when we truly Live in Process. Being totally present in the now and living our process allows all time and space to enter into us. Trying to live in the virtual reality created by a mechanistic science only fragments us and encourages us to attempt to make all processes static.

> Centuries ago, you white folks decided to go the way of science and technology. They will destroy the planet. We hope you discover this before it's too late.
>
> *Australian Aboriginal elder*

Living in Process

Living in Process is a way of living and a spiritual path. It supports and sustains a person's spiritual path no matter what that path or practice may be. Living in Process recognizes that everyone has and *is* a living process. When we follow our living process, the ancient truths will come to us un-clouded by religious beliefs that are, though often divinely inspired, finally the inventions and interpretations of human beings. Living in Process returns us to the knowing that we had when we fully participated in the oneness of creation.

Doing this work leads us into deeper and deeper levels of connection with the ground of our being. Those who practice it find that it is a practical and easy way that functions similarly to deep meditation and moves us beyond what we have believed is possible. When we trust our deepening levels of awareness, we find we come to knowing and healing at often untouched levels of our being.

Living in Process is about spiritual remembering. Living in Process is about shedding old destructive patterns, beliefs, and behaviors. When we live fully spiritually, physically, emotionally, and mentally in harmony with ourselves, others, and the planet, we are Living in Process.

Living in Process is a deep spiritual commitment of being at one with one's life. This spirituality does not take us out of our life or ask us to rise above it. Rather it plunges us more fully into life and asks us to participate, while recognizing that our primary relationship is and always will be our relationship with all process.

Remember, God is a process. My process is God.
God is more than my process.

To live in process we must encompass all that is. Judgmentalism, provincialism, and rigidity remove us from the wholeness of all life and thus interfere with our spirituality. Being one with nature helps us to deal with the illusory virtual reality of our technological world and helps us experience our process.

When we are living our process, there is no we-they, me-you. We do not have the need to judge, separate, or be holier-than-thou or know "the only true way" when we are Living in Process. Who is to say that a blade of grass is less spiritual than we are? When we deny the sacredness of the land or of anything, we deny it in ourselves.

Many Westerners are uncomfortable with the meditation techniques of the East. Perhaps there is a reason for that. Many of us seem to prefer active meditation to passive meditation; we meditate while washing the car, cleaning the stove, or walking in the woods. There is no one way to meditate. The heart of meditation is to allow ourselves to move beyond ourselves. When we live our process, all of life is an active meditation.

In the West, our mechanistic, antiprocess science has wanted and even demanded that God be solid, static, and stable. When we are Living in Process, we may ask ourselves questions like, What if God is the void? Can we accept the process of the void? Perhaps we have become so outer directed that we are losing the ability to experience God, whatever our definition is. We have reached a point where we can relate to something or someone only if we can touch it and bounce off it. Going into our own process often means entering the void.

Living in Process is a sacred trust. It teaches us that no matter what is going on within us, everything is all right. When we honestly own where we are or what is going on inside of us, we can move on. Happiness and freedom are not only possible, they are our birthright. We are in the hands of our Creator, and those hands sustain us.

Our stopped and blocked processes are the real enemies
of peace. I feel that my place in the peace movement is

centering more and more on helping people find their core of living wisdom within.

Diane

The wisdom of the world is available to us and within us. We must remember our noble potential. We have choices and we are responsible for the choices we make. Life is an opportunity to move us toward nobility of being and spirit. We need to focus on what we know deep inside and what is possible.

Living in Process is about the common, everyday living of our spirituality no matter where we are or what we are doing.

BRIDGING THE BODY–MIND–SPIRIT SPLIT

In order to approach spiritual maturity and develop and support our spiritual growth, we have to bridge the mind-body split that is so entrenched in our society. We have separated body from mind and spirit, and have progressively learned to ignore the wisdom of our bodies. We have cut ourselves off from the vast stores of information in our bodies and lost the balance of the whole of our beings.

Our minds are extraordinary and can participate in marvelous processes, <u>and</u> when they are not balanced with our bodies and our spirits, they can become insane tyrants feeding on their own thought processes.

Charles for some reason decides that his wife is upset with him. He then starts searching around for what he could have done to upset her, and as the day goes on, his list grows. By evening, he is angry with her for being "angry" with him!

His mind has gone off by itself and become discon-

70

nected from his body and spirit. He has stopped *feeling* his love for his wife in his body. He has left his spiritual knowing; he cannot control what is going on with his wife <u>and</u> if he can return to his center, everything will be all right. He is running around with a disembodied mind gone amok. Many of the difficulties that we make for ourselves can be traced to our disembodied thinking.

When we split our minds and our bodies and our spirits, we create what Morris Berman, author of *The Reenchantment of the World*, calls a "disenchanted world." We lose the magic and the "livingness" of the world. We stop participating in the world around us.

Our bodies have so much information for us. They store memories current and archaic. Our bodies help us remember more than we believe we can remember. Our bodies warn us of danger. They tell us when someone is lying to us or when something is not quite right. The seat of our intuition is in our bodies and a total-body knowing is much, much different from a "head" knowing. We need to have open communication among body, mind, and spirit to Live in Process.

Recently, I was talking with a new friend from Indonesia who wanted to know about the Living in Process work. He was asking me "how you do it." I find this a difficult question to answer in a few sentences over dinner.

I know this man to be a very spiritual man and a very intelligent man. I ventured a guess that he might not be as strong in the area of being in touch with his body and knowing his feelings as he was in other areas.

I shared with him that one of the most important skills for doing the Living in Process work is "noticing."

71

"What do you mean by that?" he said.

"Notice what you're feeling and honor it. Stay with it," I answered.

"What does that mean?" he said.

I could see that I needed to back up a step. Many people are simply not aware of their feelings. They have become so thoroughly disembodied that they literally do not know that they *have* feelings. In modern society, we are encouraged to live in our minds and not in our bodies.

When people don't know their feelings or don't admit that they have them, we have to start at the most basic level—learning what feelings are.

"I know that you love your wife," I said. "You say you do and I believe you do."

"I do," he replied.

"Now, when you say to me that you love your wife, be aware of what you're feeling," I said.

"Nothing," he said.

"Now see if you can remember the time when you looked at her and you felt the feeling of love move through your body," I suggested.

His smile played across his face as his body remembered the feeling of loving his wife.

"Now, that's feeling," I said.

"Our feelings are our friends. Love, anger, sadness, or fear may all be doors into our Living process. Without them, we may not be able to access our inner spirituality," I said.

He understood.

When we split body and mind, or when we split body-mind-spirit, we become imbalanced as human beings.

Living in Process, then, is an action spirituality that evolved from our beings expressing a spirituality that permeates all things. Living in Process evolved out of the present needs of individuals to heal and address the demands of today while reaching back through the eons to a deep, deep knowledge of the spiritual that was planted in the DNA of our ancestors' ancestors. Living in Process is a spiritual living made possible only with full participation in life. All is process. Process is all. Spirituality cannot be separated from the process of the whole.

We can use any number of substances or processes to shut off our feelings, which in turn shuts off our most direct access to our spiritual knowing. When we split our wholeness, we split spiritually.

Chapter 4

BASIC TRUTHS
FOR LIVING
IN PROCESS

The process of my life is what is important. The content is interesting. <u>And</u>, it's the process that needs to be honored.

We are not a thing. We are not a personality. We may have a personality; we are not our personality. When we think of ourselves as personalities, we mentally conceptualize ourselves as a static, unmoving, unchanging given. We then project this tendency onto others and our environment—to control life and to make life static. At some point in our evolution as human beings, we developed the notion that if we could just make ourselves and everything around us stay the same, we would feel safer. Unfortunately, trying to make ourselves and our world static has had just the opposite effect. We have become more and more anxious and more deadened.

It's an insult to the Creator not to be who I am.

Not only are our personalities and psyches evolving along with our spirituality, our bodies, too, are always changing. We treat our bodies like our houses, assuming that some day we will get them exactly the way we want them, and then they'll stay that way forever. When we accept our bodies as ever changing, we have many more options for participating with them and for keeping healthy. However, when we view our houses and our bodies as static—or wish they were—we remove the possibility of participating in the process of being. We feel alienated and isolated.

We are so focused on stasis that we spend much of our energy trying to be "safe." For example, buying insurance, getting vaccinations, making our environment permanent, creating building codes. We try to impose a fixed pattern on everything, finding out as much as we can about a new experience before we do it, so there will be no surprises. When we're trying to static our process, we *hate* surprises! When life does not conform to our attempts at control, we call it chaos. Yet, often, what we perceive as chaos is only the natural unfolding of process—or an unnatural unfolding of the process we have set in motion by being estranged from our spiritual selves. Unfolding does not necessarily follow a set pattern. Unfolding changes directions as new information is discovered.

There is a kindness and a gentleness that develops in the way we treat ourselves when we recognize that we are an evolving, emerging process. We are not necessarily changing because we're sick or bad. We are changing because change is the nature of who we are. We may be getting better or getting worse—<u>and</u> the very nature of life is not to be stagnant. As we begin to perceive ourselves as a process, we see what happens when we turn in on ourselves and shut down. We also see how we blossom when we allow ourselves to expand and evolve into a process being whose options and potentials can be revealed only as the process unfolds. We are a kaleidoscope of possibilities. We may sense some of these possibilities up front. Others may emerge only when we take the next "right" step for ourselves and open to the possibilities as they emerge.

Living in Process

Options are our wealth.

We can never know what all our options are. Options emerge as we move along our path of life. Yet, we will always have options. Part of our responsibility in life is to see that we do have options. We never have only one choice, although it may seem that way at times, and we never have only two choices, again sometimes difficult to see. It is our responsibility to stop, look, pray, and ask for the vision to see our options. Options are our wealth and facilitate our living our process.

God grant me the willingness to allow myself to be changed.

We're tempted to see our relationships like we see our houses or our bodies, as an "it" that we can "work on," "fix up," and get in place so that we can then get on to bigger and better things. We often treat ourselves and our relationships as if they are machines: "just give 'em a little tune-up once in a while and they'll be fine." We tend to forget or want to forget or need to forget that all relationships are themselves processes in which we must participate if they are to live and grow.

It was 1:00 A.M. when I heard a rap on the door and a voice saying that my friend had called and that she was in labor. I had been in a dead sleep and instantly hit the floor running, saying, "She's coming!" I stopped myself, wondering how I knew "she" was a she and then quickly dressed and headed to Colorado Springs in the wee hours of Christmas Eve.

When we arrived, my friend was in the birthing room and all of us—the mother-to-be, a longtime friend of hers, the midwife, the doctor, the nurse, and I—settled into the process at hand. The women there all attended to my friend's birthing process completely. I was astounded at how easily we all became a well-functioning team with the baby and the mother as the center. The midwife and I moved in as a coaching team. There was no ego in the room, all was a living process. There was no competition, no "left-braining" it, no uneasiness. We were all there for the same thing—to support and help the mother and baby.

I loved the way that we all just naturally worked together using knowledge that seemed to come from deep within us. As we kept tuned to the deep-process knowledge within us, we knew what was needed. Clock time lost all meaning. The mother was wonderful! She kept focused on the task at hand and accepted the help and support that was there for her. The whole experience was an affirmation of living our process. All any of us could do was be totally involved in the process of labor and delivery. That involvement required full participation.

There was a point when my friend moved from labor to delivery and the MD told her that she needed to push down. For some reason these directions were not in sync with the process. My friend had, it seemed, mastered labor, and this now was something new. She was not getting strong pushing cues from the baby even though the MD had said that she needed to push. She became confused and then started to question whether she was "doing it right." She lost touch with her process.

For a moment, the ease of the process was broken. The midwife and I quickly moved in and reminded her to trust her body and just do what her body wanted (truly a very deep process) and she moved right back into the process of labor and delivery. Although this was a slight problem, I found it to be a good learning about what happens when we leave the process and get into our heads, thinking instead of participating in our process.

At 6:58 A.M., a beautiful new female being entered the world. She shouted her arrival and wriggled her newness as she was rubbed with warm towels, while lying on her mother's belly. We were all so excited. She immediately nursed when put to the breast, screeched her protest when removed, and clearly pouted, all within twenty minutes of coming into the world. I couldn't help being totally aware of the whole person in that wee little body. We had all participated in a miracle on the eve of miracles.

I learned so much that night. I learned that birthing is the ultimate model for process living. Truly living a process requires all our being, attention, and participation. Clock time ultimately has no meaning at all. Deep living processes are very intense. Thinking can and does stop a process. I drove home knowing that the process is the miracle and the miracle is the living process in which we can all participate.

Living in Process means that each person and each moment is unique in itself while being embedded in the entire process of the All.

Everything around us is a process and is in process. We need only to participate to find out what each process is. Our work, our communities, nature, the planet, the universe are all in process together. Human beings are not above nature. We *are* nature. We have the possibility of being a consciously participating part of nature. We will never break through our feelings of loneliness, estrangement, and isolation until we recognize that we are not separate from nature. We are nature.

We can never save the trees in the rain forest until we realize we are the trees in the rain forest.

When we say, "It is good to be in nature," we may have moved a step away from our isolation <u>and</u> we *still* see ourselves as separate. As human beings, we are part of the natural world. As an old Canadian Indian medicine man says:

> We humans were the last to be created. We are the newcomers here. We have a lot to learn from the other animals. They were here first. They know more. . . . But the rocks— the rocks have been here for a very long time. We need to learn from the rocks.
>
> *George Goodstriker, Kainai (Blackfoot) Elder*

When we recognize that we are nature, we develop a very different picture about the planet and the environment. When we recognize that all things come from the same source and go back to that same source, we see the connectedness of all process. When we see ourselves as participating in all process and recognize our common origins, some troublesome aspects of life disappear.

> We all have the same mother and the same father.
>
> *Phil Lane, Sr., Yankton Lakota Elder*

If we all have the same mother and the same father, then we are all brothers and sisters. How can we look down on, feel superior to, or even kill our brothers and sisters? If we see all races, all people, as participating in the process of life on this planet together, we see the possibility of enriching our knowledge, our wisdom, and our spiritual growth, as we listen and learn from those unlike ourselves.

> You are part of us now. You came to this land of our an-
> cestors and we welcomed you. We knew that you would be
> coming. You have tried to kill us off, but can't. You see you
> are part of us now. For 40,000 years our ancestors have
> been buried in this land. Their blood is in the rivers. Their
> bodies feed the land. You have drunk the water of the
> land. The blood of our ancestors is in you. You have eaten
> the fruit, the vegetables, the meat of the animals who have
> fed off this land. All of those foods have been fed by the
> bodies of our ancestors.
> We are brothers and sisters. We welcome you as family.
> *Reuben Kelly, Australian Koori*

We are a process. We are not things. All beings are processes that have the opportunity to participate with one another. When we know that we are part of a greater whole, and life can only be that way, then hierarchy, domination, exploitation, isolation, and estrangement become meaningless.

We are a process. Our relationships are a process. Our children are a process. Our communities are a process. Our work is a process. Our organizations are a process. Our society is a process. The planet is a process. The universe is a process and all is a process.

Back in 1981, in the last chapter of *Women's Reality*, I raised a question about the essence of what some of us call God. At that time, I could see that what we humans and some of our religions had tried to do was to make "God" static. I believed that needing to believe that something was constant in an ever changing universe was something human beings had done in order to try to feel secure. That's when I began asking, "Would a static Creator create a universe that is ever changing?" It's still a good question.

What if what we call God is also not a thing but a process—a process in which we participate? Are we ready for that experience?

I never cease to be amazed at the profundity and the simplicity of my spiritual experiences. These experiences are often where I know oneness and also experience a deep knowing of process.

I AM THE BANK

One such experience was very mundane and yet very profound.

Some years ago, I lived in Boulder, Colorado. Since I traveled a great deal, I often drove the highway between Boulder and the Denver airport. In fact, I knew this road like the back of my hand. As the road leaves Boulder heading toward Denver there is a small hill to be climbed. When one reaches the top, looking back offers a breathtaking, sweeping view of Boulder, the Flatirons, the front range, and the Boulder Valley.

Further ahead toward Denver, on the right-hand side of the road, there's a small earthen bank. Part of the bank had been removed to build the road, to make the climb more gradual, and to keep the Boulder-to-Denver traffic parallel and level with the traffic going toward Boulder. (We do have the urge to tidy up nature, whenever possible!) I'd passed this small bank many times, noticing it, I suppose, as I neared the top of the hill, yet, never realizing that I had any relationship to it.

On this particular day, I found I had to acknowledge that we were in a process together. The bank had let go, slipped, and was covering a major part of the road. Traffic was backed up, and it looked as though I might miss my plane. My life was being affected by the process of the bank. As I sat there, I realized that the bank had always been in process. I hadn't even noticed. For goodness knows how long, it had been letting go. It didn't just let go all at once. No, each day a little root had dried up here, a rock had shifted there, a piece of dirt had crumbled, a plant had blown away, a drop of rain had penetrated further. For a long time, the bank had been moving toward the process of sliding onto the road.

Waiting there in my car, I realized that we were the same. Both the bank and I were a process. We were the same, and we were different, and we were definitely inter-related. We may have been oblivious to each other's processes, _and_ we both were a process, and we were now in each other's process together. Who could have believed that a falling wall of dirt could have taught me so much about myself and all existence?

When you are ready, come to me. I will take you into nature. Nature can teach you everything you need to learn.

Rolling Thunder, American Indian Shaman

As we begin to see ourselves and our universe as a process, we can experience the oneness that surrounds us, that is with us, and of which we are a part.

I am my process. And I am more than my process. You and your process are more than your process. My process is God and God is more than my process. God is your process, and her process, and his process, and the process of the planet. And the Creator, the Great Mystery, is more than all our processes.

Seeing ourselves as a process, the universe as process, and the Great Mystery as process are simple yet profound experiences. For many of us, the idea of life as process and ourselves as process echoes down the corridors of our being into long-forgotten, rarely visited chambers . . . and yet . . . somehow, down deep, there is a remembering. However, lest we begin to believe that living our process has nothing to do with everyday living, we need to remember that the reality is that living our process *is* everyday living. Let me share a letter from a German man who has been doing this work for some time:

> As for my "Living in Process," I learn more and more that I don't need to make things happen, as (I believed) I did in the past. I used to believe that when I noticed any feeling, I had to get active to make any changes, especially when I felt uncomfortable. I'm learning that this old pattern costs me a lot of energy and that Living in Process is a lot easier. I need only to feel my feelings, to accept my feelings, not to want to change them or have them go away. And then, changes come all alone.
>
> Last fall in Altenmarkt (European training session in Germany) I had a process where I was reminded that sometimes I feel like I am living in two worlds, the world of Living in Process and meetings (Twelve Steps of Alcoholics Anonymous) on the one side, and all of the rest on the other side. I know this feeling especially when I feel uncomfortable in the materialistic world. Then I felt I was living in many worlds. Now I have come to believe that it doesn't matter which world I am in. For me it feels good to

live my life wherever I am, to be on my way. And I know
that life feels easy when I am on my way, and that it feels
heavy when I am in my self-will or trying to control it.

Claus

All is process.

Process is not personal and not impersonal. It just is.

BASIC TRUTHS
FOR LIVING IN PROCESS

Over the years, those of us who have been attempting to live our lives in a
process way have discovered basic truths that have emerged. Knowing these
basic truths makes learning a new way of living easier.

I share these truths in the hope that they will gently lead us all into
new pathways of living and growing.

Please note that these truths are not understood in one day, nor do
we learn to live them easily at times. Each of these truths is itself a developing process. As we grow, learn, and expand, we move into deeper and deeper
levels of awareness and functioning. My experience is that as we do this
work, we continue to develop depths of functioning that we couldn't have
imagined earlier. Most often, I feel as if I have just begun.

Honesty

In order to Live in Process, we have to become honest with ourselves, with others, and with our God.

Honesty is not as easy as it seems. We live in a society that has become enured to dishonesty to a point where some of us are confused about what honesty really is. We expect dishonesty from our public leaders and are not surprised when we get it. Yet, real honesty, at times, seems illusive and out of reach—almost shocking. Many of us may believe that we are honest people, <u>and</u> as we start looking at our ways of being dishonest, we may be horrified.

For example, I had always believed that I was a very honest, straightforward person, and others certainly saw me that way. Then, as I began to do this work, I discovered little dishonesties about myself, like not saying that I was too tired to do something or that I just didn't want to when someone asked me to do something I couldn't or wouldn't do. Sometimes, I would just agree and do it, and be resentful.

Recently, Paul was with a group of visitors who had spent a long day touring Hawaii. On the way home, they talked about going to a movie. Paul was tired and didn't want to go to the movie, <u>and</u> he said nothing. Instead, he became more tired and grumpy. Since he is trying to learn to be honest, he finally spoke up and said that he really didn't want to go to the movie. Everyone said that was okay, and interestingly enough, some others spoke up and said they didn't want to go, while others did.

Later, Paul mentioned how good he felt that he had

spoken up. Indeed, after he had been honest about what he was feeling, his mood shifted and he was comfortable to go or not.

Often when we are honest, our feelings shift.

Paul's example is a simple one and looks easy on the surface, <u>and</u> it isn't. Paul's not accustomed to being in touch with his feelings, so that was difficult for him. In addition, he liked the group, wanted to be with them, and wanted to be accepted by them. Saying what he wanted and didn't want was a risk for him. Still, he felt so much better when he did. Sometimes the honesty required to be honest seems like such a little thing that we convince ourselves that we don't need to bother. These little dishonesties with ourselves are quite costly and they add up.

Back in the 1960s we went through a "being-honest phase" that was interesting and certainly an attempt in the right direction; still it wasn't too helpful. Many of the attempts of honesty back then were "honestly" telling someone what was wrong with *them*. We have now learned that honesty begins and ends with ourselves. We need to keep the focus on our own honesty and let others take care of themselves. Actually, cleaning up our own act usually proves to be more than enough for most of us.

In order for me to be honest, I have to be in touch with myself and my feelings. I have to know what's going on with me. I have to be in contact with my internal information system.

Also, when we are learning honesty, we need to learn to be honest in all our affairs. We can't cheat on taxes and use the excuse, "because everyone does it!" We need to return too much change given accidentally. We need to admit that we creased the car in the parking lot. We need to clean up our act. We also need to be gentle with ourselves, and realize that honesty is a growing, ongoing process that will grow and change as we do.

As we begin to be more and more honest about little things, we discover subtler and often more important areas where we have been less than honest. And, even when we find this budding honesty difficult at times, we begin to feel better and better about ourselves. We are giving ourselves the gift of self-esteem. We begin to realize that not being honest, or trying to "get away with something" is much too costly. We find ourselves being honest about the strangest things, not to stay out of trouble or to please others; we are being honest because not to do so would damage our soul. Spiritual living is not possible without rigorous honesty. We come to a place where nothing is worth our integrity, and we live out of our integrity happily and serenely.

As we start on this path of honesty, like all processes, we do not know where it will lead us, <u>and</u> if we are committed to the path we will never be disappointed. We also discover that keeping ourselves honest leaves us little or no time to focus on the honesty of others. They will have to see to that themselves. We do learn, however, to be less supportive of the dishonesty of others.

Noticing

To Live in Process we must notice ourselves and our environment and ourselves in our environment.

Noticing, being in touch with our bodies, feelings, and knowings, and learning to trust our perceptions are necessary for Living in Process.

Some may call noticing, *awareness*. Noticing is more active than awareness. We need to notice how we feel. We need to notice what is comfortable, and what is uncomfortable. We need to notice when deep feelings are coming up and honor them. We need to notice that everything we do and that everything that happens to us happens in context, that we are surrounded by other people who also have a process, and also by plants, animals, and a planet that also have processes.

Noticing is the absolute baseline for Living in Process. We cannot grow and change unless we are able to notice. There is no possibility of change unless and until we can admit where we are. We don't need to figure out and understand what is going on for us. Figuring out and understanding are not noticing. They come from the part of our awareness that is easily manipulated and controlled by the illusions around us, ultimately doing us no good at all. Our healing level of knowing, accessed through our body, takes us to levels of knowing that can never be reached through our rational mind. Often, what we need to do is "wait with" for this deep knowing to emerge.

Around every corner is the opportunity to notice. We can notice those little connections that make life alive. Sometimes all we have to do to experience abundance is to notice.

Basic Truths for Living in Process

A GARDEN OF NOTICING

Our daily activities have so much to teach us about noticing. I learned such a great process lesson while cleaning up my yard in Hawaii.

Having a yard in Hawaii essentially means hacking back the jungle. In the islands, the lovely philodendrons that we so carefully nurture and tend on the mainland can develop leaves almost three feet across and can climb and completely suffocate a tree.

The yard often becomes a raging jungle between our visits. Added to that, I have great difficulty hacking, hewing, pruning, and killing plants, and it is a difficult situation at best.

I have seen various approaches to yard work over the years: my overly cautious approach; a friend's ex-lumberman's approach (hack, stomp, chop); another friend's cutback approach (just cut everything back); the Hawaiian "haircut" approach (prune everything to within an inch of its life); and my son's Swiss-German friend's approach (strip away everything so the ground is *neat* and *clean*).

As I stayed with myself and what was comfortable for me and what seemed respectful of the plants (weeds and all), I learned some very important lessons about Living in Process.

One of the ways I "arrive" in Hawaii is to get the house and yard in shape. The weeds between the house and the river have usually grown so thick that we can hardly hear the river. Since there is little more than weeds in that area of the yard, the "haircut" or the hacking and hewing method seems okay. I let one of the hackers and hewers do that part. On the other side of the house, however, the garden is a different story. It has been planted in pink ginger, salmon ginger, red ginger, spider lily, several varieties of haleconia, tree ferns, orchids, you name it; it's clearly not an area for hacking and hewing. When we first arrive, it always looks like the only possibility might be the haircut method, yet that approach doesn't make sense with all the lovely plants in the garden. Orchids, for example, don't do well when cut back.

So, I picked one small area and I just stood there and looked at it to see what I could see. It's amazing what one can see by just looking and not just plunging in. As I stood there noticing, I began to spot some weeds that were choking the garden. I have a special fondness for weeds—seeing myself more as a weed than a hothouse flower—so I wanted to move respectfully.

Then, after careful consideration, I began to pull some of the plants that I was sure were weeds. I've found it a slow process learning what are weeds in Hawaii and what are not—and, is there any such thing as a weed?! I realized how important it is to look carefully, as friends had just slaughtered an orchid and a flowering tree while I was looking the other way.

As I pulled out the big, obvious, overgrown weeds, I realized that this process was uncovering plants that were not visible before. That meant I needed to stop to look again. As I looked, I saw some special haleconia I didn't even know were in the yard; I also began to see smaller versions of the parent weeds. So . . . I went after the next layer. Again, after this run-through, I felt more confident in recognizing a small group of weeds. Then, I began to see some bigger trees and bushes I hadn't "noticed" before.

They had been so surrounded by weeds and bushes that their presence wasn't obvious. So, I had to stop to look again. I have always been opposed to cutting down trees, but after the two initial passes, I began to see these trees differently. I like the African tulip trees, but they were coming up everywhere. They were crowding out some of the ornamental plants and overtaking the garden.

Then, I had to stand up and look again to see which trees needed to go and which could stay. When I cleared out some of the underbrush, I could see that two big African tulip trees were stunting the growth of a majestic old poinciana that needed space and support.

As we cut back a tree that tends to spread and take over like a vine, I discovered a very rare hibiscus with a blossom that looks like a bellflower and is so delicate. I had never seen it before!

And so it goes. Neither the hack and hew method nor the cutting-nothing method really works well for me or for the garden (a dualism?). I took each step of the process one step at a time. It's not possible to be present to everything in that piece of garden all at once—at least, not for me with my untrained eye. So, if I just do what I know how to do, then wait with, the next steps become obvious and I can take those steps. When I have done that, I wait with again and the next steps emerge.

In working with the yard this way, I was aware of how centered I felt. I didn't accidentally destroy a precious plant I didn't want to lose. I didn't just get the job over with. I didn't let myself become so intimidated with the enormity of the job that I became paralyzed and did nothing. I didn't take anything out until it felt right to do it. I didn't have a preconceived notion of what the garden would look like, or what the process would be, *and* I made new discoveries all the time, feeling very centered in the process.

As I reflected on this gardening process, I realized that it was a great metaphor for life and being in process. And . . . the whole thing was great for my body. What more could I ask? I felt grateful for my life and my process and the process of the garden and the planet and the opportunity to be a part of it all.

TO NOTICE, WE MUST LEARN TO BE
IN OUR BODIES

We hear a lot about being "in the present" these days. One of the ways that we can be in the present is by noticing our bodies and what we're experiencing. Being in the present also helps us with noticing. Like many aspects of a living life, noticing and being in the present are circular.

In order to notice, we have to "get back in our bodies." We need to relearn the ability to listen to our bodies. When I was in graduate school studying psychology, I realized that I had come to believe that awarenesses and feelings were in the ether, swarming around my head someplace. No one ever said this *exactly*, <u>and</u> I do believe it was implied. I had the same idea about memories. In fact, in neurology and physiology we even learned about mapping memories in the brain. Imagine my surprise when I actually started working with real people and discovered that their feelings, awarenesses, and memories were stored in the body and only later "came to the brain"!

Often, I have found the question "What are you aware of?" to be a total conundrum for some people. When I asked that question, I might as well have been speaking Martian. Like the term *process*, there is just no association.

Then, I start with something simpler. I ask people to start with simple body sensations. I ask them to begin to notice when they're tired, when they're hungry, when they're full, or when they need to go to the bathroom. Many of us have lost touch with the most basic of bodily awarenesses. Most of us have learned that great energy has been wasted *not* knowing when we are tired.

Then we move to feelings. What do you feel? So many people believe that feelings are in the head. If we believe that, then we look for an answer in our mind and try to *name* the feeling.

Many years ago when I was practicing as a psychotherapist, I was seeing a German couple together so they could try to work out issues in their relationship. At one point, I saw something move through the husband's body—like a wave of energy. I stopped and said, "What was that?"

"What?" he asked.

"Something just went through your body," I said.

"Did it?" he asked.

"Yes," I answered.

"Amazing," he answered. "I wasn't aware of anything."

Later in the session I *noticed* the same phenomenon and named it—as something—not interpreting it.

"I think it's a feeling," he said. "Will you work with me?"

Later, he told me that no one had ever "noticed" anything, especially himself. He felt that he had been trained not to be aware or notice, and he had no skills for either.

As we worked together, he slowly reclaimed his feelings and awarenesses. He realized that he was gay, and that the marriage was destructive to him and his wife. They divorced and both are now happily in long-term relationships.

Slowly he had become aware of who he was and what his life path was. His life continues to work well for him as he "notices" feelings, awarenesses, and knowings.

As we learn to Live in Process, our noticings become subtler. We begin to "feel" when someone is being dishonest with us; usually we feel it in our solar plexus. We can then do what we need to do. Awareness of dishonesty is *never* in the head. It is in the body.

Then, hopefully, we will begin to feel our own discomfort when *we* are dishonest. In fact, as we get clearer, we find it just isn't worth it anymore to be dishonest with ourselves or anyone else. Dishonesty simply costs too much to indulge in. <u>And</u>, we have to notice before we can hope to change.

As we notice more and more, we become aware of old feelings, sensations, and memories that present themselves to be worked on and healed. When this level of noticing exists, we are well on our way to living our process, doing the work of our soul, and healing whatever needs healing.

We have come to know that we have many more levels of awareness than we use in what we call normal life. As we start to trust our noticings, we may become aware of intuitions, hunches, and sources of information and levels of consciousness not previously available to us. The beauty of Living in Process is that these awarenesses do not emerge until we are ready to handle them. Even though we may not believe we're ready, our inner process has a way of knowing what we need when we need it.

A word of caution is in order here. Early in our attempts to notice, we may appear to flip-flop like a superball—our noticings bouncing all over the place. Usually, this kind of confusion occurs when we're not really in touch with our body or our inner knowing, and our thinking is getting in between them. At these times, we really cannot trust our perceptions. After a while we will see that if we continue to focus on our noticing, we will be able to feel when our perceptions are accurate and when they are distorted by our own biases and confusion. When we sense we are confused in our perceptions, it is best not to act on them.

The following saying has saved my sanity more times than I care to remember.

When in doubt, don't.

Basic Truths for Living in Process

Our perceptions may have become so distorted with our disembodied thinking that we really cannot rely on them at times. This is when we need trusted friends and people who are clearer than we are with whom we can check out our "crazy thinking." Over time, our perceptions will become clearer and more reliable as we do our work.

We must remember that learning to notice and getting clear noticings takes time. We have learned to be so out of touch with ourselves and our world that now we have to learn how to crawl before we can walk.

Alone Time

In order to Live in Process, we absolutely must have alone time. We need time to settle down and go within ourselves to be able to notice.

Many of us have a fear of being alone. Often, we equate being by ourselves with being lonely. Often, that's when feelings of fear and feelings of being a failure as a human being begin to surface. There's a reason for whatever feelings begin to come up, and if we can simply honor those feelings and go through them, we will learn a great deal about ourselves.

All too often, we get busy, immerse ourselves with others, use our favorite distractions to avoid dealing with our emerging feelings. Unfortunately, these sidetracks never really work and the feelings will keep coming up again and again, often stronger and in a different form.

Alone time allows us to be with our self. However, some of us don't know that we have a self. When no one else is there, we think that nobody is there at all. Living in Process helps us become acquainted with our self so that we can move through and beyond that self. Through alone time, we can learn that we are not isolated and alone. Alone time allows us to reconnect with our spirituality and have a living experience of being part of the Oneness and All That Is. When we are in touch with our self, we discover that through the self we are connected with God, our Higher Power, the Creator, and the Great Mystery. We are never alone. Paradoxically, it is our time alone that affords us the opportunity for this reconnection. It is through our alone time that we learn that we are never alone.

By alone time, I do not necessarily mean a ten-day silent spiritual retreat—although, that might be nice, too, for those who need it! Living in Process is about participating in our everyday life, not retreating from it.

The opportunities for alone time appear a million times a day in our everyday life, if we do not "stuff" ourselves with clatter and chatter.

One of my favorite alone times is during the process of waking up. I have been given the wonderful gracious gift of being able to awaken easily and gently no matter what time I have to get up or what time zone in which I find myself. For me, the waking-up process is one in which I tune in, listen to my insides, listen to my spirit, and wait with the unfolding of my life.

I have been tempted not to take my alone time upon waking, because this is a time I also have with my husband to check in with one another. However, I have found these waking times so precious that our lives seem to work better if we both have alone time beside one another first and then share. I go into myself, and he does his meditation and readings. This works for us. When my children were younger, alone time early in the morning was more difficult. Still, I did find that when I needed it, I would wake earlier than usual to have those few moments.

Washing the dishes or cleaning up can be good alone times when we can be with ourselves. Walking the baby, or dog, or taking a walk ourselves can be serene times to tune in to ourselves and listen to our spiritual beings. Some people like to refinish furniture or wash the car. I have noticed that Westerners seem to do much better with a meditation that is also "doing something."

True alone time has the quality of "waiting with," definitely not "waiting for"! We are participating with our lives when we are waiting with and we are expectant, present, and open to hearing and seeing and feeling on many levels.

Some of us may have to take time to learn to participate in alone time. We are so accustomed to chatter, to fillers, that silence and calm may be foreign to us. When we first begin trying to have time alone, we may feel anxious and restless. We can use these times to go into our obsessive thinking patterns, our worry, and our need to figure things out. These "escapes" go very deep and are difficult to handle. Often, we use these mechanisms to avoid ourselves, our inner feelings, and our inner connection with our spirituality. It's important to be aware of the feelings that are coming up, to honor them, and to go through them.

Brenda Ueland, the wonderful woman writer from Minnesota and author of *If You Want to Write: A Book About Art, Independence, and Spirit,* used to say that writers should walk at least six miles a day alone and spend a lot of their time "moodling—long, inefficient, happy idling, dawdling, and puttering." Most of us may feel that we cannot do this, <u>and</u> we can do something to have alone time.

When we make space in our lives for time alone, awarenesses, thoughts, ideas, connections, and intuitions begin to flood in. We connect within and we connect beyond, both of which are absolutely essential for Living in Process.

Participation

In order to Live in Process, we simply must participate in our lives. By participation, I mean being active in our lives and not being an observer. So much in modern society invites us and requires us to remove ourselves from our lives. We have come to worship the myth of objectivity and have come to equate objectivity with nonparticipation. As I said in Chapter I, my curiosity about the Twelve-Step program of Alcoholics Anonymous helped me learn the difference between objectivity and nonparticipation.

My experience in learning about AA shifted me from an observational worldview to a participatory worldview. I began to see that if I wanted to "get" life, I had to "do" life—fully, completely, with dedication and commitment.

I came to see that my educational training had all been focused upon taking me out of participation, out of life, and training me to observe, analyze, and usually judge life. I could see that addictions, obsessions, attachments, and dysfunction were all excellent ways of removing me from myself. These were all escapes from intimacy with myself, with others, and most frightening of all, from my spirituality and my God. The myth of objectivity had reduced me to a shadow of life while leaving life unlived.

I learned that the purpose of what had paraded as objectivity in my training was in truth an attempt to gain a kind of clarity that did not distort people or the information from them, which is a very good skill. That kind of clarity does not come from being divorced from myself, my feelings, my being, and my spirituality or from nonparticipation. Clear awareness comes only from being completely in touch with and present to all aspects of my being. I saw that in order to be that clear, I had to do my own personal and spiritual work and heal. As I did my healing, I came closer to myself and my spirituality and slowly learned not to contaminate my perceptions with my own distortions. This kind of clarity had nothing to do with "objectivity" or nonparticipation, as I had been taught. It had to do with full participation leading the way to clarity.

PASSIVE PARTICIPATION

No discussion of participation would be complete without mentioning passivity. Passivity, of course, is the opposite of participation, and it is much more.

At a core level, our passivity arises from our being nonparticipants in our lives, and then expecting someone else to do our lives for us. This, of course, eventually leads to our feeling like a victim and throws us back into the old victim-perpetrator dualism.

As we expect others to take care of us, or as we become so fearful of doing the wrong thing and indulge in the illusion that we can control others and what they think and feel about us, we become more and more passive. Passivity is weighty. Passivity is exhausting to those around us. I have a friend who can get caught in his passivity cycle and when he does, being around him feels like having a huge, dead octopus dropped on my head with the tentacles hanging down to the floor. Others people's passivity can kill us if we don't learn to step away from it. Our passivity can kill us if we don't learn to step away from it. Passivity is the ultimate nonparticipation.

Trish was recently talking with me about how she sees Elizabeth as a person who participates in life. Elizabeth travels a great deal and finds herself in a wide variety of situations from luxury hotels to very rustic retreat centers. Trish observed the difference between Elizabeth's participating lifestyle and her own and others' passive lifestyle.

When Elizabeth arrives somewhere, she gets busy and

makes a home for herself. She sees what's available that she can use, being respectful of others and their needs, of course, and what isn't available. She takes some time scouting local junk, secondhand, and discount stores until she is comfortable and at home in her surroundings. When she leaves, she donates what she acquires to the place, if they want it. Or she gives it away. The practical is always in the service of the important.

Trish said that she saw herself and others waiting for someone else to make them comfortable. They looked to the facility to have what they needed—when they had rented it the way it was!—and if it didn't, they complained. They looked to the organizers to provide for their unknown and unarticulated needs, and complained if they weren't met. In their passivity, they did not see that their own comfort and ease was their responsibility.

If we are participating fully in our lives, we see that our needs are met, while at the same time being aware of and respecting others' needs, and the needs of all around us—the earth, the rest of nature. When we get into the passivity-aggression dualism, we wait and don't get what we need and then get angry and walk all over everything and everybody to *take* what we want. The passivity-aggression dualism is closely related to the victim-perpetrator dualism.

Participating in our lives offers us another option. Ironically, we can't *not* participate. That's why I call it the *myth* of objectivity.

The Bhagavad Gita points out that activity is inherent in human nature. Sloth is simply "wrong activity."

> *No man shall 'scape from act*
> *By shunning action; nay, and none shall come*

Living in Process

By mere renouncements unto perfectness.
Nay, and no jot of time, at any time,
Rests any actionless; his nature's law
Compels him, even unwilling, into act;
(For thought is act in fancy).

When we're out of touch with ourselves, and we shut off from our feelings and our spirituality, we tend to feel and be isolated. Unfortunately, isolation breeds more isolation, until we become mere observers of our lives. Our "myth of objectivity" supports the belief that we *can* be objective and that it is desirable to be objective. In order to try to be objective we remove ourselves from ourselves and make ourselves objects to be observed, and we withdraw from the other and the world around us and make the other an object to be observed. When we remove ourselves, we have stopped participating in our life. We are acting life, not being life.

One of the ways we "act" life is by scanning.

Doris came to realize that she had lived her life in fear. She was a "scanner." She was always on the alert to see what was expected of her, how others were behaving, and what she needed to do to be safe. Her scanning, she believed, was what kept her safe. On the outside she appeared competent and efficient, but she knew that it was only her constant vigilance that kept her safe.

Doris had stopped participating in her life. She was watching her life, trying to figure out the correct response and then do it. She was a reactor, not a doer.

We have the great possibility of participating in our life and in all life. When we expend our energies to withdraw from ourselves and from all life, we are going against our very nature. What is the meaning of life? Quite simply to live it! This does not mean that we live the life we think we *should* live. This does not mean that we live the life our parents, family, friends, bosses, teachers, ministers, or mentors *think* we should live. Each of them has enough to do to fully participate in his/her own life. Our participation will determine what our lives are, and this, after all, is what we need to know.

Each of us has the responsibility to do our spiritual, emotional, and personal work so that we can become clearer and clearer about who we are and what our life is about.

To live is to participate.

Only in participating in our life can we discover what it is. Only by participating with others can we begin to know who they are and experience the intimacy that is there for us.

Life is not abstract. Life is not a thought. Thinking and trying to "understand" often confuse us and result in paralysis. Only as we participate can we learn.

Spirituality is participation.

We cannot experience our spirituality by thinking about it. If we are open as we follow our process and live out of our process—in Buddhism, this means doing the next right thing—we can truly learn our place in the universe. Participation does not mean keeping busy or just doing. In fact, we may keep busy, overwork, jangle in our minds, or push activities in order *not* to participate in our lives. Avoiding our process is not unusual in a materialistic culture.

To participate, one must have time for solitude and reflection. We then can find our reality expressed in our body and in our feelings. In fact, feelings tend to be the door into our process. Whenever we respect and honor our feelings, we are participating. Respecting and honoring our feelings doesn't mean that we have the right to dump them on others. Often, when we have strong feelings, they may have nothing to do with the situation at hand, and they are only the door inviting us into our deeper work (see Chapter 6).

As we participate in our life and the life around us, we begin to see that life is about learning, and in order to learn, we need to make mistakes.

> The Creator designed us to learn by trial and error (participation). The path of life we walk is very wide. Everything on the path is sacred. What we do right is sacred—but our mistakes are also sacred. This is the Creator's way of teaching spiritual people. To criticize ourselves when we make mistakes is not the Indian way. To learn from our mistakes is the Indian way. The definition of a spiritual person is someone who makes thirty to fifty mistakes each day and talks to the Creator after each one to see what to do next time. This is the way of the spiritual warrior.
>
> *Don Coyhis, Mohican*

How far we have come when we realize that we are not mistakes, rather, we make mistakes. I heard one old-timer say, "Remember, God doesn't make garbage." What an insult it is to the Creator not to live out our process!

As I participate in my life, I begin to see my spheres of participation. As I live my process, I begin to respect that others are a process and that they *have* a process. Their process may not always be to my liking, and it may not be the process I would have planned for them, and it is *their* process. As I respect my process, I begin to respect the processes occurring in greater and greater spheres and see that I am related to these processes. What is happening in Bosnia or Africa or the Middle East or anywhere in the world is somehow related to me and affects me. As I learn to participate, I come to see that I exist in context. Living in Process means that we recognize and accept that we do not exist in isolation. We are part of a larger whole.

Wholeness and Context

We can and do exist only in context.

We exist in context. We are part of the created order. As we participate in it we know who we are. Learning to accept and honor this basic truth is key to Living in Process.

As we learn to live our process, the reality of our living in context takes on more and more meaning. When we accept that we live in context, we know that we are part of a larger whole. We begin to see that we are always in community, and we also see that as we grow spiritually our communities expand. We become one with all creation.

Living in community is essential if we are to understand the context of our lives. Everything is linked and part of the same creation. There is no hierarchy. When we try to put ourselves above creation, we are participating in spiritual suicide and the destruction of the planet.

All is sacred.

We can have peace and harmony in larger and larger contexts if we do our work. Becoming an adult implies recognizing that we have responsibilities (the ability to respond), and that what we do and do not do affects other people. When we do not recognize that we are part of a greater whole and that all of our actions and nonactions have meaning and repercussions, we are arrogant and self-centered. Some of us have been parented in such a way as to believe that we are the center of the universe and everything revolves around us. This experience is very sad, for ultimately it robs us of our connectedness and our experience of being embedded in a reality much larger than ourselves.

Even though we exist in context, we also need to know that each person has a unique and important place in the whole scheme of things. There is no need for us to want the same things or to do the same things. We all have different paths.

I have a dear friend who is a very spiritual man. He is a delightful, intelligent, and, at times, intellectually challenging friend. Very successful in his chosen profession, he is respected and liked by those who know him. Yet, he often says that he feels that his life is a failure—even though he is quite settled into and happy in the life he has built. He lives in a culture where the expectation is that one will marry and have children and "carry on the name," and he has not done that. (Actually, I suspect that he might be a "terror" to live with on a day-to-day basis.) As it is, his life makes sense—as he is living it. He has the opportunity to rejoice in what his life *is*, which is pretty good. Yet, he is haunted by what he believes his life *should* look like.

He has succumbed to the cultural pressure toward sameness. When a culture pushes toward sameness, individuals tend to feel threatened if others are not doing what they have chosen to do and they will put pressure on others to conform. This pressure is even stronger if those who are conforming are not really doing what *they* feel they need to do. The truth is that each person's path in life is purely a matter between that person and their spirituality. Each person's path *is* their spirituality.

Living in context does not mean that the context need have the power to dictate to us what our path or the form of our life must be. As we come to recognize our process, begin to live that process, and are open to and participate in all processes, our paths will unfold before us. When we're operating in tune with our spirituality and our process, we make choices that are necessary for our growth and learning, and no one—not even ourselves—can dictate what that path will look like. Clearly, the path of life is not the same for everyone. When we try to force ourselves into someone else's agenda for us, we become zombies, slaves who work <u>and</u> own nothing because we do not own our own process. We must trust our individual path, our own process.

Some might say that trusting your own process sounds self-centered. It is anything but. The result of Living in Process is that we become acutely aware of and responsible to the context of our lives. Some of those who want to control our lives may feel rejected or take our living our path as a personal affront. What we are doing with our lives is not dependent on what they do with theirs. Let me hasten to add that trusting our process does not mean that we are harmful, or inconsiderate, or do not meet our responsibilities. Living in Process simply means that our primary relationship is our relationship with our spirituality. When we are living our process and living in context, we are acutely aware of the responsibility we have to all life and all processes.

We are the environment. We are nature.

Remember, we can never save the trees in the rain forest until we know that we *are* the rain forest. When we speak about being *in* nature, we have not quite yet learned that we *are* nature. Native people wisely recognize that they have a living, pulsating relationship with the earth, for example. Everything we eat comes from the earth. The clothes we wear, the houses we live in, the cars we drive all come from the earth. We are not above the trees or the rivers. We all live in context with one another. As we learn to Live in Process, we have a growing experience that we are one with and have the possibility and the necessity of participating in the processes that are all around us. As we learn, know, and experience that we can exist only in context, our feelings of aloneness begin to disappear. We can reconnect with our spirituality, which is our participation in the wholeness of all our context.

Living in Process means always moving toward greater wholeness. When we reduce our world, eventually it vanishes. We experience a wrenching of self when we slip out of our process—our oneness with all things. At these times of fragmentation, it is important to know that the living process has not left us. We are the ones who back away from our own Living in Process. Also, paradoxically, when we are trying to hold on to something or someone or control the process, we feel separated. As we live our lives more and more in process, we experience less and less separation from anything and everything.

We sometimes feel physical pain as we feel the silent groaning of the trees in the Black Forest striving to survive the acid rain threatening their very existence, or the cries of the earth when bulldozers penetrate her. Some may say, "I don't want to feel this. I'd rather be numbed. I'd rather not be free. I'd rather be a slave." Yet, the essence of being human is to experience all within the wholeness—and this also includes the healing, the ecstasy, and the profound bliss of oneness. Ultimately, feeling the pain of the trees or the earth or of other people can never compare with the magnitude of the painful experience of being separated from our living process. Opening ourselves up to the awareness that all is process can bring us back to the oneness of which we inextricably are a part.

Life is so constructed as to be unmanageable.

It is not that it *becomes* unmanageable and can be made manageable again. Life is designed to be unmanageable, and it is "managed" by the Great Mystery. Why put an inexperienced kid in the driver's seat when we can have a master at the wheel? Our responsibility is to participate in life. When we participate in and experience the life we have in all its fullness, we learn the lessons we need to learn. The Creator's role is that of the celestial hand that occasionally shakes the paperweight with the snow in it to see that we have the experiences we need.

Pain is inevitable in physical existence. Yet, much of our suffering we bring upon ourselves and much of the suffering of the world we bring upon each other by not realizing that we are all part of the oneness.

Truth is not static.

There are many levels of truth available to us. Our movement toward truth is not static. Our ability to perceive truth changes as we do our work, and as we grow and evolve spiritually. We need not to make our perception of truth static. When we recognize that we are all on a path toward truth, we can respect our and others' place along that path. The issue is not where we are on our journey. The issue is that we are *on* our journey.

Human existence dictates limitations. We probably do not have the capacity to know ultimate truth. Our teachers can share what they have come to know for themselves, and it is just that—what *they* have come to know. Each of us has equal access to the possibility of knowing the truth. We must look deep inside to find the path that is ours, and then trust it and ourselves.

Living in Process means moving beyond judgment. What is, is. The ultimate issue is not whether something is right or wrong. It is what we do with whatever comes our way. As in the Zen Buddhist way of looking at the world, there is "right" action, <u>and</u> this view of rightness is not on a right-wrong dualism. Many people try to make the concept of truth static out of fear. For the dysfunctional person, "right" is static. For the person who Lives in Process, rightness changes and evolves as we evolve. A Living in Process rightness is not self-centered, it is not judgmental, and it is not disembodied. This kind of rightness comes from being one with all life, and it springs from our experience and our very beings.

Willingness to Take Responsibility

Another key to Living in Process is the willingness to take responsibility for our knowing, our own internal truth, our healing, and ultimately, for our lives.

We have become convinced that we are not responsible for our own lives. Somewhere along the way we accepted the notion that we are the result of the sum total of all the things that have happened to us, that we are helpless reeds buffeted by the winds of circumstance. In the process, we have relinquished all our personal power to anyone and everyone who has "done something to us," and become sorry, victimized creatures whose only hope for healing is to strike back and become perpetrators to those who, we believe, have victimized us. What a pathetic and sad state of affairs.

When we Live in Process, we take responsibility and ownership for our lives. This does not mean that we are to blame for what has happened to us. In fact, this means that we spend little or no time in blaming at all. When we Live in Process, we recognize that terrible things may have happened to us, most of which were completely out of our control. Then, we see our issue as focusing upon whatever we need to do to heal from our experiences and glean the learnings there for us so that we can get on with our lives.

We may have been raped, abused, coddled, or spoiled as a child. This is our reality. Our question is, What do we need to do to heal and learn from these experiences? When we focus on the other person, what he/she did to us, and getting even, we become a perpetrator and, in the process, move far away from the Creator and our spiritual selves.

Taking responsibility for our lives means accepting the reality of our lives, healing, learning, integrating, and moving on.

Living in Process

We have a concept and way of functioning in Living in Process that is absolutely essential to living this way, quite radical and revolutionary, and totally empowering. We call it staying on our side of the street.

STAYING ON OUR SIDE OF THE STREET

The concept of staying on our side of the street as we go through life is one of the key foundations of Living in Process. It is also one of the major differences between Living in Process and the current culture. Since the current culture tends to be externally focused and supported by a science based on information gathered by the sense organs (observation), this necessarily requires that the information gathered be external.

When our main source of information is gathered externally, then external sources become our modus operandi. Interestingly enough, this orientation results in individuals feeling like victims. As we said before, when we feel like a victim, this reinforces our tendency to scan and look outside ourselves to find out what is causing our upset. Whenever we believe we are a victim, we are giving away our personal power. It is as though believing we are a victim actually drains our being of its power. This draining is like a small gas leak in a car. The leak may not be too noticeable, yet it drains off the fuel to power the machine, and explosions are always potentially possible.

Victims will become perpetrators. This external focus sets up a dynamic that is destructive and difficult to break. The most effective process for breaking through it is learning to stay on our side of the street. Staying on our side of the street is very difficult for most of us because in our culture taking responsibility for ourselves and our part in any situation means we immediately believe we have *caused* the situation (cause and effect) and are therefore to blame. Cause and effect and blame may be good concepts in mechanics; they are less than useful in living.

I would like to give an example from my own life to help clarify this concept.

A few years ago, I learned that my genetic father was an American Indian. I had never known the man, as he and my mother had separated before I was born. I always felt that the father who had raised me was my true father. Therefore, I had little or no interest in finding out about my genetic father.

However, when I learned that my genetic father was American Indian, this information seemed important. I had always felt like I was Indian, and my Indian friends had all told me that I was Indian. Even native people in other parts of the world insisted that I was a native person. However, as far as I knew, I was not Indian at all and I went out of my way not to mislead anyone. Therefore, when the information came to me through an aunt that my father was Indian, suddenly, trying to find my father and get more information about this side of the family became important.

A little background here will help clarify. My father who raised me married my mother when I was three years old. He and my mother had gone to grade school and high school together, and he had always been around. However, I could remember "before" they were married, when I had lived with my mother and my great-grandmother. My father who raised me tried to adopt me, <u>and</u> that was not possible without consent from my genetic father, and he could not be found. The father who raised me did not want me to know that he was not my genetic father, so we had a family secret. My mother had been told she would never have children because of a horseback injury and she almost died in childbirth, so I was it for them.

As I look back, I remember knowing "before" my father

who raised me as a child. I also remember being introduced when I was a child as the Willeys' stepgranddaughter, which I filed away.

In college, when I wanted to get a passport and needed my birth certificate, my father who raised me, who was usually very mild-mannered, raised a ruckus and said that the U.S. government would have to accept an affidavit from him as to who I was. My mother quietly took me aside and gave me my birth certificate. She told me that my genetic father had gone off to find work during the Depression when I was born, and had never come back. I asked no further questions. I honored the wishes of my father who raised me.

Recently, I have tried to trace my genetic father, get information about his family, and learn more of my roots. The roots have been fairly easy to trace, <u>and</u> my father is a phantom! If I weren't here, there are times I feel as though he never existed. We have searched and re-searched and come up with very little information about him. We have no middle initial, no birth date (a year, perhaps), and no Social Security number. He may even still be alive. Yet we find so little.

During these times of hunting, there have been times when I've felt frustrated and depressed. Once, when we were in Arkansas heading out on yet another search, I was sitting in the backseat (and my husband and secretary were in the front), and I began to indulge in feeling like a victim. "Why can't I find him?" "Why is it so hard?" "Why is this *happening* to me?" I was working myself into a muddled slump—handing out my personal power by the bucketload!

Then, I stopped. Wait a minute. What's my part here? I halted the downward spiral and took a look at me.

I was a very curious child. Almost nothing missed my scrutinizing eye. I was curious about everything. Why had I not pursued the matter when I was introduced as "the Willeys' stepgranddaughter"? Normally, I would have asked a million questions, <u>and</u> I didn't. I had to take responsibility for that.

In my mind, I could just hear a chorus of people saying, "You were only a child. That's too much to expect. Don't be so hard on yourself." Rubbish! The reality is I did not pursue it, and that reticence was not like me. The whys were unimportant.

As I sat there, I began to remember "before" my father who raised me. I had never explored those memories either. When I was in college and my mother told me "the family secret," I didn't pursue further information. There would have been no harm in quizzing my mother since we were alone together, <u>and</u> I did not do this. I felt loyal to my father who raised me and did not seek further information.

About fifteen years ago before my uncle, my mother's brother, died, he came to visit and said that he thought my father had come to eastern Colorado (I was living in Colorado at the time). I did not pursue the information he gave me, and remember thinking that I did not want any more financial burdens at the time. Of course, I had no information whatsoever about my genetic father's financial situation. Before my father who raised me died, he talked some about marrying my mother and wanting to take care of me. I could have asked for more information then. I remember thinking, "After he dies, I will find out about my genetic father." And, I didn't. I was busy and put the search on a back burner until almost everyone who might have some information was long since dead.

Now that I've learned to stay on my side of the street, I've come to perceive the entire situation from a different angle. No longer a victim, I realized I had made choices. I had made decisions. And now I wasn't really liking the consequences of those choices, *and they were mine*. As I took responsibility for the decisions I had made, I could feel a plug securely affixing itself into the hole in my being and the soul-leaking stopped. I no longer felt like a pitiful victim being put upon by an ungiving world. The world might be ungiving, and that was irrelevant to the issue at hand. No one had given me information, and *that* was irrelevant to the issue at hand. I had not pursued the information I had been given when it was given, and that was very relevant. I could feel my personal power returning.

Staying on our side of the street does not mean that others have not done something wrong to us. Others may have done terrible things. That's their issue. They have to deal with what they have done—or not, as they choose. All I have to deal with and clean up is my side of the street. That's enough.

Staying on our side of the street does not necessarily mean that we have *done* anything. We may not have done something, or there may have been nothing we could have done. In that case, staying on our side of the street simply means focusing on what we need and what we need to do. Maybe we need to go into the deep sadness that we have of a horrible experience. As we go into that sadness, or even rage, our process will take us where we need to go to heal and learn. Maybe we need to feel the regret that we feel that these incidents are the reality of our lives. When we focus on ourselves and what we need, we are staying on our side of the street. When we focus on others and what they have done to us, *we* deprive ourselves of our healing and our learning. No one else can deprive us of these treasures. Only we can do this to ourselves. Massive healings and learnings can take place when we stay on our side of the street.

KNOWING

Another aspect of taking responsibility for ourselves is taking responsibility for our own knowing and our own truth.

All of us have deep wells of knowing within ourselves. Securely hidden within our DNA are resources and wisdoms that far outdistance our current knowing.

All of us possess a wisdom that is beyond our imagining. We have truth hidden deep within us. We may have to learn mechanics and technology, _and_ wisdom and truth are embedded deep within us. We only have to get out of our own way and access what is already there. The very act of taking responsibility for our own truth and our own knowing opens more doors of connection with the All That Is—our true spirituality. Doing our inner work of healing, having alone time, cleaning up our act through noticing and honesty all pave the way to our inner truth. A big part of our task is to trust that it is there for us.

> *Living in Process cannot come from our head or our understanding. It can come only from living.*

Often, we say to ourselves, "I'll be glad when things settle down so I can get back to my life." Surprise! This—whatever this is—is our life! Living in Process does celebrate the meaning of an ordinary day, and yet each day is also unique and exquisite.

Living in Process

I am not here to create a crisis or prevent one.

Creating a crisis is a way of generating false feelings to prove that we are alive. It also gives us the wonderful adrenaline high that we often confuse with aliveness. Later, we feel exhausted. When we are truly living our process, our aliveness is more than enough. Exuberance and extravagance are related. Extravagance has nothing to do with materialism. Extravagance, like participation, is linked with spirituality. Living life fully is extravagance. It is important to live abundantly within one's means. Abundance is intimately related to pace. Our lives develop a pace, a rhythm. Often that rhythm seems to have no relationship to what we think we need or what we're sure we want. Look again. Check it out. There may be a higher knowledge and awareness at work.

We need to be so tuned in to the present that proving something—anything—becomes irrelevant.

When Living in Process, innocence, openness, inquiry, curiosity, and the ability to see the new, the redeeming in everything, are absolutely essential. We have so much to learn, and even knowing that it is all there inside of us is often not a great help when we want to live in the future, or in the past, or try to control the present. Living in Process is living in the present while respecting and owning our past and honoring that we have a responsibility to the future. When we are present in the moment, we bring the accumulated wealth of our past to that moment. When we participate fully, we can only be in the moment. Yet, when we live the moment, we are fully mindful that our actions have implications for the future. We experience our lives as an ongoing process, not a series of isolated events. In Living in Process our life is full of mistakes, opportunities. When we are open for learning, we don't punish ourselves for our mistakes, nor do we allow others to punish us for our mistakes. We consult with our Creator and move on.

Basic Truths for Living in Process

Living in Process is normal life, <u>and</u> we have created a system where normal life is not easy. Some say, "If I listen to myself, I won't be able to function in the 'real' world." What we call the "real" world is illusion made up of abstract concepts, half truths, and lies. Perhaps we have been trying to make sense out of a system that doesn't make sense while the world of our experience does.

In *Mutant Message Down Under*, Marlo Morgan quotes the Australian Aborigines as saying that all people in Western culture have become "mutants." We have left what the Creator created us to be and strayed from the path we were created to journey upon in intimate relationship with all beings and all creation. The Aborigines say the alcoholics and other addicts are probably the most spiritual people among us because they have not been able to tolerate this mutant reality. They see addicts as trying to alter reality to get back in touch with their true spirituality. This is a good example of how our chosen "solutions" frequently not only do not deal with the problem at hand, they compound it. Native peoples the world over are urging the human race to return to ourselves.

> The core of our personal power lies in self-knowledge and self-defining; when we know what we think and feel, we can take responsibility for our lives, we can be open and accepting of life, we can make respectful, loving choices for ourselves, living each day fully. We can be *well*.
>
> *Jeanne M.*

Living in Process is rooted in and connected to making conscious choices. We are actors in our life, not just reactors. When we do react, we recognize that the reactions are ours and take responsibility for them.

For example, I sometimes get feedback that someone has said this or that negative comment about me. I can't control that. I've learned that I'm powerless over what others say about me, think about me, or try to do to me.

I am, however, responsible for my reaction. My reaction is mine. I may laugh, I may feel threatened, I may feel fear or anger, or I may shrug and walk away. The closer I am to my spirituality, the more likely I am to shrug and walk away, knowing that eventually whoever made the comment will have to deal with their issues and I will have to deal with mine. All I need to do is keep my side of the street clean.

When something—anything—does come my way, I need to remember that I have choices. I need to wait and not react on impulse. I need to be aware of my feelings, do my work, wait with what I need to do, even check in with someone I trust before I act.

Time changes all perceptions.

We need to give ourselves time to settle in with our perceptions and get clear before we make choices.

BEING RESPONSIBLE FOR OURSELVES

Another aspect of taking responsibility is being responsible for ourselves.

When I am Living in Process, I do not think that my process is the only one around. Quite the contrary—I clearly know that I am part of a much greater process. This knowing helps me want to take responsibility for myself, my actions, and my commitments.

Living up to our agreements and honoring our decisions even if we have changed, or changed our minds is the tuition we pay in life so that we end up feeling good about ourselves. All this is freedom and responsibility.

Basic Truths for Living in Process

OWNING OUR BEHAVIOR

Living in Process is not designed to get us off life's hooks.

Some people would like to use the idea of Living in Process to justify doing whatever they feel like doing whenever they feel like doing it. Nothing could be further from the truth of living our process. Not doing what we don't "feel like" then becomes confused with self-centered laziness and/or self-will. Work does not necessarily interfere with Living in Process. *We* interfere with Living in Process.

Living in Process does not mean that we don't work, or that we are not responsible for our lives. We need to take ownership of our behavior, our decisions, our thoughts, and our feelings, even when we're not clear. I sometimes hear, "Well, I wasn't clear when I decided that or when I did that," frequently implying that we then do not have to take ownership for our decisions and/or our behavior. We lose pieces of ourselves when we don't take responsibility for ourselves regardless of our "state" when we made these decisions.

There is nothing in Living in Process that is contrary to taking responsibility for oneself. In fact, Living in Process means that we *do* take responsibility for ourselves. It means that we are aware of, responsive to, and respectful of our process and the process of others. When we are truly Living in Process, we have no illusions about our process being the only process around. We cannot truly live our process unless we are tuned in to the process of the world around us.

None of us ever experienced the sweet taste of healing by going from one self-centered behavior to another. There is such a difference between one who is just taking care of herself or himself and someone who is aware of the self and of her or his needs while also being aware of others and their needs and respecting both.

Living in Process means that we are responsible *about* our work. If we have agreed to do a job, we do it. We do not agree to do a job and then not follow through because we "don't feel like it." We don't not do our job because we would rather hang out or play. We may need to take time off or take a rest, <u>and</u> we do not expect someone else to support us or take care of us, while we do nothing. We negotiate what we need and take responsibility for what we need.

When we do not do our part, or when we do not make our contribution, when we do not meet our commitments or try to get out of a commitment because we have changed our minds, we do not feel good about ourselves—even if we get away with it. We may make mistakes while we are trying to learn to be responsible for ourselves, and our mistakes are our tools for learning. Often, we have moved so far from our Living in Process that we cannot shift into full living overnight.

As I said earlier, living up to our agreements and honoring our decisions even if we have changed our minds is the tuition we pay in life so that we end up feeling good about ourselves. We may try to renegotiate a commitment, <u>and</u> even if it is not negotiable, we still feel better because we have taken responsibility for our decisions.

Responsibility is the ability to respond fully and participate in our lives. Blame is irrelevant. Participation is the door to responsibility. Responsibility is the pathway to freedom.

Dualism

In order fully to live our process, we have to be able to move beyond our illusionary perception of dualism, which may be one of the most difficult—and not impossible—tasks we have ever attempted.

Dualisms are a figment of our imaginations. We create them in our minds, and therefore, we can let them go, and move into a new perception of the world and a new way of living in it if we choose. We always have the power to choose.

What are dualisms? Dualisms are made by mentally setting up a pair of false opposites. We resort to dualisms in order to simplify and explain a very complex world, giving us a false sense of understanding and control. We resort to dualisms because we have lost our connection with our spirituality and abandoned our participation in the wholeness that is our birthright. In our fear and anxiety, we try to oversimplify a very complex universe. Dualisms are our creations and our illusions. They are not real. In our estrangement from participating in our spirituality and wholeness, we seek to simplify and control, and neither work.

When we think and see our world dualistically, we think in terms of male-female, good-bad, in-out, up-down, or victim-perpetrator. We use dualisms to simplify a very complex world and then we attempt to live there, trying to destroy anything that does not fit into our simplistic view.

Take one of the most accepted dualisms we have created, male-female. This one looks self-explanatory. And it is not! Reality is just not that simple. There are whole ranges of male-female. There are female persons in male bodies and vice versa. The Jungians say that we all have male and female in each of us. Spiritual teachers teach that the soul is neither male, nor female, nor both. We have people born with no genitalia—many more, I understand, than are made public. And we have people who are born with both female and male genitalia—again, many more than we are told; the decision is often made in the delivery room as to how to handle the situation. The male-female dualism is just not as simple as we would have it be. Indeed, maybe the furor over gayness has little to do with the issue of sexual identity and a lot more to do with an attempt to hold on to a simplified worldview that gives us the illusion of safety and control.

The great Indian saint Paramahansa Yogananda taught that dualisms are a given of the material plane. I take a slightly different perspective. I see dualisms as a given of the way we have attempted to understand the material plane, but not an inherent characteristic of the material plane of existence.

For example, when Western Europeans thought the world was flat, they reduced it to a dualism of two directions, north-south and east-west, and their conceptualization of their world was explained as flat and two-dimensional. After the great European sea voyages, they had to revise their conceptualization of the planet as three-dimensional and later as multidimensional in relation to the universe, and universes.

We are now facing a similar shift in the way we see ourselves and the way we participate in our lives and our spirituality. Moving beyond our attachment to dualisms is one of the major shifts we have to make.

If we give up our illusion of dualism, we will be forced to fall back on our deep spirituality—of a world in which we can participate with a power beyond our comprehension. If we have created dualisms to simplify our world and feed our illusion of control, we have done a great disservice to ourselves, our God, and the world around us. We have severely underestimated our ability to comprehend and to be fully who we are—a part of all creation.

We've been stuck with our dualism. When I was a child, we had construction toys called Lincoln Logs that we could use to build square or rectangular log cabins. They were really two-dimensional, not flexible, and were quite limited in their scope. Yet, they were fun and helped train us to fit into a two-dimensional world. Unfortunately, our world is more multidimensional. I see dualisms as being like the Lincoln Logs, or building blocks of our society.

When we are on a Lincoln Log dualism, we really have only that building block to deal with. We can run from one end of the log to the other, <u>and</u> we are still on the log. For example, I have seen people move from "Should I stay with my job?" to "Should I leave my job?" They run frantically back and forth from one end to the other, and they are stuck. Another example is the male-female dualism mentioned earlier. Many therapies and spiritual paths focus on trying to find a balance *on the dualism*, making an assumption that the dualism is a given. This trying to find a balance or middle point will never work. It is the dualism itself that is the problem.

The issue is not trying to find balance in the dualism. As long as we do that, we keep ourselves stuck in a limited two-dimensional world and alienated from our spirituality.

One of the most common dualisms I see in people who come to participate in the Living in Process work is arrogance-worthlessness. They are either arrogant, believing they are special, unique, and better than anyone, or they feel just horrible and believe that they are the most terrible people in the world, or they alternate between the two. All dualisms have a fulcrum on which they spin and turn. These fulcrums are usually the characteristics we think of as dysfunction. Clearly, the fulcrum around which this dualism turns is self-centeredness. Initially, most people believe that they need to find a balance between arrogance and feeling awful about themselves. When they try to balance these two, they stay stuck in two dimensions.

My suggestion is to jump off the dualism. For some, this seems like jumping off into the void, and maybe it is. We keep asking, "What's the third option? What's the third option?" The third option is always going inside and seeing what the truth is for you. When we tap into the inner process that is our being and that connects us with the All That Is, we no longer need to define our world in dualisms. Dualisms become irrelevant, because we have the spiritual base that allows us to trust that we do not have to simplify and try to control our reality. We are free in our spirituality. We are participating in our process and are one with the process of the All.

As we confront our cherished dualisms and jump into our wholeness, we can live our process.

MOVING BEYOND DUALISM

According to Hindu thought, nature and the material world are inherently dualistic. Yet this has not been my personal experience, nor my experience when I'm with native people throughout the world who participate in the wholeness of nature. Perhaps the Hindu sages meant that until we shift into operating out of our own process we have a tendency to *perceive* nature and everything as dualistic. Dualistic thinking does, indeed, oversimplify our universe and keep us stuck, because ultimately—like in staying with our job or leaving it—we usually don't want to move toward either end of the dualism! It shorthands reality and misses the essence.

Some time ago, I participated in a dialogue with Susan who was well schooled in Jungian work. I had always had an uneasiness about Jung's approach, and we often explored Jung's ideas and my discomfort. The following is a letter I received from her, and what she's writing about is what I call the "third option."

This morning I was reading an article written by a Jungian friend on the emerging feminine, and I am back at my usual syntheses. At first glance, I admit, Jungian thought looks like dualism; Jungians are always talking about the opposite, even *pairs* of opposites. Actually, they are really talking about the third way. For Jungians, health is the *reconciliation* of opposites. That point at which one is able to see that they are not opposite at all.

The real difference, for me, between your thinking and Jungian thinking is not on the issue of dualism, but on the whole approach to how one lives in that spot which is the third way. Jungians see it as a tension point. They see the psyche as struggling continually to maintain that balance and yes, that *is* dualism because the psyche can fall off in either direction. If it isn't dualism, it's exhausting! With process, with a system shift, one has a new vision of what *is*, in which opposites are irrelevant, and the struggle isn't necessary because one doesn't go back.

Another point of truly important difference (in which your ideas seem so much more natural than Jung's) is how one gets to the third way in the first place. In the article, my friend writes, "But unfortunately we cannot make one what we have not previously divided." (I include the "but" because it will say worlds to you.) This is really the gospel according to Jung; what he called "The Process of Individuation," or coming to consciousness, means first seeing the differences (dividing the opposites) and then seeing that there really are not differences of opposites, but aspects of the same thing.

For me, that awareness is "Anne's <u>and</u>"; it is present from the beginning. It's part of our knowing and seeing, a reality we can apprehend without dissecting it.

A year ago I was making notes for our first training session on my attraction to thinkers who see that third way: Thomas Aquinas, William Blake, Jung, G. K. Chesterton (paradox), Anne Schaef. I have always felt truly at home in the "Moor Eeffoc-y" side of life, and searched for writers who validated that. I loved Chesterton because he knew, and had the courage to write that the teapot was bewitched.

At this point (in my letter) I am groping for the verbalization of something I have always seen out of the corner of my eye, but which eludes me if I look straight at it (with the intention of saying what it is). For me it is the real reality.

This year doesn't seem to have brought me any closer to articulating it. What it has done is allow me to begin to reclaim it. Like Jung, I don't believe it, I know it, and I have allowed the system and other people to shake that knowledge (including one Jungian analyst—imagine a sensation type analyzing an intuitive—who said I needed to be kept in reality). I can't make a tidy ending, so I'll just end. . . .

Moor Eeffoc, by the way, comes from Dickens, via Chesterton. It is *Coffee Room*, written on a glass door, and seen from inside the room. For me, it is the irrational, intuitive reality, seen from the inside. For passers-by, it seems to be a coffee room. Those of us who live on the inside know it is that magic place, Moor Eeffoc.

Susan

Susan was struggling to make dualism understandable and to move beyond it in her thinking. She loved the work of Jung, and yet was fascinated with my not trusting his focus on dualism. She—and Jung!—try to solve the issue with a balance of the dualism, which, as discussed earlier, does not work. Also, she is uneasy with the reality being not the differences of opposites but the same thing. We do not need opposites to get to the one. The light is *not* defined by the darkness—even if we believe it is!

Living in Process pushes us further than this conceptualization. It pushes us to the third option, which is moving beyond the dualism, not referring to it, and then defining ourselves and our world out of our own living process. The third option means *not* retreating to either end of the dualism, going inside instead, to see where your feelings take you. A challenging opportunity.

Dualism is fodder for the mind. It does not and cannot reflect our reality. Whenever we relapse into it, we lose our participation in our process.

Soul-Level Healing

SEEKING, ACCEPTING, AND FOLLOWING IT THROUGH AS FAR AS WE NEED TO GO

Living in Process is a path of healing and learning. Human existence being the way it is, our learning possibilities often come as woundings. On the TV program *Saturday Night Live*, there's a skit about a little boy who's hyperactive. He's always hurting himself. His mother dresses him up in padding and a helmet and ties him to a jungle gym with a bungee cord. He's always running off, coming to the end of the bungee, and getting snapped back, essentially unharmed, to the jungle gym. I tend to think of all of us as being much like that little boy. The Creator has fixed us up to be ultimately safe, given us a jungle gym as a sturdy base, and tied us to a bungee cord. The bruises we get are often of our own making. We keep running and getting snapped back until we finally get the point and start learning the lessons we need to learn to walk the path of the soul.

Of course, there are things that just "happen" to us in living life that need to be healed. We do not "create" all our situations for learning, at least not consciously. And, all situations in our life are opportunities for healing and learning. As I said earlier, at some ultimate level, the issue is not whether we have been molested, beaten, spoiled, or overindulged. *We* are the ones who have to deal with whatever our life is and has been. Our issue is to do the healing necessary so that we can get the learning and become whole and move on and live our life fully. Focusing on what others have done to us is useless. We need to have the commitment to do what we need to do to heal and move on.

Basic Truths for Living in Process

WILLINGNESS

Willingness is an important word here. Nothing positive can happen in our lives unless we are willing. We have to be willing to go to any lengths to heal. We have to be willing to plumb the depths of our inner selves courageously, to be ready and open to learn whatever is there for us. Life will present us with many opportunities to learn. I have seen some who stubbornly refuse to gather the learnings there for them. Yet, life still continues to present them with opportunities for learning the lessons time and time again. Unfortunately, each time the opportunity recycles, it seems to appear with more force and more intensity in order to get our attention. I see this increase in intensity as one of the ways that our inner process loves and cares for us. It gives us every opportunity to heal, grow, and learn. We can choose not to take those opportunities, and they will just recycle with more intensity the next time.

Sometimes, all we need is the willingness and our inner process will do the rest. Yet, willingness is not just an act of will. It is much deeper than that. By willingness, I mean an openness to face courageously whatever we need to face to take the next step in our journey. Often, our fear is so overwhelming that we're afraid that we won't be able to handle the information we learn about ourselves. Yet, in the end, all of this information is inside of us and it's *our* information. Getting clear about it, whatever it is, and working through the healing is what life is about. I find that it is often our mind and our *thinking* about horrible illusions that make our healing difficult, not our reality. Ironically, as we truly probe deep within ourselves and face our learnings, we find that our connection with our spirituality gets stronger and stronger, and we find we have the immeasurable support and caring to do whatever we need to heal.

Often, I find that many people underestimate themselves and become satisfied with a quick fix. Once they're feeling better, they're not willing to go to the depths within themselves required to truly heal themselves at a soul level. They will feel a little better, give up some of their harmful and dysfunctional behaviors, and back off, accepting existence rather than true living as enough.

Accepting a half life is not what Living in Process is about. In this work, there is an acceptance of wherever one is, while at the same time believing and knowing that we can have and are meant to have an abundant, fully alive life. In Living in Process, we have the possibility of embracing the process of full healing and full spiritual living. We see in those around us, lives changed and people living a complete, happy, and serene life, and we believe that this fullness of living and complete healing is possible for us all.

In my earlier career as a psychologist and psychotherapist, I came to see that the field of psychology did not believe that anyone can completely heal. They can go through endless psychotherapy and work on themselves forever, <u>and</u> underlying the whole field is a belief that no one ever really changes. Unfortunately, this actually limits what is possible.

Louisa, an Austrian woman, had an experience that illustrates this underlying assumption. She went through a period when she had some "emotional problems." As a result of this, she was hospitalized in a mild form of what we would call a mental hospital (a psychosomatic clinic) for several months as an inpatient, then was released as "cured and much improved." She did not agree with the diagnosis <u>and</u> did not yet feel "sane." She came into the Living in Process work facing bulimia and other eating disorders, as well as her other work. However, after meeting with the training group for three weeks during the year, meeting with her regional peer group every month, and going to Twelve-Step groups for eating disorders, she felt much clearer and quite functional.

In order to get a job, since she had been receiving disability, Louisa had to have an evaluation and go through a job-placement process. She had been a teacher when she became totally dysfunctional. She did well on the tests and interviews, and they recommended that she get a job as a secretary! She was stunned and said that she wanted to go back to teaching. She was told that because she had had "mental problems," she could not go back to her old job. She pointed out to them that she had followed their recommendations and been declared healed by the doctors in their system. (She had just added on the Living in Process work to *feel* healed herself.) They again reiterated their position and she was dismissed.

When I heard her story, I remembered that when I had worked in that system, the underlying belief was that no one ever really healed. They recommended drugs, psychotherapy, psychiatry, and counseling, and pushed people into those modalities. And, they did not *expect* people to heal and did not *believe* that they could. This was the major reason I left the field.

My experience with the Living in Process work that I was developing was that people could heal from *anything* if they were willing to do their work and stick with it. This deep healing, regardless of what the wound is, has been my continued experience in this work.

The only requirement is to have the willingness to do our work and to have the commitment to follow it through as far as it takes us. As we heal, we move into a freedom and responsibility we could not have previously imagined.

In the chapter on healing, I will discuss in more detail the specifics of the healing work in the Living in Process work.

ANCESTORS, SPIRITS, AND ANGELS

I have come to know that each of us has someone or something available to help us. Some people talk of ancestors who are present to offer support and guidance. Some talk of the power of our DNA and its gift to us. Others speak of angels or guardian angels. Still others refer to spirit guides. I even have one friend who calls his guiding, protective forces *spooks* in a half-teasing, familiar way. Whatever we call them, most people would admit that something is there when we need it and we can call upon it when we need it. Sometimes we may feel that there are a gentle pair of hands holding us up and sustaining us as we try to walk our path. At other times, we sense an unconditional love enfolding us. Whatever is there and whatever we want to call it, we can ask for help and we will receive it, although, perhaps not always in the form we imagined—yet help is there. Often, it is the asking that we find the most difficult.

We need not confuse these guardian guides with God or the Great Mystery. They are not the same. There is a whole universe of beings with whom we can communicate who are available to help. Often, we say that we are praying to God, when what we are asking is help from our guides. Perhaps this is yet another way we delude ourselves into believing that we can know the Mystery or reduce it to workable, human terms. Who knows?

As we do our work and live our process, we find ourselves connecting more and more with those previously unknown and unimagined forces. In our fear and personal constrictions we have so limited our lives. The willingness to make a commitment to go as far as we need to go with our healing, one step at a time, breaks through our false prisons and sets us free.

You shall know the truth and the truth shall make you free.

Jesus of Nazareth

Trusting–Relinquishing Our Illusion of Control

One of the most debilitating of the characteristics of dysfunction that we learn in human existence is the illusion of control. I have said in the past that any societal system that is built upon the illusion of control is a dysfunctional system. Unfortunately, most modern societal systems are built on the illusion of control. Control is so integrated into our society that very few people can even spot it. And, those who do, see nothing wrong with it.

Yet, the illusion of control is deadly. Our belief that we can control people, places, events, and things is a serious threat to our physical health. The stress we put on ourselves trying to control ourselves and others destroys our bodies. The stress we put on ourselves trying to control relationships destroys our bodies. The stress we put on ourselves trying to control money, business, economics, or our security destroys our bodies. Our security and our health come from participating in our lives and living them, not from trying to control them.

Giving up our illusion of control is one of the major steps we take toward our healing when we begin to learn to Live in Process. When we start making the shift out of a controlling way of living and begin Living in Process, the world looks different. It is as if we have put on a new set of glasses, and nothing ever quite looks the same again. The shift is internal as we forsake our attachments and begin to put our spirituality, our living process, our healing, first in our life. In spite of ourselves, we begin to see the world and participate in it quite differently. We come to know at a very deep level that we cannot compromise with our living process because our living process is God.

Living in Process

When we Live in Process, we are responsible for our actions and the consequences of our actions. As we accept responsibility—abandoning the roles of victim and perpetrator—we embrace our personal power and merge with the infinite power of the Great Mystery. As I said earlier, people who see themselves as victims are constantly giving away their personal power, which can be thought of as a leaking away of the soul. If we choose to be victims, it's as if we have cut a hole in the bottom of our souls and our soul is gradually being depleted. We need to have our personal power intact to be able to connect with the infinite power that is available to us. We are free to do otherwise—and there are consequences.

Ironically, as we take responsibility for our lives, admit whatever we have done, do whatever feeling work or deep processes we need to do, we shift internally and our personal power and connection with the infinite grows. We are not here to be perfect. We are here to participate and grow. We are here to become who we are. Whatever happens in our life, however difficult it is, it is always an opportunity for growth and learning. We can learn from whatever presents itself to us.

Living in Process is freedom and justice starting at
the personal level.

I have often said that Living in Process is living a life of faith. One of my favorite historical figures is Martin Luther, who led the Protestant Reformation. He was a man who certainly tried to live his faith even when it took him in directions he was reluctant to go. I like that. Living in Process is developing the ability to trust the process of life, knowing that it will give us what we need while offering us opportunities to grow and heal. We may not always understand immediately why our lives are taking the turns they're taking. Yet, if we wait with openness, usually the learnings and the knowings will come to us when we are ready to receive them.

Trusting our process does not mean that we are passive. It is anything but. Trusting our process means that we trust that we have a deep inner process that is connected with the Infinite that guides and protects us. We can be one with the Infinite, and when we are, we are truly living our process.

Trust is not something that we can will. Trust evolves as we do our work and again and again experience that we have some deep inner sense that guides us truly. I believe that our most profound sense of trust emerges as we do our deep-process work. (Deep-process work will be discussed in detail in Chapter 6.)

As we go deep inside, respect our inner process, and learn to go where it leads us, we heal. The more we have this healing and deep spiritual experience, the more we trust. The more we trust, the more we know that we are not alone, and that much more help is available to us than we had realized if we were willing to make ourselves available. The more we know that this help is always available, the more willing we are to go deep inside. We have leapt off the limitations of dualism into the sphere of possibilities.

These nine truths and guides, then, are the doors to Living in Process. They ask much of us, and give much in return. They are best learned and practiced in a community setting along with others who are attempting to live their process, and they are general principles for living. Those of us who are living our lives in this way can be mentors for beginners.

And, Living in Process is a way of being that is known to and belongs to all of us.

Chapter 5

WHAT WE KNOW AND HOW WE KNOW

LEARNING, THINKING, AND DECISION MAKING

> The senses are contradictory and deceiving. We never look at anything with our senses. We look with our feelings. Only our feelings can be trusted.
>
> *Alex Pua, Hawaiian Kapuna*

We have taken a quick look at learning and teaching in order to try to establish a baseline for understanding process. We have also touched on knowing what we know. Now, I want to explore knowing, learning, thinking, and decision making in more depth as they relate to living our life in process.

What We Know and How We Know

KNOWING

Deep inside each of us there is a knowing that functions as a gyroscope for our lives. A gyroscope is a spinning mechanism that seeks to maintain balance in several planes simultaneously. We have such a balancing mechanism in us. When we get off balance, if we can listen, it tells us that we need to get back in balance and reconnect. We are born with a sense of an internal balance that will tell us exactly what we need at each and every point in our lives if we only retain the ability to hear and to listen.

> To be deaf to the voice of the spirit within is to be crippled, a burden to others for as long as you live.
>
> *Morgan Llywelyn, author of* The House Goddess

One of the cruelest and most irresponsible things we can do in life is not to see what we see, and not to know what we know. We are created with this inner knowing of what we need and what is right and good. We also have inside of us the spiritual knowledge to guide us along our life's journey so that we have the opportunities to learn and grow. If the meaning of life is in the living of it, we have the opportunity to participate in our life and in so doing learn what we must know.

One woman described the deep-process work and the Living in Process as a way of learning the language of knowing. She said that she often identifies with Helen Keller, deaf, blind, and without speech in the language of intuition, feeling, knowing, and spirituality, and that her deep-process work and learning to Live in Process are like Annie Sullivan, Helen Keller's teacher, tapping out messages in her being. She is slowly learning that those messages have meaning and are a form of communication in the realms of knowing that she did not even know existed. She has been taught to communicate with her mind and she has not learned the language of her inner being.

Unfortunately, we have been taught to shut off and unlearn the most important means of communication available to us. Our schooling and culturalization have deadened us to our true knowledge. We have been taught that God is "out there," and we have been trained to look outside ourselves for knowing. As I've said before, this looking outside ourselves feeds into our belief that we are somehow victims of life and not participants in it.

We're out of touch with our inner knowing. We use anything to distract ourselves. And, our inner knowledge is still there waiting for us.

Several years ago, I was asked to consult with a group of nuns to help them decide about the admission of three women into their order. All three of these women had completed the novitiate—the training and discerning process—and it was time to make the decisions. As I sat down with these women, I could feel the tension in the air.

I let the group decide the order for discussing each woman. They left the difficult one for the last. The other two were easy and quickly dealt with.

I noticed that when we discussed the third woman, I had difficulty keeping the group focused on the task. I began to see a myriad of hidden agendas.

I. They needed new members so they hated to turn anyone away.

2. The woman in question was a friend of some of the women on the committee and in the order.

3. The woman in question had many physical and psychological problems. There was a question of how much she would contribute and the financial burden she would present to the order.

There was a great deal of taking care of each other and not speaking up honestly about what they thought.

After a long time spent in discussion and avoiding the decision, I decided to stop the process of the group, and asked if they were willing to do an experiment. I told the group that I believed that they all knew inside of them what their decision was. I asked them to stop, be quiet, and go inside to see if they could discover what they knew. Then I asked if they were willing to go around the group, and one at a time, each woman say what she knew.

We had 100 percent consensus. They all knew what the right decision was when they let themselves know what they knew. They were relieved with their clarity. Their thinking had interfered with their knowing! They decided that the woman should not become a nun and offered her a less rigorous form of being a part of the community—an associate member.

We need to trust ourselves and depend upon our deep knowing as it is revealed to us through our relationship with our Creator, Higher Power, Great Mystery. We are one with the oneness of all, and the ancient knowledge of our ancestors resides within us.

Even when others apparently have authority over us, we do not need to give our power away. We must seek our own right path. Knowing is tuning in to and respecting our feelings, perceptions, intuitions, and flashes. We need to trust what we know and respect that knowing. Living in Process affords us an increasing awareness of flashes, feelings, senses, body sensations, and memories—ours and our ancestors'. As we learn to notice them and trust them, our awareness increases, and with that comes the ability to live in our spirituality. Whatever awareness comes up for us at any point in time, we need to respect it and assume that it has meaning for us right now. Our thinking minds will probably never figure out what that meaning is, and as we notice and sit with that noticing, we will know.

I have written earlier about not trusting our perceptions until we begin to develop some clarity. Trusted friends and a community can help us with this process. And we will make mistakes as we are getting acquainted with our inner knowing. That's all right!

In order to know we must be able to discern between wisdom and information. Information is usually mechanistic and has to do with our material world. Information is usually put together and processed by our logical, rational, left brain, and communicated through words, concepts, and symbols.

Information is important to live comfortably in our environment, and it is different from wisdom. In this technological age, we have confused information with wisdom. As a result we're giving young technical wizards the status of wisdom-keepers when they simply haven't lived long enough to become wise, and their information does not emanate from the wisdom centers.

Information is helpful and useful. I recently bought a motor home and learned very quickly that understanding mechanics in order to use mechanical things is very helpful. The problem often comes when we try to apply that mechanical understanding to ourselves. The laws of mechanics do not apply to processes.

Wisdom takes time. Wisdom is processed with the whole being

and comes from our place of knowing. Wisdom is knowledge that has been tested with time and has the patina of the ages upon it. We often find wisdom in the proverbs of a culture. I have recently noticed in this age of information how few young people know the proverbs of their culture. Proverbs are one way of passing on the wisdom of the culture.

One of the issues we have to face in life is how to distinguish our knowing—our process, the voice of the Infinite—from our self-will and what we think we want. Because our minds are tricky and quick, this is a tough one, especially for persons who have been trained in linear mechanistic thinking. It is so easy to convince ourselves that our will is God's will for us. We can easily fool ourselves.

Our inner knowing never gets us in trouble. We may find that following our inner knowing will not always be easy, and actually, it may be quite difficult at times. Yet, it is almost always accompanied by an inner peace, a cosmic sense of relief. On the other hand, following our self-will almost always results in pain, struggle, confusion, disorientation, and stagnation.

> Sin bravely so that grace may abound.
>
> *Martin Luther*

Yet there are times when we seem to need just to crash ahead with our self-will and be ready to glean the learnings. This approach may not always be pleasant, <u>and</u> when we do it enough, it usually proves effective in bringing us the lessons we need to learn and grow.

LEVELS OF TRUTH

I mentioned levels of truth earlier. Now, I wish to explore them in greater depth.

We go through different levels of truth as we move into our knowing. What may have been absolute truth for us last week may no longer hold true for us this week. That is because our life is a process and we are a process. As we affirm what is true for us today, we are ready to move to a new level of truth. Only by completely embracing where we are can we move on.

One grave mistake we can make is to assume that the level of truth that we are on is the ultimate level of truth, or that our grasp of it is the ultimate. By grasping and holding on, we prevent ourselves from participating in the process of our inner knowing and moving on.

Levels of truth can be confusing especially if we try to make them static and are able to see only one or two fragments of the ongoing process at a time.

I tend to think of levels of truth as being similar to a sine curve.

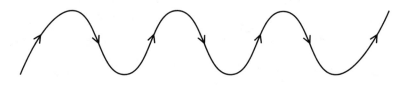

We can understand levels of truth better if we use an example. Let's take the issue of understanding and accepting gayness. There is an ignorance and phobic attitude toward gayness in our culture.

The first level of truth would be people who know nothing about being gay. This stage of development is often called heterosexual blindness by those who are gay. At the first level, we do not use slang words to depict gayness or even recognize that there are gay people around. There is an absence of focus on gayness.

At the second level of truth is an awareness of gayness that is frequently followed by a personalized homophobic response. Terms like *faggot, queer, homo,* and *dyke* are often used with a significant level of negative and hostile energy. Clearly, the awareness of gayness is producing some un-processed deep feelings and they come out in behaviors that are often nega-tive and mean.

If we continue to do our work and move to our next level of truth, our attitudes and behavior change. As we become more aware, we usually move into a stage of being more open-minded and sensitive. We are aware of the weight of being gay in this culture and we want to be supportive. We would never use derogative terms and are offended by them. This level would be the third level of truth.

As we move to the fourth level of truth, we have worked through more of our issues and have a comfort with gayness. At this level of truth, we might even joke around in a loving way about being a faggot or an old dyke.

There are fascinating aspects to the levels of truth. For example, as we grow and learn, we may go through many levels of truth on various is-sues. If we become fixated on one level of truth, we often become combative and mean.

Also, if we look at only one level of truth in and of itself and see it as isolated, we can delude ourselves into believing that it's the *real* level of truth. We can also set up a dualism with two consecutive levels of truth and try to live in that dualism.

One of the most fascinating aspects of levels of truth is that every other level of truth can *look* similar behaviorally and they can be eons apart. For example, using the illustration given, level two and level four both use terms that are emotionally laden to refer to gays. Yet, the emotions and the levels of awareness are quite different. And, to the unknowing person, they may look quite similar. Both level one and level three don't use the terms, and they, too, are quite different in scope and awareness.

As we move along our levels of truth, we have compassion for those who are traveling through levels we have experienced. Conversely, those on the earlier levels of truth are not aware of the other levels and tend to be more rigid and judgmental.

The more levels of truth we get through on a specific issue, the fewer people are with us and the less support we have. Indeed, we may experience more attack from those of earlier levels.

Life may be nothing more than moving through our levels of truth for one issue after another. Who knows?

All learning is self-learning.

As we explore ourselves we can know more about our place in the universe. Self-learning cannot be done with our logical minds. All too often, what we learn about ourselves with our logical minds is an illusion and a virtual reality, not our real knowing.

We are capable of knowing much more than we think we can know.

Ultimately we need to see what we see and know what we know.

Perhaps we often only tap into our more primitive brain structures, resulting in our compulsive and ritualistic behaviors, and our higher brains are our process selves.

LEARNING

How then do we learn and why do we learn? Good questions.

Learning should never be based on forgetting what we know.

A meaningful life is surely one that allows for learnings that evolve slowly.

Learning is different from gathering information. Learning may involve the gathering of information, and often when this is true, it's still the *process* of the gathering that's more important than the information itself.

Now let us return to the story of Mr. Kelly, the Koori elder and friend of mine from Australia. Whenever I'm with him, I realize that I'm always learning something new, and he's always reinforcing something he's already taught me. In Chapter 2, I described his way of teaching me, to illustrate the *process* of teaching and learning. Now, I want to delve a little deeper into what that process is for me.

Mr. Kelly teaches me and others as he would teach a child. He tells a story, and he tells the same story—over—and over—and over again each time I see him. Yet, each time he tells it, he adds something new, usually where I least expect it. If I get lazy or think, "He's getting senile and keeps repeating himself," or "I've heard this before," I may miss the new building block he's adding this time, <u>and</u> I will need that block to build on when I hear the story next time. Each time around I have more understanding of what he's showing me about his world and his knowledge.

He knows that I cannot possibly get it all at once, because like a child, I have to grow into the understanding. Real understanding does not come all at once. He is not manipulating my mind. He has a master's understanding of how to teach what is most important if one has the patience to learn. He feeds me, then respects my process of chewing and digesting that must happen between the feedings. I have to let myself become more and more intimate in order to understand. The teaching is a process; the learning is a process. Both need to be gradual. The pace is respectful to us both and considerate of both our needs. The *process* of his teaching is respectful. The information is in the service of the process, not the other way around. My process learning is one of patience, respect, and caring and may be as or more important than the content he's imparted to me.

Mr. Kelly's way of teaching is so different from the Western concept of understanding. In Western culture, we try to understand quickly with our rational brain. We are constantly setting up hypotheses that we consciously or unconsciously test out, and we *ask questions* and *ask questions*. We want to *understand* what is going on, and we believe that we have a better chance of understanding if we're coming from the same base of assumptions. Most of us don't realize that we have made assumptions, and that our assumptions are also our biases. These may or may not be about the truth, and they almost never have anything to do with acquiring new knowledge.

I recently realized the worth of Mr. Kelly's approach at an intensive workshop in Living in Process. We offer intensives throughout the world to introduce those interested in this work to an experience in Living in Process. People who have heard or read about it come to have the experience of it.

Given this premise, I anticipate that some will come to learn, and most do. <u>And</u>, there are always a few who pay their money to:

1. prove that they already know how to do this work—which usually they don't;
2. reframe it in terms of their own biases;
3. fight with it and attack;
4. come laden with so many assumptions, which often are premeditated resentments, that they can't let themselves experience anything that doesn't fit into their assumptions;
5. prove their hypotheses about this work, whatever those hypotheses are.

All of these agendas inhibit the possibility of learning. We cannot learn something new if we think we already know it. We can't learn something new if we have to reframe it into something we already know. We can't learn something new if we have to disprove it before we experience it. When our minds are closed, learning cannot take place.

Rarely do we come with a genuinely open mind. Often, our search for new information takes the form of, "Is it this *familiar thing*? Or is it that *familiar thing*? Or is it an unfamiliar thing that needs to be understood through a familiar thing?" We frequently do not allow ourselves an open mind and therefore miss many possible new learnings when we have to force new possibilities into familiar structures.

Understanding takes time. Understanding is like the taming of the fox in Antoine de Saint-Exupéry's children's classic *The Little Prince*. Understanding is a process, not an event, and it is not possible unless we are willing to take the time and effort to "stay with." Understanding is Mr. Kelly's giving me time to digest and chew.

This process of understanding and learning also applies to understanding ourselves. We cannot understand ourselves with our left brains. Understanding ourselves and our world is a process. In order to understand both, we have to live both—not think about both. In order to live, we have to deal with those forces that keep us from ourselves, from the attachments and all the things we use to numb our awarenesses. We cannot live fully if we are masked from ourselves.

I believe the kind of process described above is directly related to peace—peace within ourselves and peace among ourselves. Rarely, if ever, do we get peace from our rational minds. The kind of understanding I'm describing here has to come to our rational minds through our inner knowing, and this kind of knowing takes time.

Learning can come in many forms and from many places. We can never know ahead of time what our learnings will be or who our teachers will be. For example a very important teacher for me recently came from nature.

I had a very interesting experience with a snake at a Zen Buddhist retreat center deep in the canyons of California. Indeed, our teachers are all around us if we choose to accept the learning. It was bag-lunch day—i.e., cook's day off—and a friend and I had walked downstream to spend the day on the smooth boulders by our favorite deep pool. The rocks there are amazing. They have been worn smooth by endless years of spring melts and they are curved and sensuous. On each big boulder, there are at least a million possible places for sitting, and positions for sprawling and reading. I find that even the slightest change of my nude body brings in an entirely new sensuality. Just molding myself to the rock and it to me is an experience that speaks of many places, times, and lovers. It is a knowing of infinity within finiteness as the rock and I get reacquainted. I have been there many times and it is always new.

My favorite sitting place is right next to a small waterfall by a big, deep pool. I had settled in comfortably, reading a good book, and only moved as one muscle or another needed adjustment. After some time, I felt the need to look around me, and there in the big pool, treading water, so to speak, and looking me right in the eye, was a three-foot snake.

Now, snakes always evoke a certain speed in me, and before I knew it, I was at the top of the rock (safer there, of course) having screeched "Snake!" The snake continued to look at me and then swam under the rock. Since that rock, about the size of my VW van, was clearly no longer safe, I jumped across the waterfall and crouched on the rock on the other side of the stream—again clearly believing I was in a much safer place. The snake came out, hooked its tail in a rock just under the water, and floated for a while facing me. We both seemed safer when we could keep an eye on one another. Of course, at that time, I believed that only I was keeping an eye on *it*.

While I sat there trying to decide whether I would abandon my turf to the snake, wondering where its family was and how large it was, and generally stewed, the snake swam—that always gives me the creeps—to a smaller rock in the middle of the pool, crawled on it, and began resting and sunning. I stayed in my crouch for a while and then, deciding that I was safe, as the snake was in plain sight, I crawled back to my favorite rock and picked up my book, checking frequently to make sure I had the snake in a direct line of vision. Of course, we all know that snakes are safer when seen.

As I watched the snake, I realized that it was doing the same thing I was. It was keeping an eye on me, *and* it was sunning on its favorite rock. Like me (or perhaps *I* was like *it*), it made small movements to adjust to the rock, catch the sun, be more comfortable, or whatever. We were not so different. As the afternoon wore on, we both quit watching and seemed to become more involved in our own processes.

I left before the snake did. And after I jumped over the waterfall, I stood on the rock on the other side and bid it farewell. How simple it was to see the similarity. I was able to let go of the fear, and not deprive myself of a perfect afternoon because of control and turf problems. I learned to be one with a snake, of all things. The day truly was more because of the snake. I was more because of the snake. It taught me that I can't prescribe my teachers. Only learn from them.

Living in Process

When we know that we are part of the process of the entire holomovement, anything and everything becomes our teachers.

We have made the assumptions that learning must come through the senses and be as devoid of feelings as possible. As Alex Pua, the old Hawaiian elder, stated in the beginning of this chapter, our senses, which lead directly to our brain, probably cannot be trusted either. And yet, although our emotions may get muddled, our feelings are generally more reliable than our thinking. And, if we would be honest about it, our feelings are less amenable to our confusion and distortion than our thinking.

Our clearest approach to learning starts with our experience and knowing. Often, we have knowings and awarenesses in our body that have little or nothing to do with our thinking. Our deep process is one of the ways we bypass our thinking mind and go directly to our being, which is where all real *learning* and *healing* take place. When we start with our experience and knowing, our knowledge is embodied. Embodied knowledge is the language of the soul. We can relearn the language of the soul, of our being, of our wisdom through our deep process and our process living.

When we start with concepts, we become disembodied. However, after we have come through the body and our being, we can then bring the knowledge up through the body to the brain. One of the ways we "fix" our learnings is to give them concepts and language while fully realizing that all concepts and language are not real and are, at best, mere approximations of reality. The problem is that, when we start with our minds, these concepts and language have little or nothing to do with our experience and inner knowing and often lead us away from our knowing.

SEARCHING FOR CUES

Often, in native cultures we hear, "Don't ask so many questions. You white people ask so many questions. Just watch, listen, and wait. You'll learn."

When a native person says this, she is not suggesting a disembodied searching for cues. Native people are suggesting that you take in information and weigh it with your inner knowing. Asking questions requires left-brain activity, and the resultant information goes directly into the left brain, bypassing any filtering or balancing functions of the inner being. Information learned in this manner is suspect and unbalanced.

As we discussed before, Westerners tend to be extremely external in their identification, and consequently they look for their major information from sources external to themselves. This external focus actually supports a victim mentality since the major forces of influence are seen to be coming from outside. This method of learning tends to result in a society of "con artists" who are always looking outside of themselves to see what they want, who they are or should be, what is expected of them, and how they should behave to get what they want. Those persons whose learning is based upon external cues do not have the skills or language for internal communication, or for checking out the information they're getting with their internal gyroscope. They have forgotten the lost language of internal knowing. Unfortunately, people who try to base their lives on external cues and manipulating the environment for their needs are usually quite angry and unhappy because *they* have become lost in the process. Fortunately, these skills are not gone forever, though they may be deeply buried.

One trainee discussed that she suspects that she's incapable of learning what she needs to learn when she's not present to herself. If she's going through a particularly difficult time, when she is going through that time, all her skills may be used up in coping with the situation at hand. It's only when she is through the state of turmoil that she has the opportunity to look back, sit with herself, go inside, and wait with the learnings. Too often, we become impatient to know the learnings of a situation and we leave the situation emotionally, and then we miss the learning situation because we are simply not there. Often, what we have to do is live whatever the present is and trust that when the learnings come, we will be available, and we will notice them.

THINKING

Living in Process is moving without thinking.

Moving without thinking does not imply not being present. In fact, moving without thinking implies being totally present.

> My mind is a dangerous neighborhood. I don't dare wander in there alone.
>
> *John*

> I've been in recovery long enough to know not to trust anything I think.
>
> *Anonymous*

Lest we begin to get defensive about our thinking and start to believe that thinking is getting unfairly accused, let me quickly say that thinking is not bad. It is a gift of the Creator, and the Creator does not make garbage. It is what we do with our thinking and the sequence of it that gets us into trouble.

INTERPRETING

Interpretations are one of the major trouble spots in our thinking. Interpretations are nothing but unverified hypotheses that start with our brains and are not balanced by our inner knowing. They're almost always based on abstract theories and concepts that have nothing to do with real people in real situations. Interpretations may be interesting, <u>and</u> they have nothing to do with inner reality.

What We Know and How We Know

When we try to interpret the actions of others, their motives and the reasons for their behavior, our ideas may be very rational and logical, <u>and</u> they usually do not make any sense from an inner-being perspective. Frequently, we're trying to fit others into our concepts and theories so that we feel more secure.

There is no way that we can truly know what's going on with another person. That information is just not available to us. It may not even be available to them at that time. To let ourselves believe that we know is total arrogance.

The same is true when we interpret ourselves. We are bypassing our deep process and our inner knowing, and functioning in a disembodied head. When we interpret, we are almost always trying to construct a "theory" about what is happening so we feel more secure. Interpretations are attempts to explain, understand, or know why. Often, this very process of needing to know why or believing we know why takes us away from whatever is being triggered in us at a deeper level. When we stop our process with an explanation, we rob ourselves of the deeper knowing that will come if we stay with our feelings and go into our inner beings. Interpretations are like mental drugs that keep us from our process. We do not need them, they are not helpful, and they can be extremely harmful when our desire is to approach our inner wisdom.

Often, after we do our deep-process work, we may have awarenesses and almost always those awarenesses are not anything we could have come to by thinking. The awarenesses reached in our deep process ring with the wisdom of our being.

I have been brought up to believe that my mind is my Higher Power.

Brigitte

How sad that our minds have been put in such a position. We have made our thinking sacred and worshipped it while misusing it.

Living in Process

When you are in your mind, you are out of the flow.

Interpretations are violent and destructive no matter how well-meaning they may be.

NEGATIVE THINKING

Negative thinking is a characteristic of people who have lost touch with themselves. Interpretations are a form of negative thinking. Negative thinking is a form of contagion that can poison almost any environment. Our very thoughts become a thin film that coats and weighs down everything that it touches. Unfortunately, negative thinking feeds on itself and results in downward spiraling.

How is negative thinking different from critical or evaluative thinking? Very simply, negative thinking has a charge to it. Because negative thinking feeds on itself, it begins to take on a life of its own. Negative thinking glues itself to us, prevents us from seeing the separation between what we're thinking and reality. When we are "in" it, we cannot see that anything else exists. Negative thinking becomes reality to us, and we are completely incapable of getting enough distance to see that our thinking is not reality.

Often our thinking determines our reaction to information. For example, a few years ago in the Living in Process network a rumor emerged about the advanced training. The rumor, quite simply, was that if people had dropped out of the advanced training, they would have to take a year of the basic training before they would be allowed back in the advanced. Not true, and frankly not that big a deal!

For those who did not get into their negative thinking, the rumor didn't ring true, or they checked it out, or they thought they'd check it out, and they went on to bigger and better things. For those who indulged in their negative thinking, the rumor became a trigger for unleashing unprocessed feelings. They used it to fuel their negative thinking, which then self-generated all kinds of other negative possibilities, and they were off and running. This familiar way of reacting is a good way to give others control of your life.

There's another incident I'd like to share as an example of negative thinking.

In the break between the intensive and the new year's training in New Zealand, the group decided to take a little excursion together to visit the Waitomo Glowworm Caves, which I just love and think are one of the most beautiful experiences in the world. The group members had arranged accommodations to fit their budgets and all was in order. At the last minute, Anaru, a Maori elder man in the training, came in and announced that he'd called a local *Marae* (Maori meetinghouse, eating house, and gathering place) and we would be welcome there and could stay there.

After much discussion, the group decided that it was what they wanted to do, and they were able to get out of their other reservations without penalty. There were discussions of it being cheaper and saving money, and we also discussed that the *koha* was a gift given to the *Marae* and was not seen as "paying for" this or that. Rather we were bringing what we could give and we could take from what is there according to our need. Anaru had said that usually we get *kai* (food), but the vegetarians had better bring what they needed, as *Marae* food tends to be meat and starch.

When we got there, we discovered that the elder was a lovely old man who has severe congestive heart failure, and that the *Marae* was new, sparsely equipped, built on family land. Basically, it was his family of five who ran it and who greeted us. Our group had put together a very generous *koha* and obviously expected certain things in return.

Very quickly it became obvious that they had not prepared dinner, and in fact, I saw that they'd not had enough warning to prepare for thirty-five people. From my past experience, I know that it is embarrassing for a *Marae* not to have abundant food, so I quickly said we would love to do dinner ourselves and we invited them as our guests. Amazingly enough, we were able to put together a lovely meal of salad and fish and chips, and it was fun. The *Marae* family all enjoyed it, as did we. We even had money left over from the money freely chipped in for meals.

Then the negative thinking started: We weren't getting what we'd paid for. This wasn't such a great place to stay. The hostel would have been a better value . . . and on and on. Some people seemed to have lost sight of the possibilities in the situation and slipped into their negative thinking. The *koha* is not a pay-for-services arrangement as Westerners think. It is a free giving of what we have.

On the positive side, I noticed that the *Marae* did not even have its paintings and carvings up yet. Our *koha* might be adding to that, and they would be there for generations to see—maybe they could be part of us. I was immediately glad to see that we could make a contribution to a new *Marae*.

In addition, the elder who had congestive heart failure asked if we could help him. The doctors and nurses in the group offered consultations. The elder also knew I had helped Anaru with his back, and he asked if I could help. He told me that he wanted to live longer, as he had accomplished only a third of the work he was here to do. I told him that I believed that the Creator, through Fools Crow, the great healer and spiritual leader of the Lakota Sioux who had made me a pipe carrier and healer, could heal him. I told him that I would be willing to use what had been given to me and call upon them for healing. He had given me a gift by simply asking me to use what had been so freely given to me. How can one put a price on that?

Thinking negatively leads us to believe that we didn't get what we expected . . . that we see a poor return on our investment . . . that things are costing more money than we had expected . . . that we feel resentful for giving our power away to Anaru . . . and on and on.

Thinking positively, we see an opportunity to contribute to a new *Marae* . . . an opportunity to share personally with a Maori family . . . an opportunity to work together cooking and cleaning up with a local family . . . an opportunity to listen to an elder . . . to offer healing skills from our group. And, most of all, we were given an opportunity to become part of a *Marae* in a very important and historic area of New Zealand. This meant we could return to the *Marae* anytime, because we had participated in the process of being formally "called on," therefore becoming a member of that *Marae* as long as we lived—or longer!

Beauty is in the eye of the beholder.

Ugly is in the eye of the beholder.

Negative thinking could have ruined our experience at the *Marae*. Negative thinking has a deadening effect upon the possibilities of life and constricts our living.

Living in Process

MAKING UP STORIES

Often, when we feel afraid—or even just feel something—we make up stories about what's going on with other people to justify our feelings. Instead of just staying with our process and doing our deep-process work to discover what really lies behind the feeling, we retreat to our thinking. In the absence of any "real information," we find ourselves making something up, and we use this story making to relieve our tension. This is a very good example of where we are offered a door into our deep process, and we use our thinking as an escape that confuses and muddles us even more.

Some time ago, Louis started focusing in on what he calls *making up stories*. Making up stories is a particularly dysfunctional way of thinking. In the past, one of his favorite "stories" was that someone did not like him for some reason. The person he was focusing upon may have been so tied up in himself that he was not even aware of Louis. What was actually going on with this other person was irrelevant to Louis in his story making.

Given this trigger, the ball gets rolling. A whole slew of feelings, thoughts, and behaviors can follow. He can feel scared. Get angry at being ignored. Become concerned that he has somehow upset the other person—who may be oblivious to his existence! And so on, and so on, and so on. His thinking gets very busy: he isn't good enough; he's too crazy; things will never be okay; he might as well give up right now.

Then the behaviors start: he withdraws so as not to get hurt more; he has a chip on his shoulder for having been "wronged"; he pouts; he protects himself with fear-generated behavior and keeps his guard up. His life becomes totally involved in his "story."

In the meantime, the focus of his attention may just be getting on with his life.

An important learning for Louis now is that he's been able to label these "stories" as stories that he's making up in his head. He is now very quick to see that they are part of his thinking and that he can slip into them at any time. Any of us can. Since he has labeled this process as *making up stories*, he zeroes in on the process very quickly and rarely "indulges" anymore. In fact, we laugh and talk about his "stories" a lot.

The effect of Louis's naming this process as story making and owning part of his obsessive mind tricks and his taking responsibility for his thinking has done wonders for him and his relationships. These episodes still happen on occasion. <u>And</u> he picks up on his process quickly and calls someone to talk about it, and he can then let his stories go. When we are not clear, so much of our life consists of stories made up by a soggy mind.

I believe that much of what the court system handles, especially in civil cases, are probably stories made up by distorted thinking. Because the stories are made up, the person making up the story then amasses a mound of evidence—probably much of it fabricated—to "prove" it's true. From what I've seen, the key here in general is that there are people who don't want to take responsibility for their decisions and their lives, so a big part of their story is making someone else responsible.

Story making is not unusual. Politicians do it when they have international or national conflicts; tennis commentators do it when they're trying to apprise the television audience about why a particular person is playing a certain way—laced with interpretation, of course; and researchers do it to explain just about everything.

When we accept that distortions can occur as our perceptions move to thinking, that makes us feel less confused about our distortions. Information may come into us clearly, <u>and</u> as we move it into our thinking we can confuse, contaminate, and confabulate, and leave reality.

One important part of personal and spiritual growth is learning and continuing to do the necessary inner work so we do not *distort our perceptions*. Our best safeguard against distorted thinking is our deep-process work and checking out our perceptions with a community we can trust.

BEING OBJECTIVE

I want to say a bit more here about the myth of objectivity. Although I've mentioned it earlier, I want to reemphasize its importance here. Objectivity, as it is used in our society, implies complete nonparticipation. In order to be objective, we remove the self from the self and make the self the object to be observed. We also remove self from other in order to make it the object to be observed, whether it is another person, animal, plant, the earth, the planet. When we remove ourselves from self and other, when we leave the oneness, we then feel free to manipulate, exploit, and use up what we perceive as other, for it has no relationship to the self.

In many circles, objective thinking is seen as the highest and purest level of thinking. This myth of objectivity is touted as value-free, when in actuality, it is valueless.

Open, nonjudgmental thinking is possible, <u>and</u> it is not possible when we remove ourselves from ourselves and the other. It is possible only when we are willing to deal with our own feelings, do our own deep-process work, and open ourselves to a place where the oneness is a reality to us.

We can be clear when dealing with people and situations, and the way to do that is to do our inner work so that we are not projecting our issues on someone else. Once we have done our work, the thinking that we have available to us will be less contaminated. We can't *will* ourselves to be objective.

We have been given wonderful brains and nervous systems. We probably haven't even begun to scratch the surface of what they can do. Our focus on logical, rational thinking processes and the myth of objectivity has resulted in much of our capacity for intuition, awareness, higher levels of communication, and spiritual awakening being untouched and unused. As we live our process, the varieties of thinking modalities that become available to us are far beyond our present imaginations. Thinking is not bad. It's just that we sometimes use it in unhealthy and destructive ways.

DECISION MAKING

Our major decisions are discovered, not made. We can make the little ones, and we need to "wait with" the major ones until we discover them.

Decisions are a part of everyday life. Much of what life is about is an accumulation of little decisions sometimes culminating in big decisions.

How often we force ourselves into decisions because we feel we have to, when we are really not ready to do them or to deal with the consequences. Often, we feel that we must force ourselves for the convenience of others. When we Live in Process, we recognize that decisions are a process, and that the "right" one will emerge in time if we trust the process and work with it.

When my father was seriously ill, he needed to have a repair on a painful hernia to make him more comfortable. We were given the opportunity to turn our decision making over to the authorities or to discover our own. The following is the experience my family had with my father's surgery.

When my dad learned that he had to have surgery, he was in the hospital for a myelogram. Since he was already in the hospital, the MD decided that he wouldn't send him home, because my dad might hurt himself, and he would do the surgery the next day at 5:30 P.M. All the family and my dad discussed the options and decided that we needed more information. The family decided that I should talk to some of my friends who are specialists. So I got on the horn. Then these MDs got on the phone with the local MDs. By late that evening, we had much more information, yet still not all we needed.

When my dad's MD came in the next morning, he suggested postponing the surgery until the next week so my dad could be clearer about his decision, and the MD would not be operating so late in the day; I had been concerned about that. My stepsister then asked if it could be on her day off, which was also the best day for me, and we all agreed.

We did further information gathering and talking during the weekend. We asked all the questions we could think of with local and national MDs. We processed many other doctors' opinions, other hospitals, different kinds of anesthesia, etc. Whenever one member of the family didn't process their fear and was tempted to "puke" it on my dad by becoming controlling, someone always intervened, leaving my dad completely clear to process his own decision.

By the time the day of the surgery came, my dad was very clear about what he wanted. We all felt the prayers and support of a wide network. My stepmother, two stepsisters, niece, my son Roddy, and I were all at the hospital during the whole process. My dad was so clear and unstressed. It was obvious that he had processed the information, discovered his decision, and let it go. I felt the same.

Others in the family had more trouble with control issues, <u>and</u> basically we were all fine. My stepmother was very frightened, and we could all support her in that. I truly believe that one of the reasons Dad came through so miraculously was because he'd done his footwork and then let go. He wasn't fighting his own body's healing with his own control issues. The whole experience turned out to be a healing process.

Living in Process works.

What was clear to us after the surgery was that my father came out of it more alert than he had ever been after any other procedure. We hadn't been willing to have it performed until we had processed all our questions and "discovered" our decisions. He was suffering from congestive heart failure and the form of anesthesia we would use was a major decision. If he had gone right in the next day as the doctor had wanted him to do, he probably would have had a general and perhaps not survived it.

I truly believe that our taking our time and carefully processing the decision resulted in Dad's comfort and ours about the procedure being the best possible option. Down deep I believe that we would have been able to deal much better with any possible outcome, even death, because we had processed the information and our feelings before the decision was made. Sometimes processing and waiting with decisions is time-consuming, and yet ultimately it's always economical. Decisions give us a practical possibility for practicing our spirituality. Decisions are spiritual. When we discover our decisions from deep within, they resonate with our beings.

When we have doubts, uncertainties, unclarities, we need to trust them. They would not be there without a reason. The reason may have nothing to do with the decision at hand, or it may be only obliquely related. We may not even know why we feel uneasy. Trust it. Trust yourself. Your inner process will bring you to a place of clarity. If you miss the opportunity, you will probably learn something from it and something even better will come your way.

We need to know that options are wealth, and that we always have options and choices. Even simply generating options when we feel stuck can help us discover our decision.

CREATING DRAMA

We are always tempted to engage in drama over major decisions. Drama is always good for a little adrenaline fix, if nothing else, and is readily available at any time. Often, when we're trying to make decisions, drama can give us the diversion we need to avoid our process and not see what's really being triggered. We need to be cautious with drama.

One of my friends went into his drama about a decision he needed to make. He used the event of the decision to worry, fantasize, and develop fears about possible as yet unknown consequences. Instead of living with the decision and discovering what it was, he dramatized it and tried to figure out all the ramifications and what it *might* mean. He worked himself into a complete tizzy. Soon, he had left his life and was *living the drama*.

Living the drama is living the construct, the story, the idea. We make up constructs about how we believe the world is and then we start living them instead of life. Often, we are living a virtual reality of our own creation little related to the reality of our lives. When we switch to drama, we have left our lives.

Going inside, praying, sitting with, doing our deep-process work, and waiting with are what will get us clear. If what we are deciding is important, it may take some time.

Don't just do something, sit there!

Chapter 6

SOUL-LEVEL
HEALING

No discussion of Living in Process would be complete without exploring healing. Healing and maintaining good health are an integral part of Living in Process. In the past few years we have seen miracles of physical, emotional-mental, and spiritual healing as people have learned to live their process.

When I speak of healing, I do not mean just the absence of disease. Healing is a coming to the fullness of the level of wholeness we are capable of at any point in time. For example, there is a man who is HIV positive who has been doing the Living in Process work for some time. At times, there seems to be a slow progression of his disease, at times not. Yet, his spiritual, emotional healing has been such that the quality of his life is wonderful and his life is good. He lives with and accepts his HIV-positive status and his life goes on.

In the living process of the body, the ultimate healing is enfolded in the Great Mystery. Medicines, physicians, and psychotherapists may try to help, __and__ they are, at the very best, assistants. The wonder of healing belongs to the Great Mystery, and anyone with an ounce of humility who works in the healing professions will admit the truth of this statement. It is in reconnecting with our own living process that the unfolding of healing occurs. Many years ago when the group that I work with in Europe was trying to come up with a name for this work so they could categorize it for bureaucratic reasons, one person spoke up and said, "I know. Let's call it *Schönheitsfarm*—a beauty farm. People look so much younger and healthier as they learn to Live in Process." We all had a good laugh knowing that Living in Process does not fit into the old paradigm very well, no matter what we call it.

I do know that if our inner being does not want to heal, we will not heal. We need to respect our totality. We work out our healing in our relationship with our total process. Transitory adjustment occurs at a mind level. True healing takes place at a soul level, for healing and growth of the soul are ultimately more important than the healing of the body. Real healing starts with the inner being. True healing must take place at our dynamic living process. Often, healing of the body and the psyche will follow the healing of the soul.

When I wrote *Beyond Therapy, Beyond Science*, I was hoping that it would be my definitive statement about the healing component of the Living in Process work. I hoped to present the healing component in that book and then focus on the overall concept in this book. *Beyond Therapy* presented the healing work and the actual way we work with people; and it critiqued mechanistic science and the healing professions based upon it. Now, I find I need to say more about healing and Living in Process. I have learned more and have come to see that healing continues to be a major component in learning to live our process.

Our culture teaches us to disregard our own needs and to shut ourselves off from our spiritual selves. This has resulted in a deep sense of spiritual, emotional, and physical loss that permeates all that we do and are. We disregard our bodies, escape from intimacy with ourselves and others, and are always looking for something outside ourselves to "fix" us or numb us out. The levels of adrenaline that we need just to keep going increase exponentially as we search in vain for meaning in our lives.

In *When Society Becomes an Addict*, I described Western culture as functioning like an addict and having all the characteristics of an active addiction. I saw addiction as the disease of choice and a requirement of the society we have created. And I saw the Twelve-Step program of Alcoholics Anonymous and its offshoots as the most effective tool for recovery from addictions. I still see truth in this conceptualization, _and_ I have broadened my perspective.

The characteristics of addiction are powerful elements in our culture that have affected all of us. Whether we want to call them addictions, dysfunctions, or obsessions is irrelevant. What is vital is that we recognize the pervasiveness of this dysfunction and see the need to heal from it.

As my own personal healing has deepened and expanded, so have my knowings. I still believe that addictions exist in epidemic proportions in our culture and throughout the world and that Western culture requires a high level of disassociation from the self and our Creator (our soul) in order to tolerate what we have created. We need to remember that the culture we have created has existed for a minuscule period of time in human history, yet its destruction of the planet and the quality of human life is unprecedented. We need healing at many levels.

Since Western culture has become so pervasive, and the problem is bigger than just Western culture, I now realize that we need to heal from the Technocratic, Materialistic, Mechanistic Personality (TMMP) that exists at all levels from the individual to the planetary. The TMMP can be overpowering if we look at it from a planetary perspective, so we need to start with the only place where we really can make changes—ourselves. And this means, on occasion, using the concept of addiction to explore personal and societal healing.

Living in Process

TOLERANCE FOR INSANITY

One of the characteristics of persons living in dysfunctional settings is an *increased tolerance for insanity*. People who live in the midst of dysfunction are so busy coping with existence that they lose the ability to stand back, tune in to their inner reality, and gain the perspective they need for healthy living.

To continue to produce and distribute death-producing, mind-altering agents for economic gain is *insane*. Only those whose minds are not clear, who are not living their process, who are not living their spirituality would not see this glaring truth. To continue to pollute the earth, air, and water when our lives and the lives of generations to come hang in the balance is *insane*. What will it take to see and name the insanity and begin to live differently in context?

One of the first steps toward sanity is to confront our own dysfunctional processes. Dysfunction controls us. Also, by definition, dysfunctions are mind-altering and soul-destructive. The TMMP is a disease of the body, mind, and spirit in which our minds become useless to us because they distort our thinking into confusion, convolution, obsession, and delusion. The thinking of an addict, for example, is similar to that of schizophrenics, who are described as having a thinking disorder.

Many are aware of the dysfunction in our society; however, few people have a clear grasp of the implications of the TMMP. The distorted perceptions and confused thinking of the TMMP are so embedded in our culture that it has become the norm of society and deeply embedded in our major institutions.

For example, we are no longer surprised or even concerned when politicians lie or give out mixed messages. We accept it when tobacco companies are willing to pay fines for producing a carcinogenic, addictive drug as long as this doesn't hurt their business too much and they can cut a deal with the U.S. Congress to never face these charges again. Our tolerance for insanity has reached such proportions that sanity seems frightening and unusual. One can only hope that we will reach a point where enough people return to their living process—their spirituality—so that waves of change will reverberate through all the spheres of being.

HEALING AND PARTICIPATION

Let me say something general about addictions at this point.

There are two major kinds of addictions that alter our consciousness and shut off feelings, awareness, and information from our body and spirit: substance addictions and process addictions. The former are any substance that we take into our bodies to alter awareness, such as drugs (prescription and street), alcohol, nicotine, caffeine, sugar, and food used addictively. Adrenaline, even though it is produced in the body, is considered a substance addiction when we use it to shut off awareness.

Process addictions have the same effect as substance addictions, and they are subtler and generally more integrated into the society. Process addictions teach us to become obsessed with activities such as excessive working, spending, exercising, sexing, and thinking.

Addictions are not the only way we can shut off awareness and split off from our feelings.

When we become alienated from our bodies and spirits and become a disembodied mind, certain ways of behaving begin to emerge. We become dishonest, self-centered, ego-driven, materialistic, amoral, controlling, and dualistic, which gradually destroys our spiritual base.

Whether we label these destructive behaviors as addiction, attachment, obsession, sin, dysfunction, a problem in the family, or moral bankruptcy doesn't matter. The real issue here is that we have become split off from ourselves. We have shut down our awareness of our feelings, emotions, wisdom, and spirituality and have become disconnected, compartmentalized.

The way back from unconsciousness to consciousness is through noticing and reconnecting. We have to learn how essential it is to receive feedback from all parts of our being—body, mind, and spirit.

Since we know more about addictions than we do about the TMMP, I find it helpful to use this knowledge, and I suspect that addictions are only the tip of the iceberg.

THE TECHNOCRATIC, MATERIALISTIC, MECHANISTIC PERSONALITY

The Technocratic, Materialistic, Mechanistic Personality has many characteristics in common with addictions. Let us take a little time here to explore the components of the TMMP.

The Technocrat

A native elder once said to me, "It's not that technology is bad. There is a possibility that technology could be good for everyone and everything. Unfortunately, the technological societies have not reached the level of spiritual development necessary to develop a technology that would be in the service of the spiritual and the Creator. Spiritual development must come before technology. Most of the technology we have on the planet was developed for warfare and for economic competition; it was only modified for everyday use."

What are the characteristics of the technocratic personality? Technocrats tend to function almost exclusively in their heads. Their thinking becomes disembodied and imbalanced. They move progressively into abstractions and are less and less grounded in their bodies or their beings. In fact, they learn ways to shut off their minds from their bodies and souls. This is where addictions of all types come in. The whole purpose of addictions is to shut down our internal information system, reducing us to a state much like a boat without a rudder.

The technocratic personality is an isolated personality. As we become more comfortable and occupied with our machines and our virtual reality, we become progressively disconnected with life. We live in the TV, the movie theater, and the computer. Technology feeds our illusion of control. We begin to think that we can control everything, people, places, things, ourselves, our bodies, our relationships, and the planet. In our own minds, we believe we have become God and no longer recognize or need a power greater than ourselves.

The TMMP is dishonest without the awareness of being dishonest. These persons have become so detached from their bodies that they no longer receive the usual cues from their internal information systems about their behavior that lets them know they are being dishonest. They are isolated emotionally, so they do not get the external cues that they are cut off from their process of God, becoming progressively out of touch with their spirituality and their morality. This results in a massive self-centeredness that becomes very isolating. Reality becomes a touchstone rarely approached. We cannot blame technology for these dysfunctional behaviors. We're the ones who develop them. We need to take responsibility for ourselves and our own healing, even as we see this dysfunction partially as a response to a destructive, technological world.

Materialism

Materialism is destroying our planet and our souls. Healing from it is a necessary process.

When materialism becomes our God, we become estranged from ourselves, and in so doing become estranged from nature. We no longer see ourselves as part of nature. We have positioned ourselves above nature. On the other hand we need nature—to exploit—because when we worship the material, we truly come to believe that we will be saved by what and how much we have. We become slaves to the material while believing that we are controlling it. When we separate the material from the spiritual, we begin to see our world in terms of dualism, which vastly limits our perception of reality. I mentioned that some Eastern religions believe that dualism is a fact of the material world. That has not been my experience. As I have learned to Live in Process, I have seen myself and others move beyond dualism back to wholeness. Dualism is a virtual reality that results in distorted thinking.

Materialistic solutions for spiritual voids will never work.

Mechanistic Science

Mechanistic science has become the major religious belief system of our technocratic society. We have come to believe that salvation lies in technology, and most modern technology is based in mechanics. We have come to see people and the planet as machines and treat them that way. Both can be utilized to support the economy as long as they're productive, and then discarded when they no longer serve our purpose.

A mechanistic, scientific worldview is an isolated, nonparticipatory worldview. In the dualistic views of science, medicine, and psychology we separate the spiritual from the mechanical and the spiritual from the everyday.

In a mechanistic worldview we strive for objectivity and nonparticipation and become progressively divorced from that which feeds our souls. We look outside ourselves for reality and come to believe that something external to ourselves will make life meaningful. When the material becomes our salvation, we see ourselves as victims buffeted by forces over which we have no control and with which we do not participate. As I pointed out earlier, when we feel like victims, we feel justified in becoming a perpetrator, and anger and violence are the results.

DYSFUNCTION

Although this discussion has been an oversimplification of the issues and the forces involved in creating the twentieth-century TMMP, I think we can all agree that this kind of dysfunction is an epidemic throughout the planet and is spreading quickly.

Soul-Level Healing

Unfortunately, most of the common approaches to healing in our culture are embedded in our technocratic, materialistic, mechanical worldview, and it's difficult, if not impossible, to heal the problem with the problem. Many of the spiritual, medical, and psychological approaches tacitly ignore and enable the TMMP while trying to find a solution from within the old paradigm. Because of this reliance on old models, they are unreliable and ineffective in dealing with the core problem.

I have found the Twelve-Step program developed by Alcoholics Anonymous is a good door into dealing with the addictive process generated by this worldview. Some of the criticism of AA is because it stands outside the norm. Yet, this program itself does not address political questions or confront the prevalent worldview, and it's important to know this. The program was developed by addicts to help addicts, and it works for that quite well. My experience is that recovery from addictions is one of the most dependable means of moving our being to a point of healing where we can open the door to our deep process. The paths are many. Those who truly choose to commit to walk them are fewer. Therefore, what I'm presenting here is what has worked for me in my journey and what I have been teaching others. I especially like what works.

There are many ways to conceptualize this process of dysfunction. In Eastern religions it is called attachment to the physical plane. In some Western religions it is called sin. In some medical and psychological circles it is characterized as illness, disease, and addiction. Whatever we call it, we still need to set out on our path of healing before we can begin to Live in Process.

Only recently has Western medicine begun to recognize that a very large percentage of the practice of medicine is focused on illnesses that are primarily caused by individual addictions. Alcohol, drugs (street and prescription), nicotine, food, caffeine, sugar, fat, work, anorexia, addictive relationships (battering, stress), obsessive thinking, and all their side effects account for the bulk of the practice of medicine. If we add to this list diseases that are caused or exacerbated by the practice of the addictions of the society—money, economics, power, control—such as those caused by polluted air, water, soil, overcrowding, carcinogenic agents in food, altered food sources (genetic engineering), contaminated drug products, and the side effects of drug chemicals, we have a very small number of genuine physical illnesses left with which to concern ourselves. We have come to accept the side effects and by-products of the TMMP as "givens" for illness and have lost sight of the fact that most are caused by or exacerbated by the TMMP or addictions.

Western approaches to healing have tended to view the individual out of context as an isolated, germ-carrying entity that can be treated singularly. This approach to healing ignores reality. In Samoan medicine, for example, whenever a person goes to a healer, that healer immediately focuses upon context: What is happening in the family, village, community, the whole society, that has pushed a normally balanced person out of balance? Imagine what would happen in this culture if the illnesses of the individuals were viewed as the thermostat of the culture. Imagine what would happen given the blinding evidence that nicotine causes cancer, if all physicians insisted that regardless of economics, tobacco must be banned. Imagine, if you can, a culture where the government, the institutions, and the organizations exist to support the spiritual growth and health of the individual and the society, and that all major decisions are made not on the basis of economics and money.

Whatever we call this dysfunction is not important. It's all the same process. However, the solution cannot come from the old paradigm. Our healing will come about only as we return to our wholeness and make a complete paradigm shift.

We can learn vast amounts of knowledge in the process of healing our inner being if we can make ourselves available for those learnings. The very process of equality means we all share the dysfunction of the society, and participation is the key. Dysfunction is always a disease of isolation and withdrawal (objectivity). The process of healing reawakens our deep human memory of participation. We cannot heal in isolation. Full participation in all of life is the ultimate healing.

PRELIMINARY HEALING

First, we must do some preliminary healing before our dysfunctional store abates enough for the living process to be experienced.

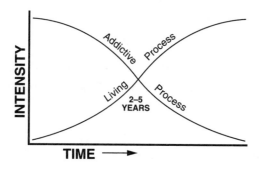

As we see by this diagram, when we first start confronting our TMMP, our awareness of our living process may be almost nonexistent. We have lived so long in a dysfunctional society, so many around us are dysfunctional, and our tolerance for insanity has become so enormous that we may have no awareness of our living process. However, in spite of this lack of awareness, I have yet to meet anyone who has managed to completely destroy their living process (spirituality), although many have gone to great lengths to do so. Early on, as we begin to heal, it may seem to us that we're only our dysfunction. And, do remember, our living process is there waiting for us. As we do our healing work, we will get little glimpses of sanity. The first time we experience clarity and being one with our spirituality, it may scare us to death because it's so unfamiliar. Yet, as we continue to heal, we will spend more and more time in our living process and less in our dysfunctional TMMP. It may take two to five years of healing before we experience real clarity and oneness. Once we do, though, we never want to go back to where we've been.

As we continue to do our healing work, our worldviews shift, and so does our way of living. We learn to live at one with our spiritual selves, and experience living the way our Creator intended for us.

As TMMPs and as human beings, we never completely give up our dysfunction. We may spend less and less time there, <u>and</u> it is often just beneath the surface. Since we live in a culture that reinforces and even demands dysfunction, we are always being invited back. This, of course, does not mean that we have to accept the invitation.

The fact that people are willing to move toward something they can't remember experiencing is one of the miracles of healing. Another miracle is that no matter what we have done, our living process is still there. The deep knowing of these miracles may help us return to a knowing of the deep compassion for All That Is.

To heal, we need to participate in a program that confronts the TMMP and is healing for us. Participation is key to making the much needed paradigm shift. The Twelve-Step program may be a door for some. Please remember that I am writing about my own experience here and the experience of those with whom I have worked. There are other paths to get to a place of being available to learn to Live in Process. I simply don't have much personal experience with them.

There is no doubt in my mind that the recovery program is divinely inspired, and if practiced in all aspects of one's life, it can result in major paradigm shifts for both individuals and society. We must also remember that, like all spiritual programs, it was developed by humans, and is practiced by addicts as best they can. One of the greatest wisdoms of the program is the saying, "Take what you like and leave the rest," leaving the ultimate relationship between a person and that person's Higher Power (spirituality). The best that some groups hope for in recovery is adjustment to the system and not total spiritual health and healing. Others develop an openness that allows them to move beyond mere "recovery."

Gloria wrote this letter to me about recovering from a long-term obsessive process. I share it with you as an example of one woman's path for healing. From it, we can get a feel for the everydayness of this kind of healing.

I was lost. Yesterday I realized the emphasis in this sentence should have been on *I*, not on *lost*. Something was missing in me and it seems to be what I think of as *I*. Now I feel alive again. There again. Present to myself in a way that allows me to be present to and caring toward others. Some fog has lifted from me. It is very strange to be so aware right now of the difference in the two states of being I have experienced this week.

I think perhaps where I have been is "in my dysfunction" as you say. And I have not had till now such a clear sense of what this means for me. It is my version of alcoholism. (I read *Broken Promises, Mended Dreams* and had no trouble finding the parallels between myself and the woman alcoholic in that story. Weird! And useful.) I don't need another person, an outside event, a substance, an object. I can get crazy all on my own (which seems quite weird to me). Hating myself. Being hard on myself. Feeling horrid. So confused that to say I am unclear is a gross understatement. Spinning around inside myself. Totally distrusting myself. I feel as though something else has taken me over.

I can also today see quite clearly how different I am when I am in that state and when I am going along in my more usual state. It occurs to me that being fully alive may be a spectrum, not an on-off condition. I have been "nonliving" the last three weeks. And now I am alive again. It may be I can be and will learn to be more fully alive. And I know that where I am right now, I have some degree of aliveness. And it is a place (like the bad state) that is familiar to me. In the last few years, I have spent more time in the alive state and less in the nonliving.

And still the "nonliving" can descend on me seemingly out of nowhere. And seems to stay with me till it is ready to leave. I remember you spoke of our friend and said not very much of her is available. When I am in my nonliving state, not much of me is available either.

One of the things I hated about those three weeks was I wasn't learning anything. I didn't know what was going on with me. I tried to stay with where I was and to be open to the learning, and I got so upset with myself that I wasn't learning (part of my dysfunction is being judgmental and dissatisfied with myself, right?). What I am thinking now is it may not be possible for me to know the learning while I am "in my dysfunction." And that when I come out of it, I may then be able to discover what there was to be learned. There sure (in retrospect) doesn't seem to be much point in trying to stay with that state until I learn what I am supposed to be learning. It is as though I am incapable of learning when I feel like that. Everything is too distorted for me.

Now in the last few days, I am knowing the learnings, understanding better where I was. Still not sure how to help myself during these times. Leslie and my friend Cathy tell me it sounds like letting-go time, surrendering. And one of the things I am learning is that no matter what, under no circumstances am I willing to surrender, to let go. I am just rigid about this.

Soul-Level Healing

I read something in the Emotions Anonymous big book which fit for me. There is a difference between believing in a Higher Power and having faith in a Higher Power. I do believe there is something or someone much greater than me. And I have no (zero!) faith that that Higher Power will help me, will take care of me. It seems somehow wrong, bad, sinful for me not to keep trying the best I can to help myself when I feel down. Letting go seems like giving up. And anyone who gives up, who doesn't even try, deserves to stay down. I am sure this doesn't make sense to you. And I think it is some part of what goes on in me. I know it just doesn't feel okay to me to let go, to turn myself over. It just seems the "wrong" thing to do.

Anyway, I am feeling mostly happy now. Feeling good most of the time with an occasional relapse, where before I was feeling bad most of the time with an occasional remission.

Each night I look back over the day and see what I have to be grateful for. My version of praying for now. And each morning I pray (to no one or nothing in particular—just pray) for openness to my process and the process of the universe, for willingness to learn what I have to learn that day, for willingness to let go, for help.

And I wonder what to name my dysfunction. To call it my left-brain process doesn't seem to be quite accurate. And it disparages the good parts of my left-brain process. There is a particular aspect or process in my left brain which is sick. And it is quite tangled up with my emotions. I am powerless over my feelings sometimes. I am powerless over my thinking sometimes. And there is some combination of some aspects of my thinking and feeling which is my dysfunction.

I don't think I am trying to evade or deny by searching for the name. I, too, (I remember you saying this about yourself during the September training) want to be precise with my words. I think the distinctions of particular words affect me, my experience, my feelings, my thinking, my understanding, my knowing. So, I continue to seek a word that names my dysfunction for me. As I see my dysfunction more clearly, I know better which words fit and which don't. I get closer to naming it, more precise. And I believe each time I get closer to the naming of my disease, my healing is helped in some way.

Gloria

Gloria is very articulate in expressing her experience on the path to healing. We all have to face our dysfunction on the path to healing, and the process of naming it in a way that functions for each of us can be very integral to moving on. We always need to remember that each stage is part of the process of healing. When we attach to any stage, we become stuck.

I have found that a certain amount of healing and letting go of dysfunction must occur before we are ready to even see the door to living in our process, much less walk through it.

We need to begin to make the shift from a nonparticipatory to a participatory worldview and start to take responsibility for and function more actively in our lives. We need to let go of the substitutes for living that we use to shut off our awarenesses and the connection with our spirituality. We need to begin our exploration of the Living in Process truths discussed in Chapter 4. We need to remember that healing is a process, not an event, and that learning to trust the process itself is important learning, as vital as the specific healing. In fact, the healing process may be the vehicle to learning about our living process as our living process is healing to us.

Whatever we call it, we need to remember that we live in a culture that demands dysfunction. The purpose of dysfunction is to keep us out of touch with our own living process. Our dysfunction keeps us from fully experiencing the pain of the isolation, dishonesty, illusion, and self-centeredness of living in the world we have created . (See *When Society Becomes an Addict*, for a further explanation of these concepts.) Whatever we call this process, the meaning and the process is the same. We are removed from our spirituality.

Dysfunction is learned. Whatever is learned can be unlearned. Dysfunction keeps us in the ritualistic behavior of our lower brains. We can do and be better.

As individuals give up their dysfunction and move into healing, the deep processes that were held down begin to surface. These processes are always trying to surface for us, <u>and</u> our dysfunction may keep us so busy and "numbed out" that we stay completely unaware of our processes requesting to be healed.

DEEP PROCESSES

As we grow and develop, we have various experiences that affect us. Some of these experiences affect us quite traumatically and some only slightly. Often, when we experience these events, we do not have the skills or maturity to handle them. These memories, experiences, sensations, and knowledge are held within our bodies, ready to move into awareness when we are ready to heal them. This is one of the miracles of human existence. In our bodies we have the storage of all the events that we need to learn from to become whole. When I think about this miracle, I am truly in awe. Everything that happens to us or that we do is our personal educational material. It is carefully geared to our needs and is in exactly the form we need to provide us with the essence of individualized learning. We also seem to hold archaic memories in our DNA, which we may have the opportunity to heal.

Our bodies and beings hold these experiences deep inside until we have reached a level of awareness and maturity to work through whatever we need to work through in order to move through our soul's journey. I think of these deep processes as bubbling around inside of us in a big cauldron. Occasionally something bubbles up—like the mud paint pots in Yellowstone National Park—and we have the opportunity to focus on and go into that deep process, heal, and glean the learnings. My experience is that anything can be healed in our deep process regardless of how traumatic the event or how deep it is hidden. If we can have the trust to honor the deep process when it comes up and the willingness to go into it and go wherever it takes us, we can heal from anything.

Sometimes, we do not notice a deep process when it comes up, or we don't feel ready to deal with it, and that's all right. In the loving wisdom of our inner being, it will recycle and give us as many chances at it as we need. Each time it resurfaces, however, it does so with more force to get our attention. In our denial and resistance we may experience this recycling as an attack or failure. It is anything but. It is our inner being, our Creator loving us and giving us every opportunity to heal. The very fact that it is making itself known is an indicator of how strong and aware we have become and that we have whatever we need to deal with it. If we miss it, it will come up again.

DOORS

There are many doors into our deep process:

1. tears;
2. a rising feeling;
3. an overreaction or emotion too intense for the situation at hand;

4. picking a fight with a spouse or others as a distraction;

5. an urge to indulge in our favorite addictions;

6. a fleeting thought or awareness;

7. a song that won't get out of our mind;

8. something entering our sphere that tries to lull us or trick us into believing that we're experiencing the "good life";

9. pain;

10. depression;

11. deep happiness.

These and other doors suggest to us that we have a deep process that is ready to be worked. Usually all we have to do is stretch out on a mat or something similar, abandon thought, and wait. It's good to have someone sitting with us, as deep processes sometimes become intense. When we sit with someone in deep process, our role is to be with her as she goes where she needs to go. It is none of our business where she's going, and completely inappropriate for us to think we know where she should go.

Usually the door into the deep process has nothing to do with what the process is eventually about, and it is the door to getting there. Often, our doors to our deep process are persons who set off our triggers. Remember, they are gifts for us to do our deep-process work, and the actual process probably has nothing to do with them.

For example, if we have a strong reaction to someone, feel wronged by them and want to "get" them, what is coming up for us probably has nothing to do with the person or the incident at hand. That person may be a gift to us and an invitation into our deep process. Our reaction is usually the opportunity to go into our deep process and heal old wounds and old, unfinished processes. The person who triggered our deep process is usually irrelevant for us. We can, however, choose to focus on that person and, in so doing, miss an important opportunity for our healing. The choice is ours. The opportunity is ours.

Louise was afraid of her deep processes. Whenever she would feel one coming up, she would become very resistant, gritting her teeth, and was not willing to go to the mats and stretch out and see what came. She had been through many types of therapy and was considered a therapy "failure."

It was suggested that she honor her resistance and stretch out and see what came up for her. She was willing to do that. She stretched out to see what would happen. She moved spontaneously into some raging and some crying. (Deep processes should never be pushed nor should techniques be used to elicit them. Someone, anyone, may sit with you while you do your deep process, and their job is to be with you, to stay out of your way, and to keep you safe if you start thrashing around.) After this, Louise became calm. She came back to the group looking serene and peaceful.

When she shared, she told of the rage that came up when it was suggested that she honor her resistance. She had never been told to honor her feelings and had always tried to be a "good girl" and do what others wanted. Her rage then dissolved into pain as her tears poured out her years of not honoring herself. She could feel the sadness and see the destruction of herself she had caused in not honoring herself. Years of self-abuse flashed before her in remembering the myriad of ways she had tried to be good. She then came to a peace in knowing that she had honored her resistance and that she was taking a tentative step on the road to healing.

Soul-Level Healing

In Louise's case it was the process of the process that was important. The process of honoring herself led to her healing. The resistance (content) was not that important. That she honored it and went where it led was. Slowly, over the years, Louise has begun to trust her deep process.

Our deep processes are the major way we have of bypassing the rational illusion of control of our left brains so that we can go directly to our inner beings where real healing takes place. No one ever healed from understanding or insight. Both can be interesting. Yet, neither heals. True healing takes place somewhere deep within the recesses of our inner being where only our deep processes can penetrate.

Many people have tried to develop techniques to access and work with our deep process. Unfortunately, these techniques often rape the psyche. Unfortunately, often, the only major learning gleaned from techniques is to trust the technique or the therapist, and little or nothing is learned about trusting our own process. The therapist becomes the "god" for the client, and the technique becomes the "god" for the therapist, removing both from the healing of their spirituality.

Our deep process, ultimately, is the magic door that opens the way to the bottomless pool of our spirituality. In learning to trust our deep-process work and to trust what comes up, we learn to trust our living process. Living in Process is about facilitating our own process even when it's going in a direction we do not understand, never thought of, or thought we wouldn't like. Trusting the unfolding of our deep process teaches us to develop a life of faith while at the same time healing old wounds. Our inner being is very efficient and usually manages to accomplish more than one thing at once.

DEEP PROCESSES ARE UNIQUE

Not all deep processes are painful, which we might expect in our negative thinking. Some are quite joyful, funny, or serene. We are, after all, filled with variety, whether we know it at all at this moment.

John was often depressed and fearful. He saw his life as fairly miserable and lived it accordingly. He truly believed that his deep processes would be more of the same, and he wasn't sure that he wanted any more of that. One day in the group meeting, he was feeling restless and irritable, snapping at everyone. Someone in the group said that they were not willing for him to "puke his process" on them and asked if he was willing to go to the mats. He stomped off to the mats, obviously not happy about the situation and not asking anyone to sit with him—he'll show them!—and depriving himself of the support he could have had.

On the mats, he moaned, he groaned, he sighed, and he whined. After a while he seemed to develop a rhythm and pattern: moan, groan, whine, sigh; moan, groan, whine, sigh. A few snickers went up from the group as he continued to do his deep-process work.

Suddenly, John started laughing. He laughed uncontrollably. He rolled around on the mats. Others scurried to hold up mats and keep him safe. The group felt the urge to join his laughter, and everyone joined in for a while. Then, he became quiet and peaceful.

Later, when he shared, he said that he was initially "pissed off" to be "told" to go to the mats. "What did they know anyway?" This is a good example of how we distort what others are saying or have said when we have "work up" and haven't done it! He felt "pissy" when he got to the mats and he certainly wasn't going to ask anyone to sit with him after the group had "treated him so badly."

Then, when he got into his rhythm of moan, groan, whine, sigh, he realized after a while that this was the pattern and structure that he had set up for his life. Not long after that, the hilarity of this choice struck him and he convulsed with laughter. What a ridiculous life choice. When the group members spontaneously came to support him and make sure he was safe even though he had not asked for help, he was touched and filled with gratitude. Some bubbles of laughter were still there as he shared his deep process.

We never know where our deep process will take us, <u>and</u> if we are willing to let it lead us, it is always interesting.

Deep processes can be about anytime, anyplace, anywhere, and anyone. We don't even need to know what they're about for the healing to occur. Deep process is much more than catharsis, <u>and</u> a catharsis may occur. Deep process is more than "getting the feelings out," <u>and</u> feelings may lead into a deep process. Many feelings may be deeply felt during a deep process, <u>and</u> deep process is much more than feeling feelings.

We must remember as we move into our deep processes, no deep process will come up that we are not ready to deal with. Indeed, the fact that it is coming up is an indicator that we have reached a level of strength, maturity, awareness, and spiritual growth that we are able to handle whatever is there. The fact that a deep process is coming up is a compliment to our spiritual growth, although we may have difficulty seeing that at the time.

We seem to have an internal thermostat that regulates what processes come up. If we do not want to deal with a deep process when it comes up, that's our choice. Our inner process (the Creator) is very forgiving, and will simply bring it up again and again until we deal with it. I need to reiterate, however, my experience is that each time we push it down and do not deal with it, it comes up harder (maybe even more painfully) the next time until we ultimately pay attention. We do cause much of our own pain. Our suffering and exhaustion seem to be directly related to blocking our process, as does much physical illness. The Creator does, it seems, want us to heal. In doing our deep processes we learn to honor our process.

HONORING OUR PROCESS

To honor our process is to live life fully.

A word needs to be said about forcing processes and blocking our processes. Frequently, we have had people come into this work who have been well "therapized." They have experienced any number of techniques used to force their process. I think of techniques as similar to the use of forceps in the normal delivery of a baby. You may get a baby, <u>and</u> it may be damaged. You certainly don't learn anything about trusting and honoring your own process, which is the ultimate reward. As stated earlier, you may just learn to trust the technique and the technician—not your own process. Such people can go to the mats and "process at will." This is not deep-process work! Nor is it the work that can heal and transform our lives.

There are others who block their process and avoid it at all costs. They will do nothing until they are completely brought to their knees, and maybe not even then. Blocking our process and forcing our process are two ends of the same dualism. It spins around the illusion of control, which is one of the main inhibitors of our spiritual journey.

The actual process of our deep process teaches us surrender. Only when we allow it to carry us wherever it wants to take us can we get the full meaning of deep process. When we force, block, think about, or try to control our deep process, what we actually learn about is forcing, blocking, and the inhibiting aspect of thinking, all of which ultimately are about control. We do not get the deep lessons of the process—and there are always lessons—and we do not learn, ultimately, to trust our process. Only in the deep surrender and letting go do we learn to participate in the process that is the All.

Soul-Level Healing

We cannot choose to be alive partially or partially choose to be alive.

The deep process of the oneness invites us all. This surrender can never happen just in our heads.

SOUND

Sounds are important in our deep process. Many of us have never made our sounds. We have been told to be quiet and we have complied. In our deep process, we need to make our sounds, whatever they may be—moans, groans, screams, yells, laughter, whatever rises to the surface. Our sounds need to be expressed, <u>and</u> there is much more to sound. At times, it seems as if our sounds are like nets with grappling hooks on them that snag the festering poisons in our body and soul and pull them out to be neutralized and healed. As we express them in our deep process, we are free of more than the tone. These tones cannot be prescribed or predetermined. We have to find and let the process itself express our sounds in our own way. Our sounds may be an important contribution to our full healing.

As we do our sounds, more and more they seem to reflect the sounds of the universe, <u>and</u> this may not be true in the beginning of our deep work. We need to start with where we are.

STAYING IN THE PRESENT

Staying in the present with your deep-process work means that you stay with whatever is coming up for you in the present. This can literally be anything—from any time, from any place. If we truly trust our process, we go where our deep work leads us. We do not predetermine where or what that will be.

We have learned from our experience, and from observing and hearing others, that when we have an agenda for or against anything in our deep-process work, we are being confronted with our control issues. The first step is to look at our illusion of control. The old therapy paradigm is an approach where someone, the therapist or the client, determines what one needs to work on—or not work on!—and sets about doing it. That approach has nothing to do with the paradigm out of which this work emerges. I see that old paradigm as violent and abusive. It may work for some. That is not for me to say.

In this work, we have experienced that Living in Process and our deep processes have an inner wisdom that moves much beyond our thinking and understanding. *Being in the present* means we trust that wisdom to bring up what we are physically, emotionally, and spiritually ready to work on. The "governor," if you will, is internal to our deep process. It is not external to us, as our thinking can be when we are thinking dysfunctionally. It means being open to whatever our process is bringing up for us whenever it comes.

I have learned that my deep process, while sometimes painful, is always loving and caring of me and moves toward healing. Even when our processes are hard, or the information coming up is difficult, there is a gentleness that the "I" of our personality would not afford. This experience of gentleness teaches us a great deal about trust and faith—faith in the wisdom of our process.

There are no constraints about your deep-process work and what it can or should be about. You may, from time to time, get a response from the group that you seem to be pushing your process, or blocking your process, or having an agenda for your process. Remember that this feedback offers you the opportunity to take a look at what is going on with you, especially around control, which is a biggie in early healing. If it doesn't fit or feel right, after you have openly looked at it, just go on. You might not be ready for the learning, or it may be someone else's issue.

Some people have come to believe that their deep process is a way back to their connection with the Creator. They use it almost as a form of meditation. Others have the experience that their deep process always leads them back to themselves and thus to their connection with God.

Connie had become increasingly aware of her negative thinking and the disastrous effect it was having on her life. Once she began to notice her negative thoughts, it seemed as though they were everywhere. "I'm not good enough," "I can't do that," "It won't work," "I don't like her," "It's raining today. Why can't it be sunny?" "My car isn't running right, it'll probably break down," "I'll never get any time off" . . . and so it went.

After a period of noticing her negative thoughts, Connie decided that she would do one of three things if she had a negative thought:

1. she would talk with someone;
2. she would pray;
3. she would go to the mats and do her deep-process work.

She began to realize that her negative thoughts were her doors to her deep-process work, and she found herself more and more "taking her negative thoughts to the mats." The results were miraculous! Her contact with her spirituality increased exponentially. Her negative thoughts decreased in the same way.

DEEP PROCESS OPENS DOORS

The more I do deep process and the more I listen to others report on their deep process, the more I realize that we have just begun to scratch the surface of it and what it can do.

When most people start doing their deep-process work, it is usually tied to their current life and its problems related to childhood issues.

As shown in the diagram on page 177, my experience is that as our healing progresses and we begin to spend less of our time in our dysfunctional process and more time Living in Process, we then begin to have deep processes that move beyond our personal healing issues. Actually, this phenomenon occurs very easily simultaneously with our own healing work and simultaneously with other healing work. Suffice it to say that many levels of spiritual and emotional growth and healing are taking place during our deep-process work.

Often, people come out of their deep processes with powerful spiritual truths experienced on a profound level. This experience of spiritual truth is so different from and much more potent than learning about it with our heads.

We always check in with where we are and what we are feeling during the group meetings. Sometimes there is something in someone else's check-in that will trigger a deep process for someone even when there seems to be no relationship between what is said and our own deep process. It is important to have a safe place with support to do our deep-process work when it comes up. Sam felt pushed to the mats by some intense feelings that arose during someone's check-in at a group meeting. She plunged to the mats and went into a deep process that was very intense and lasted about an hour and one-half.

In her process, she envisioned herself as a man and was a physician on some battlefield. Her association was that the scene was during the U.S. Civil War. She had done this Living in Process work long enough to know that she did not need to focus on who, what, when, how, and why. She needed only to get the learnings from the deep process.

In her deep process, she was aware that she was surrounded by carnage and destruction. All around her were young men with limbs blown off, holes in their guts, their heads blown open, and screams, moans, and crying every-where. She had no medicines or bandages left, and every-where she looked there was pain and suffering. As she looked at the carnage and the bodies, each one became personal to her. She could see each one as someone's fa-ther, brother, or son—as *her* relations—each and every one. She could no longer see them as "others."

She let herself move through feelings of horror, help-lessness, rage, and impotence. Time and space had no meaning for her. Some time later, she came out of her deep process looking tired and peaceful.

She was appalled by the horror and intense feelings she had experienced. She said that before the Living in Process work she would not have believed that she could have en-dured such intense feelings. When she reached a point where she thought she would explode, her process slowly brought her out of it.

When she shared her deep process, her sharing was so intense that many went to the mats to do their own work. Yet, she seemed to have found a peace and serenity that was beyond description.

She ended her sharing by saying in a voice that seemed to echo down through the ages, "I came to know with my whole being that war can be no more. I can never partici-pate in anything that has anything to do with war." We knew that she had learned something at a soul level.

Sam had done deep-process work that seemingly was not just about herself, her life, and her personality. Her deep work seemed to be about healing on a more cosmic level. We never completely know what our deep process will present to us.

Living in Process

Deep process really is an act of faith—faith in oneself and in the living process. When we participate, we are relearning to be gentle with ourselves and with one another. Our deep-process work helps all the processes of life integrate. Living in Process includes deep process and is much more than deep-process work.

One of the miracles of human existence is that we have all things and all times available to us. On the one hand our bodies store memories of everything that has happened to us so that we can return to these memories, or processes, to heal them when we are strong enough and ready. <u>And</u>, on the other hand, we seem to be able to draw into ourselves all experiences (past lives, the holomovement, all consciousness) in order to heal what we need to heal. The more I work with my own and the deep processes of others, the more I am open to the possibility that when we do our deep work, we are not only healing ourselves, we are moving into the All That Is (the holomovement, the oneness) and healing within and beyond ourselves.

At times we experience a compression, or an enfolding (à la English physicist David Bohm), of time and space in deep process. We find that we exist in many dimensions of time and space at the same time, and return with wisdom we could have never figured out in any other way. Some people think they go into previous lives. This concept may be much too simple for the phenomena experienced. We almost seem to go into the holomovement, the oneness, and pull out whatever we need to heal.

All of the uproar about "false-memory syndrome" collapses in the face of understanding deep process. The issue is not whether something did happen or did not happen and who should be punished or not be punished. The issue is healing! What does that person who goes deep into herself need to do to heal? No one outside that person knows. Only in the depths of the deep process of that person will knowing and healing be possible. In fact, often the knowing comes after the healing. And, I have never seen healing, when worked through in the depths of our process, involve trying to punish someone else. When the focus is on ourselves and the healing we need to do at a soul level, we do not distract ourselves with what others have done or what they need to do. They must tend to that themselves.

Children seem to take to deep-process work naturally. They know deep-process work. We have a two-and-a-half-year-old who started coming to the Living in Process group when he was in the womb. He is very easy with the deep-process work. The other day he was fussy and grumpy at breakfast, he didn't like the food offered, and he was unhappy. After a little of this behavior, he said, "I'm going to the mats!"

He flopped down, cried awhile, raged awhile, and then got up his happy, sunny self. His mother says that he does this often when he's upset. He's learning very early to take responsibility for his feelings. Children who do this work do not give away their personal power very easily, if at all. I have imagined a time when all homes will have a deep-process room designed into them like bathrooms and kitchens, and families can grow up knowing that all of them do their deep-process work when needed. This dream, of course, has already started to manifest.

A word of caution here. I believe we all know deep-process work and it is natural for us. And, because we have moved so far away from it, we now find it helpful to have the support of a group or community when we are first relearning how to do our deep work.

THE RELATIONSHIP OF
DEEP PROCESS TO LIVING IN PROCESS

Healing is not going to be directly proportional to the amount of time spent in deep process.

Healing is directly related to learning to Live in Process and doing deep-process work as it comes up.

All true healing is at a cellular, DNA, soul level. Relief and adjustment will not last and will cause more problems than they can possibly cure. Ultimately, the only solution for those who seek mere relief and adjustment is drugging themselves until they are completely out of touch with the mur-murings and thundering shouts of the soul. Then, simply existing, not liv-ing is the obvious result.

Living in Process is a form of healing that is integrated into all as-pects and at all levels of our being.

As one person put it, "Living in Process is more than just waiting around to experience psychological orgasms."

Living in Process is not a work or technique. It is a way of living our lives—a soul living. When we Live in Process, our old issues and unfin-ished deep processes are the possibilities we have at our disposal to learn to Live in Process. As we accept our unfinished processes and do them, we learn to live our process at the same time.

HEALING OLD WOUNDS

When we Live in Process, no matter what has happened within our experi-ence of the oneness, we have the opportunity to heal from it. There is no such thing as just getting by. Symptom relief and adjustment are dead-end concepts. Whatever horrors come up in our deep process (regardless of whether we can attach it to our present lives or not), if we are ready and will-ing to face them and go through them, we can experience healing at a level that is beyond our wildest imaginations. We must be willing to see what we see and know what we know.

Some people have horrible dreams, thoughts, feelings, and impulses. These just are! They all offer possibilities for our healing. As long as we do not run from them, deny them, or hide them from ourselves and others, they are grist for our healing mill. They are there for a reason, and if we trust that reason more than we trust the dreams, thoughts, feelings, and impulses, we can go into them and use them as access to our process of healing. These fearful and maybe even horrible images become the doorways to healing the soul if we let ourselves know that they are not real and do our deep-process work. If we act out on these impulses or images, we poison our soul and its connection with the All That Is. The common dualism here is avoiding-denying, or acting out. Like most dualisms, both lead to self-destruction.

Remember we are the only ones who can injure our souls. Others can torture and destroy our bodies, attack our psyches, and take our land and our money, but we are the only ones who can damage our own souls. Our souls are under our protection.

When we accept whatever comes up for us as possibilities for learning and healing, we can do what we need to do to heal. When we con ourselves and others, we destroy our souls. Others can support us, _and_ we have to do it ourselves. No one can get to our core except us. What has happened to us has happened to us. What we have done we have done. Ultimately, we must own and take responsibility for our part in all our behaviors. Whatever has happened or whatever we have done is part of our experience. They make up the person we have to work with. It is up to us what we do with what has happened to us. As each of us does our work and heals from the life experiences we have had, we do not have to allow those experiences to be repeated in our lives, and we are less likely to inflict these same behaviors and our responses to them—hate, anger, fear, dishonesty—on others.

As I often say, when we stay a victim, we become perpetrators. As we do our work, we break the intergenerational chain of perpetration. We clean up our DNA.

Sometimes, it almost seems as if our deep process is healing the past, healing our ancestral DNA, or even healing the holomovement, the oneness. As more people actually do their deep-process work, we may experience a planetary healing that is beyond anything we can imagine.

Here is a letter I received from Sandy, who experienced healing at this deep cosmic level.

> I would like to share with you an experience I have had in
> my deep work:
>
> I had a process a year ago in which I had a knowingness

that my family (those who lived in the Cordeaux region of Australia, in the mountains west of Woollongong, 120 to 150 years ago) had taken part in the massacre of the Aboriginals who had been driven back into the gorges and valleys there.

During the November intensive last year, I had this process again. I spent days on the mats and I received a lot of pieces that have been helpful to me.

This time, I saw the killing in graphic detail, and I was one of the killers. We (I and other family members and friends) were on horseback and were circling around, cutting off any of the Aboriginals who tried to escape. We had each pulled a stirrup off our saddles. We had wrapped the leathers around our wrists and were galloping among the people, smashing open their skulls with the stirrup irons. There were people dashing everywhere, and there was blood and screaming and smoke and terror.

During this, I was aware in my process that we were all acting out of alcoholic rage, that the alcoholism that runs in my family today was just as rampant back then. I felt rage and powerlessness and a savage triumph that I could vent my impotence and fury on these people. It was nothing that they did. The law said (at least tacitly) that I could kill them, and I killed them because in doing so, I felt better.

I had a sense, too, that what I was doing was no different from all the thousands of purges, putsches, and pogroms that have happened throughout history—that they are all a result of insane alcoholic rage.

My second awareness was that, instead of feeling shame at what I was doing, I felt a soaring sense of power. The more helpless the people were that I was killing, the wider the gulf between them and me, and the greater the high I could experience. So, I took a special pleasure in killing the old ones, the women, and the children. (It was not much fun killing the adult men, because they were armed and could fight back, and the power differential between them and me was so much less.)

So, I committed murder to get power.

We were remorseless and implacable, and we didn't stop until we were sure that everyone was dead. Afterward, we smiled and said nothing. We had shared something terrible, and we knew something special, and no one ever said anything. We have kept a tradition of rigid silence and keeping secrets that exists in our family even today.

It seems to me now that power, that is to say, power or the lack of it, is what sadism is about, and ritual cult abuse. That any person who has a spiritual disease and is cut off from the power of the Creator, as I was/am, seeks power through illegitimate means—through battering, abuse, torture, rape, murder.

After experiencing this process, I asked my Creator to show me the connection between what had happened in the past and my present life. The following day, I experienced the massacres all over again (there were more than one), in even more graphic detail. I was devastated. I felt terrible pain, horror, nausea, and sadness.

Next, I was shown a vision of the alcoholism and violence in my family, passing from one generation to the next, all the way to the present day. I saw that the battering and abuse and addiction and rage had missed none of us. The sins of the fathers had been visited on the sons and the daughters. My grandfathers, grandmothers, mother, father, sister, brother, and I have all been abusers. We have battered all those around us and ourselves, as well.

I see myself now as an abuser and a perpetrator, and I remember what you said—that until we can own our roles as perpetrators, we cannot give up the victim-perpetrator-rescuer dance and move on in our recovery.

The following day I had yet another process in which I continued to look at how I experience powerlessness. I saw how all my life, I have pursued and abused illegitimate power in the belief that that was what I needed.

In my self-centeredness I have used any means available to get what I want. It's as though I needed this example of gross violence to see how abusive I was then, and still am, to see how I have been a bully and have plowed through people and over them to get what I want. I have used my size to intimidate people, or my knowledge, or my education, or my ability to lie and manipulate.

I can see now that in using illegitimate power to take whatever I want, I am a thief, I am stealing what is not mine, what I have not earned, and what is not freely given by God (or by those through whom God works).

I need therefore to acknowledge myself as a thief. When I steal what is not mine, I do not trust God to give me what I need. I am trying to steal power, rather than work for the spiritual power and inner strength that come from my Creator and from doing my work.

I continue to be amazed by the way deep process works. I do not know how it is that I participated in these events so long ago, or how I know that it is so. I accept that they happened and that I took part in them. I am grateful that I have been shown these truths, and for the opportunity to heal the past and make changes in the present.

Sandy

A powerful statement. A powerful healing. As this woman shared this process, it became clear that she was healing her DNA and also her family's DNA back to its origins.

COMMUNITY

I have discussed context and community earlier, and as we talk of healing, I want to probe a little deeper into the importance of community in healing. Healing is most effectively and powerfully done in a community setting. And, healing the soul demands a community context for complete healing.

None of us can heal in isolation.

Healing is best done in community.

We can heal. Healing is possible, <u>and</u> only we can do it. No one else knows what we need for healing no matter how "expert" they are! And, no one else can do it for us. Yet, if we do our work, we have the opportunity to heal from whatever life has presented to us. What a wonderful possibility!

How often we underestimate ourselves and our possibilities! How surprising that we sometimes choose not to exercise the possibility for healing, choosing instead to hold on to old hurts and resentments, stubbornness, and the illusion of control. Yet, we are the only ones who can let go and feed and nurture our core, our soul. Remember, only we can damage or destroy our souls.

We have to do it ourselves. We don't have to do it alone.

We have support. We need support. We are damaged in our living process when we come to believe that only one person, in isolation, can help us. When secrets are shared with only one person who is sworn to keep them, the isolation continues. When we isolate ourselves, we put our secrets, our disease, on the altar and worship them as if they were sacred, not realizing that it is in the demystifying—the owning and going into it—that the healing lies.

A participatory system offers an alternative.

In a participatory system, we are all part of a larger whole, and our participation in that larger whole is necessary to our healing. We need community to heal. We not only need support, we need to hear from one another and learn about ourselves from hearing from one another. Often, as others share their stories, their struggles, and their experience we are able to learn about ourselves in ways that we never previously considered. Even more important, we need to participate in the community, in the hologram, in order to reclaim ourselves and our self-esteem, and take our place in the universe.

The isolation of dysfunction and self-obsessed thinking takes us out of our awareness that we are a part of a whole therefore connected with all things. This isolation pushes us to forget the personal power we feel when we allow ourselves the awareness of participating in something that is much bigger than ourselves. How isolated and alone we feel when we remove ourselves from our rightful connectedness! This connectedness is the very basis of spirituality. It is only when we feel we belong and we participate in this belonging that we truly come to know our spirituality. Spirituality can have a private side, <u>and</u> it cannot, I believe, be isolated. Spirituality is our connectedness. Spirituality is our participation in a whole larger than ourselves.

Living in Process work is similar to the process of the Indian Medicine Woman, of Jesus, or of the Samoan healers, all of whom worked with those they knew and loved the most. In fact, it was this intimacy and this knowledge and the interactions that happened in community that were a large part of the healing. It was this trust that facilitated the ability to heal. Jesus and the Indian healer choose to be and to work within community. Community offers more knowledge and information than any one person can give, no matter how "objective" they may be. Yet, each person has an important and unique contribution to make and give in community.

As we heal, our communities become larger and larger, until we not only realize our oneness with all creation, we live that oneness. The Living in Process community has now developed an international network of people who are doing their healing work, their deep-process work, and their Living in Process, being as honest as they can and trying to take the freedom and responsibility to live their lives fully. Living in Process is contagious. It never leaves us, and it is supported by community.

THE PATH TO HEALING

Remember, healing is a process. We had a process of becoming wounded, and it is quite unlikely that we will heal instantly—although in the area of healing, miracles can never be ruled out.

No one really knows what another needs or what they should do with their lives. When we don't take responsibility for our own lives, others are tempted to jump in to try to live our lives for us. In situations where others are trying to control us, we need to stay on our own side of the street and see how we have set this up for ourselves. Many people get lost and confused when they're not willing to take charge of their own lives. Yet, taking charge for them is not caring. Still, if they're looking, they almost always find someone who will try to run their lives for them. Anger and resentment will then ensue on both sides and healing is unlikely.

When we try to keep ourselves or others from making mistakes, we are making a bigger mistake, and our illusion of control has outdistanced our sensibility. Mistakes are life's curriculum. When we talk to the Creator after each mistake and learn from it, we become, as Don Coyhis would say, spiritual warriors. And, we must never underestimate the injury we inflict on others, ourselves, and all things when we are trying to "help." The help we need is inside of us. The help others need is inside of them.

As children, many of us grew up in dysfunctional families of one kind or another. We developed survival skills to cope with the situation in which we found ourselves. Skills such as dishonesty, hiding, sneaking around, isolation, and withdrawing may have been our survival tools. Those skills may have saved our lives. Instead, as we are no longer children, these same skills are very often the ones that are now destroying us. At some level we still believe that our survival is at stake. And, it is! However, as we become adults our physical survival is usually not the issue as much as the survival of our soul! We need to face and go into the fear we experience at the thought of giving up these "old friends." As adults, we need to heal by claiming our own lives.

Many of us have been trained to be out of touch with our feelings and our deep process. As infants, we used our lungs and responded with our whole body. As infants, there was no distinction between ourselves and our bodies, or ourselves and our feelings. We were one with ourselves. Slowly, we learned to not breathe, not to be in touch with our feelings, and not to express them. We need to learn how to breathe again, figuratively and literally. Breathing will put us back in touch with our bodies, which will open the way into our deep process. Some say that they don't want to know what they have hidden away, and yet we already know; we're just not healing it.

There are times when deep-process work appears to be stressful to the body. Yet, not doing our deep work is much more stressful. Much physical illness is caused by stuffing our feelings and not doing our deep-process work. The body absorbs and holds unresolved processes long after they are current for that person. These unresolved deep processes wear the body down and produce great stress in our daily lives. Therefore, some of these stuffed processes need to be worked back through slowly, giving the body time to heal and absorb these healings. If we trust our inner process, it will guide us. As our bodies heal, we can go deeper and deeper. As we heal on deeper and deeper levels, we become who we really are. In fact, many people look younger and younger as they do their deep work and learn to Live in Process.

Soul-Level Healing

Ultimately, we can heal the "unhealable" and forgive the "unforgivable."

SACRED TRUST

Living in Process work is a sacred trust.

Many years ago a woman who was ordained as a minister and had grown up in a very conservative fundamentalist church did the training for Living in Process. After some time sitting with people as they did their deep process, she said that she had come to see the deep-process work as an altar call, and her sitting with them was a form of witnessing. Having grown up in the Southern Methodist church myself, this made sense to me.

Living in Process flows out of our spiritual base. It makes no difference what that base is for each person. When we come from our spiritual base, we respect ourselves, we respect others, and we respect all process. Then, we are ourselves, we are others, and we are all process.

Living in Process is being open to and a companion with the healing work of the universe. When we Live in Process, we come to know that we are all process.

Charleen shared her awarenesses and her process—moving through all the waves of influence she felt:

> To begin with, for me, major learnings occurred around Martin Luther's phrase, "Sin bravely and you shall know God's grace." As I learned to share in group, to put out what I know, to focus only on what I notice, and to ask for responses, I experienced difficulty in speaking my truth and, even more so, in being able to articulate it with clarity. Responses from others felt like judgments and criticism— something I needed to defend against or explain so that others in the group would really understand what I had said.

As I continued, I gradually came to sit more and more with the feelings, learning that the knowings I shared were heard with caring ears, and the responses I heard were given in love. This was not the enmeshed kind of love I knew from old, which now seems much more patronizing. Instead, it seemed to be a love that consisted of "here's what I see, here's what I heard, here's what came up for me as you spoke." It was left to me to decide how I wanted to use this information, which was without any judgment, enmeshment, caretaking, and perhaps my hardest lesson, and without an answer.

A challenging and fun learning was that of paradigm shifts and the myriad of possibilities I could explore either in thinking or in action. I was astounded time and again that it may be possible to see a given situation in a totally new light, to hear the same words that used to convey rigidity and "absoluteness" as inviting flexibility and spontaneity. Beyond the blinders I had been encouraged to wear throughout my life, there were choices that became alive in a colorful way that was new to me.

In previous counseling and therapy, I had become aware of some of my options: how to lighten up, play more, take more responsibility for my victim stance. The daily learnings I had in finding a bed, having a roommate, asking for help, preparing food became exciting avenues in which I could do the same activity in a new way. Usually the option at hand would be no more than adopting a new attitude. Mostly, I learned that the available options were "no big deal." They were not horrific, monumental changes that would entail great effort on my part.

As I learned to risk more of myself in a group setting, I

have gradually felt less "naked" and exposed. It is old shame and an old message that what I have to say is not important, nor is it important to spend time on. When I grew up, I was encouraged to mind what I was saying, not to be too loud, not to be open, not to invite gossip or questions. I learned in the Living in Process intensives that I do have a voice; it was unnecessary for me to find a clever or domineering way to express any sharings. I no longer needed to know all the facts to put something out in the group. In process, I did not have to wait until the "right" moment to present a check-in, or to go to the mat, or to have those listening understand precisely what I was saying.

Over the past year I have come to Boulder for intensives and trainings in different roles. I first arrived with a couple of friends, and despite feeling "exposed" in doing deep-process work in front of them, I felt supported and unjudged. At another intensive, I was accompanied by clients. Again, I had some concern that they might see another side of me. What I found was that very little energy came up for me regarding this. The clients were separate from me, accepting and supportive in the same way I was with them.

Another time my daughter requested that I accompany her to a women's intensive. There I was certainly seen in and confronted on my enmeshment with her, and I felt grateful we were both able to enter into our own processes as they came up.

I experienced a final level of exposure when I came to a training session with my husband. Once again, although very much aware of my relationship addiction around him,

I realized I could enter into my own process and carry on with my deep processes as they occurred without censoring myself. Each of these roles I play in my life as friend, counselor, mother, and wife presented me with an opportunity for exposure. Each time, I experienced an invitation for me to stretch and grow as an individual despite my irrational fears of being seen and judged by others.

I have learned to trust body memories more. In a very deep process, I was being attentive to a grieving process. It involved a white-water rafting experience the previous month in which I had nearly died. During the process, I had a lot of mucus, and did a lot of coughing and spluttering; this was followed by a sense of calmness and awareness. What I had learned from my process was that what was just part of the fun and natural course of events (falling out of a boat in white water) had actually become a near-death experience for me when I became trapped under the boat for a period of time in the rapids. I believed my process at this point to be over.

Within moments, however, I became aware that my body was leading me into another part of the process. I remember being in wonderment at this—almost standing aside to observe. I had no knowing at this point of the process. I proceeded to go through two more separate waves of feeling drowned and held down. After each part of the process, first my daughter was delivered in birth and then my son. I was grieving about how I have affected each of their lives in a dysfunctional way. Once more I felt that I had completed the process for that time and decided to lie quiet.

I was surprised to experience more processing again,

this time involving body movements. For the fourth time, I had no knowing except to stay with whatever the body was experiencing. I received a sudden flash of awareness as the retching and writhing subsided. Feeling as though I was a rubber glove being turned inside out, I saw I had been reborn, and that I could have compassion for myself, and accept my faults in a loving way.

Again I lay back, believing that perhaps I was "through" (we're talking exhaustion here), only to feel the similar sensation of going way down deep inside. I remember thinking what more can be birthed? Surely there can't be more! I rode with the wave a fifth time, having no content awareness of what the next piece was about.

Suddenly, I became aware of many generations of women in my family being reborn, surrounded by love and compassion—this being totally at odds with the staunch, stiff, Presbyterian heritage from which I came. I learned through body memory that I am part of the broader universal lineage—something that I had suspected before and never truly felt. In process, I experienced it at such a deep level that I knew I belonged, really belonged to a long heritage of women gone before me.

I felt blessed with all the gifts I received in this "birthing" process. Only by remaining with the body sensations was I able to receive the added spiritual and intellectual enlightenments that accompanied each piece. Over the last part of this year, my processes relating to body memory have involved little, if any, content at all. At first I was distressed, and felt I was missing something in my process. Talking with others allowed me to honor the body memory as just that, not discount it. Furthermore, to honor the scant, sometimes extremely quick flashes I have experienced. I almost missed them because they were so fast and minuscule. It was the body memory that allowed me to even witness the times these minute images occurred.

Charleen

When we do our work, there is so much joy and healing available to us. When our processes are aborted or stopped, we have to use all of our energy to suppress them, and we have no energy left to be alive and creative.

When I lie to myself or others, I become separated from my process.

Barb W.

We can let the healing of nature in only when we realize that we are one with nature and that the same Creator who created the lava flow created us.

When we feel superior to someone or something, it is difficult to learn from it.

As we forgive ourselves and others we can participate in all of life. We can practice boundless goodness. Or, as Anne Herbert says, we can practice *Random Kindness and Senseless Acts of Beauty*, which are, after all, what life is.

Chapter 7

THE SPHERES
OF PROCESS

Living in Process is about living in spheres—ever-expanding and ever-contracting spheres.

I would like to offer you a visual image of Living in Process. This diagram is simply an abstraction, a way of conceptualizing the spheres of process participation. Remember that abstractions, by definition, are not real; they exist only to help our brains concretize our perceptions. As Norman Jackson, a dear friend of mine, once said, "When we concretize our perceptions, we are participating in spiritual idolatry." While I hope that we will not take these abstractions and diagrams that far, perhaps they can be helpful in pointing a way.

SPHERE OF SELF

The very first sphere we want to consider is the self. Remember that the self, the individual, is not a thing or an entity. The self is a process, and is thus always moving, changing, permeating, expanding, and constricting. The self is what English physicist and author of numerous books, including *Wholeness and the Implicate Order*, David Bohm describes as a *holomovement*. It contains all that is existent within it, and it is the individual, both at the same time. Try to imagine, if you can, that this sphere of the self is so dynamic and alive that it is as busy as an atom with all its protons, neutrons, and electrons whirling within it, plus the added experience that it is constantly changing shape and colors, and moving in all directions as it remains within its integrity. The most characteristic aspect of this little sphere of activity is that it is ever changing as it moves, evolves, and develops. In fact, when you think of the protons, neutrons, and electrons, try not to think of them as concrete. They are only movement, growth, energy, and process.

Self ○

The self, as we know it, contains information from our ancestors, and that information is also continually changing, rearranging, reorganizing, and reconstituting itself in new configurations, so that genetics are destiny and genetics are not destiny, both at the same time. We are who we are, __and__ we can also change our past and our future. Time and space can limit us—a fact of physical form—while, at the same time, they do not really exist.

As individuals, we may be limited to who we think we are—if we believe we are limited—while at the same time we are limitless, as is everything else. And all of it is in constant flux. We carry a core, a nucleus, as does the atom, __and__ we are not limited by that core, because it knows no dimensions.

As a self, an individual, we do not exist in isolation. Indeed, we are always in context. To see ourselves as something apart is to set up an illusion about our reality that can only tax the human organism to madness. Whenever we try to impose logical, rational belief systems upon ourselves that do not fit with our experience and reality, we limit ourselves to only a few choices:

1. insanity;
2. shutting off all self-awareness so that we can function as zombies;
3. continuing to feed an illusion, a virtual reality, that has nothing to do with what we know deep inside of us to be true.

Just as the entire world exists in a drop of water, so each individual human being is the reflection of all of creation.

Sphere of
Family and Relationships

Every individual exists within a sphere of family and extended family. Even if we were born an orphan, we had some form of family or people who raised us and who functioned as a surrogate family. Even in the historical accounts, children who were raised by wild animals had an animal family. We all grew up in some kind of context of relationships. Many of us have several families; we have our immediate families and we may have had the families of our mother and our father. We may have had aunties and uncles who, along with their children, were close family. We may have had stepparents and stepsiblings. Whatever our situation, we had some family context of some sort. There were in our lives the possibilities of intimacy and struggles with other human beings. Miraculously, we have been given the opportunity to experience life situations that are processes, and these give us the opportunity to learn, to make marvelous mistakes, to love, to get angry, to withdraw, to come back, and to continue shaping and reconstituting ourselves.

When we are young, families and close relationships offer us an excellent opportunity to fall into the role of victim. "We didn't have the right parents. We were beaten, abused, spoiled, overindulged, ignored, never left alone . . ." Some people can get a lot of mileage out of what they did or did not get as children. As we have stressed earlier, the belief that we are a victim opens the door to embracing a lifelong victim position, and victims always feel justified in their own minds when they become perpetrators. None of us had perfect parents. Whatever our experience, it was our reality. No one except ourselves *and our spirituality* can heal and integrate these experiences.

When we're Living in Process, what has happened to us is not ultimately the issue. Healing is the issue. Whatever has happened to us in life is our experience. And this experience is the impetus we need to grow, heal, learn, and evolve. Regardless of what has happened to us, we can heal, and heal we must if we are to participate fully in our lives. Remember, we have everything we need to heal. We have only to do our work. When we are living our process, the issue is not *what* happened. The issue is what we *do* with it.

In Living in Process, we know that *we* can heal our spirit, and *we* can destroy our spirit. We are the only ones who can make that decision for ourselves.

What we do with what is done to us is the ultimate issue.

Families and relationships are where we cut our spiritual teeth so we will be better able to gnaw on the ultimate issues when we are ready.

We must remember that we are deeply affected by the family we have and by the relationships we have. In this most intimate of contexts, we have the opportunity to interact and grow. Some of us were born into families where it was a challenge even to grow up, while others had it easier. What would have been easier for some of us would not have been easy for others. It was what it was and we have been influenced by those experiences.

Some of us spend a lifetime trying to be what our family wanted us to be, while others spend a lifetime reacting to who our parents were and trying *not* to be like them. What a waste! We are *affected* by our families and relationships, <u>and</u> we are not *determined* by them—unless we choose to be. We have choices.

I have seen so many people who focus their lives on what they did or did not get from their families and relationships, giving their power away by the truckloads and then being angry at those on whom they have just thrust this power.

We are influenced by our relationships, <u>and</u> we are not determined by them.

It is important to remember that we also influence our families and friends. Quite literally the family was very different before we were born into it. Our process affects the process of the family as a whole, as well as all our relationships, just as they affect our process.

I have seen so many people who, in their thirties and forties, are having to deal with absolutely unruly parents. They have parents who have no respect for them, who treat them as small, irresponsible children, and who do not recognize any separation between their "child" and themselves. Clearly, this is a case of untrained parents. The adult "children" of such parents have not respected their own processes enough, and so they have allowed themselves to be trampled upon, and they have not put forth the effort—admittedly the effort required is extreme in some cases—to train their parents.

Since people's bad habits often become more ingrained with the aging process, these adult "children" have to take *some* responsibility for what their parents have become. I will say more about training our parents in the chapter on families. Suffice it to say that we affect and influence the processes of our family and relationships every bit as much as we are influenced by their processes. One cannot grow up and become an adult unless these two-way influences are recognized.

SPHERE OF COMMUNITY

The next sphere of influence I want to explore is the community. Most of us belong to several communities. We have our neighborhoods, our school communities, our religious communities, social communities, work communities, and possibly many others. These communities are all processes themselves. Try as they may, they can never attain stasis. In spite of our illusions to the contrary, communities are the very essence of process. Much wasted time and energy are expended seeking to keep our communities the same, which is one of the reasons that shock and sadness are expressed when someone leaves or dies. In reality, communities, like individuals, *are* processes. It is only as they grow, contract, expand, retreat, die, or change completely that they take on a life of their own.

One of the beauties of life for those of us who are older is having lived long enough to see the changes in the processes of communities and societies, and to have been around long enough to see one or more cycles of the same issues. With this perspective, one has a better chance to know that what may seem like a static reality is really a process. This is one of the reasons why the perspective of our elders is so important. They have the vantage point of being able to recognize process, and of having been taught about the processes by their own elders.

The third sphere is that of community.

The Spheres of Process

The individual affects the family and relationships, and the individual also affects the community. Clearly, our participation, nonparticipation, or level of participation affects the community in which we live, explore our spirituality, learn, and work. Also, our family affects the community. We as individuals affect the family and the community, and the family affects different communities *as a family*. Again, it is a common phenomenon that individuals refuse to admit that their participation or nonparticipation has any effect upon the communities in their sphere. As we deny our own process, we are forced to deny greater and greater spheres of processes.

One of the ways we have refused to grow up is to continue to ignore that what we do or do not do has influence and impact. We pretend to be shadow people who can slip in and out of realities, never influencing and affecting those realities. We, and perhaps our families, weave invisible webs of denial around ourselves and pretend that we are not, nor do we have to be, a part of the larger processes around us. How much we gain when our participation is inseparable from our spirituality and our spirituality is our core.

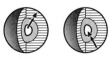

Conversely, the communities in which we live and breathe affect our families and ourselves; all are a process. Those who grew up in a Catholic religious community have a different experience than those who grew up in a Protestant or Buddhist religious community or no religious community at all.

We are affected by the processes of our work communities and we affect them. Those who work for a big multinational corporation experience a different work life than those who work in a small family business. Sometimes we get arrogant and don't want to believe that we are affected by our workplace community, <u>and</u> we are. To deny that we are affected is to deny a reality of our lives.

Just as we affect our families, we also affect our communities. How common it is to want to pull a disappearing act and pretend that we have no influence and therefore no responsibility. Yet, we do. All our communities are affected by what we do and what we refuse to do, perhaps even more by the latter than by the former. The processes of those communities contract, expand, or explode depending upon our processes and those of our families.

SPHERE OF SOCIETY AND NATION

The sphere of influence expands to the societies and nations in which we live.

The society, the nation in which we live, is a process. Again, it is not an entity, it is not a thing. Each of our nations, our societies, is a process.

Our communities are affected by what is happening at a national level. If the process of the society is a little crazy, that craziness will affect all the communities in which we live, learn, and work. That craziness will also affect our families and our relationships. And it will affect us as individuals.

When a nation decides to participate in the process of war, the processes of communities, families, and individuals are affected. It can be no other way. I was in Fiji when young men were being deployed to fight the Gulf War. I saw whole communities gathering at the airport to sing, dance, and hold kava ceremonies for their young men who were being sent off to war because their nation had decided to be a part of that war. Their little villages were personally affected, as were families and individuals, by societal decisions and turned out en masse to deal with the rupture of their community.

The Spheres of Process

The processes of nations are also ever changing. Many movies, such as *Born on the Fourth of July* and *The Killing Fields*, have been made about the processes of nations, communities, families, and individuals trying to come to terms with their decisions about going to war. Nations rise and fall. Nations forget that they are a process and try to control their processes and those of others, affecting the processes of all the communities, families, and the individuals in their care. When nations become too blinded by money economics and do not balance their material focus with the spiritual, we see economic disasters come and go in the world monetary balance.

As with all the other spheres of process we have explored, the self, the family and relationships, and the communities also affect the society and nation.

How much greater is the temptation to believe that nothing we do has any influence on the society and state. It is difficult enough to see that the society is a process. To see that we have some influence and responsibility in that process, and to see that our own process is intimately involved with that process is mind-boggling. And, yet, no matter what we choose to think, our process does affect the process of the society.

For example, in the United States—and also in many other countries—there's a rather significant number of people quietly and with great dedication seeking to recover from any number of addictions. In this process of recovery they are learning that, in order to recover, they must learn to get back to their spiritual base, whatever that may be for each one. To do that, they try to become honest in all their dealings, to do service, and to live a life directed by their Higher Power. As individuals practice these principles in all their affairs, they change—some drastically. And, they affect and influence those around them. Who knows what would happen to a nation where the numbers of those practicing these principles reached the "hundredth monkey" stage, a level of critical mass that completely shifts our view of how the world really works? What we do as individuals affects our family and relationships, our communities, and the society in which we live. Reality can be no other way.

SPHERE OF THE PLANET

Let us now look at the next sphere of process, the process of the planet. The planet is not a dead, nonliving thing. Earth itself is a process, one that is ever changing, moving, adjusting, growing new lands, submerging others, trying to live with the beings on its surface and in it. Just like individuals, the planet needs to cope not only with its own processes, it must cope with the processes of the individuals, families, communities, and societies that coexist within its sphere. We are each of us affected by the process of the planet.

Periodically, there is a current called El Niño that develops in the Pacific Ocean. This current is a broad swath of warm water that moves across the Pacific and affects weather throughout the world. For example, Washington State is usually rainy except during an El Niño. Then, the weather becomes unseasonably hot, there's almost no rain, and the ocean temperature becomes many degrees warmer than usual. The extremely warm water in the current affects the spawning habits of the salmon. In recent years, American and Canadian fishermen have been squabbling over fishing rights—who should have them, and under what circumstances—for some time. This affects individuals → families and relationships → communities → societies and nations → the planet. Presently, these discussions are moot points because the salmon are not approaching their usual spawning rivers by way of their customary route, and the Canadian—or it could be American, it really doesn't matter—fishermen can't get to the fish that go into their rivers, because the salmon are swimming through other waters.

I talked with people in Virginia, Florida, and Arizona, and all commented on how their weather was being affected by El Niño! The current, which is part of the planet's process, has affected every sphere of our existence.

At the same time, we affect the process of the planet.

The process of the planet is affected by what individuals do, by what families do, by what communities do, and by what whole societies do. None escape this process. Scientists believe that auto exhaust, aerosol products, and the freon used in refrigerators have caused the hole in the ozone layer in the planet's atmosphere. They also believe that the hole in the ozone layer is at least partially responsible for El Niño. Individuals and families have used these products. Communities and organizations have manufactured these products. And the societies related to these families and individuals have built their lives around economics that have ignored the spiritual base of all creation. All of these processes affect one another and are affected by each other.

SPHERE OF THE UNIVERSE

As you see, the spheres of influence continue to expand. The next process we need to look at is the process of the universe. What a magnificent and mysterious process the process of the universe is! Occasionally, we are privileged to catch a glimpse of it when a comet reveals itself, when meteor showers sprinkle, when the sky reveals some new wonder, or when we have a close look at our sister planets. Most often, however, the universe seems well beyond our reach. Rarely do we stop to think that the universe is a process. Yet, it is. It is ever expanding, collapsing, exploding, building, rebuilding—always in process.

Recently, a discovery was made about cosmic ice debris cast off by passing comets falling into Earth's atmosphere. Since ours is a water planet, ice debris is lucky for us, because as a planet we need water to survive. I remember that years ago an old Quaker friend who had spent a lifetime studying water said to me, "In the not too distant future, water will be one of the major issues on the planet. Who has it and who doesn't and whether there is any pure water left will be a major issue." She was right. We are only at the beginning of this issue of water, then suddenly, we discover that we are getting showered with cosmic ice that melts into water as it enters our atmosphere! Thank you! The process of the universe is continuing to provide for our needs.

Perhaps it is more difficult to see how the individual and the family affect the universe, <u>and</u> we do. We are dumping debris in space, leaving it on the planets we visit on a regular basis. In addition, what kind of germs, microorganisms, or parasites are there on the machines and people we are sending out? Typically, we seem to be more concerned about what we might be bringing back to home than what we are taking out. We are yet to know how our debris is affecting the universe.

Still we have a responsibility.

Individual actions affect the processes of the family → the community → the society → the planet → the universe. A heavy burden, perhaps. Certainly a reality.

The Spheres of Process

SPHERE OF GOD, THE CREATOR, THE GREAT MYSTERY

The last sphere I want to discuss is the process that some people call God, and others call Akua, Tane, Yahweh, Allah, the Creator, Higher Power, the Great Mystery. Even physicists believe whatever is omnipotent is also in process. It is a process. And we are affected by the process of the Great Mystery. There is something much beyond ourselves of which we are a part.

> Honey, even if you don't believe in God, can you believe you ain't him?
>
> *Woman Elder*

The process of the Great Mystery, the Creator, affects the universe → the planet → the nation → the community → the family → each of us. That's just the way it is. We are not unconnected. We are interconnected. We are inner connected. We are part of, responsible to, responsible for All That Is! This is not too heavy a burden or we wouldn't have it. The process of the universe affects every sphere of our being.

And, we affect the Great Mystery.

The Old Testament speaks of a God who "longs for His children." We hear of a God who suffers when we pull away. We have almost no words that can convey the process of the Great Mystery that affects us all and that is also affected by each of us. Yet, we do affect the process of the Great Mystery and are one with it—quite a responsibility, yet never more than we are prepared to handle. Remember, reality is flexible enough to be influenced.

My experience of contact with that process was a love so immediate and so intense that I wondered if it wouldn't blow all my electrical circuits. Yet, it was so profound and so enfolding that the process of it was beyond my meager concepts or experiences of love. Why try to describe the indescribable! Suffice it to say that we have deep within us the capacity to know and experience the process of the Great Mystery and to be one with it.

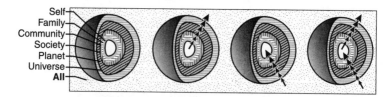

This leads us to our final diagram. Look at the sphere and know that all those elements exist separately and simultaneously. They are the same. There is no separation. They are the same. They are one. All is one.

My process is the Great Mystery, and the Great Mystery is more than my process. The Great Mystery is your process, and your process, and your process. The Great Mystery is the process of families. The Great Mystery is the process of communities and organizations. The Great Mystery is the process of societies. The Great Mystery is the process of the planet, the process of the universe. The Great Mystery is the process of the Great Mystery.

When I am living my process, I am one with God. I am one with the Great Mystery. I am one with all. I am one.

Chapter 8

BEING AN INDIVIDUAL

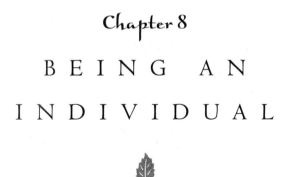

When I asked her why she fed him, she got angry, ordered
me to sit on the floor in front of her, and said, "I want you
to remember these words for as long as you live, and never
forget them: I was not feeding the man; I was entertaining
the spirit of God within him.

Nana Veary, Hawaiian Kapuna
(*from* Change We Must)

As individuals, our lives exist to be lived. We are the process of
that living. As we live our process, we become who we can be.

I remember the first time I realized that, as a female, I was born with all
the eggs I would have in me for life! Before that realization I believe that
I thought that the eggs in my body were like my other cells that get periodically changed—like an oil change—every so often. Not so! These precious
little bundles carry the genetic makeup of all my ancestors going back to the
beginning of time where we all began. These seeds have always been there in
me, and they lie there quietly suspended until the knowing comes to burst

out and jump into the void, hoping that they will journey down the tubes and into the womb where they will embed, fertilize, and grow a new being, or be sloughed off and return to our Mother, the Earth.

When I learned that my eggs were all there right from the beginning, I was astonished with the wonder of it all. This discovery was very profound for me; it filled me with sheer awe. Eggs there right from the beginning! Great planning! How could that be? What if there weren't enough? What if some were wasted? Being a child of the Depression, I devoutly hoped that there were more than enough, an overabundance, in case they were needed, which could be discarded if necessary. It's always better to have too much than not enough.

Our living process is something like the clustering of the waiting eggs. We have inside of us from the very beginning everything we need to be who we can be. We have everything we need to heal. We have everything we need to grow. We have everything we need to evolve. We have everything we need to handle the mistakes we make and learn from them. We have everything we need to realize our spiritual selves. We are like the universe in a drop of water, and we are the process of that universe.

We humans are creative and have devised many ways not to live our process, _and_ sooner or later, we long to return to the process of ourselves.

LEARNING OUR PATH

As human beings we have to acknowledge that we do not exist in isolation. Unfortunately, we so easily forget that we exist in context and that there is no way to understand ourselves in isolation. We are connectedness. We are unique. And we exist in context.

Being an Individual

EXCUSES

We live in a world of excuses. We live in a world that demands and makes a profession out of our demanding of ourselves that we be less than we can be. How often we use the phrase, "I'm only human" meaning "I'm less than human." Perhaps, as Frederick Franck, the great artist and author of *The Zen of Seeing*, would say, "We have taken our baser selves and called that human."

When we keep giving ourselves and others excuses, we are not living in a way that honors ourselves as who we are. Recently, I have noticed a rash of what I call denigrating-being-human phrases: "What about human frailty?" "It's not humanly possible." "I'm only human." Frequently, these phrases are linked to others such as, "Well, I'm an alcoholic, what do you expect?" Or, "I've been lying all my life, why do you expect honesty of me now?" "My whole family lies." "I told a priest sixty-two years ago and his reaction was so strong, I learned not to tell the truth."

We have defined being human by its lowest common denominator and have developed a complete armory of reasons for us to accept ourselves as less than we are. Acceptance of the self seems to have come to mean accepting, condoning, and settling for ourselves as the least we can be. We seem to be so fearful of being "too hard on ourselves" that we lose touch with our possibilities. We have other options:

> I was at the American Indian Science and Engineering Society conference, and I was acutely aware that there was an expectation there that people could be honest, considerate, caring, and nondestructive without judgment. One example of this attitude was when one of the elders got up and spoke to the entire group after there had been some vandalism. To paraphrase, he said, "Some things have been stolen or damaged. We don't do things like

that. We don't take what doesn't belong to us, nor do we damage things, especially if they are not ours. We can only assume that those people who did these things have not been taught right and they need our help, prayers, and understanding."

What a different way of looking at the world! All was voluntarily made right.

I remember many times saying to people that we are much more accepting of others as they are than we are of ourselves. We must never lose sight of the divinity in each of us. We are all connected with the holiness of all creation. We all carry the possibility of living in a way that does honor to ourselves and our species. We can participate in and with the Divine because we are one with it. When we forget this connection, we are not in touch with reality. Our sacredness just is. It is not up for question.

BEING A WRONG

It is a small step from giving ourselves excuses about our behavior to focusing on what is wrong with us. Often, because of our training in mechanistic, scientific models, we tend to think of ourselves as machines. We just want to diagnose what is wrong with us, fix it, and get on with life. When we get into this way of viewing ourselves, we become very self-centered. Indeed, it is an important process, a good process, and a necessary process to see what we are doing wrong. Unfortunately, we often go about using this information to promote misperception and misunderstanding. We begin to believe that if we make mistakes, we *are* a mistake. And if we do something wrong, we *are* a wrong. We focus on the negative. When we jump into the negative, we begin to teeter between the unhappy dualism of either being grandiose or worthless. In all sincerity, we may focus on the "worthless" end of the dualism or we may flop from one end to the other, both of which effectively keep us from the Divine. Remember, when we move into dualism, we fragment ourselves, stay stuck, and do not experience our wholeness.

At times like this we forget what it means to be truly human. We forget that being good doesn't mean being what we *think* is good, or what we *think* other people want us to be. Being good is the process of tapping into that deep well of goodness that is our heritage, our birthright. We may be weak on hope. We may have come to believe that we are hopeless. We may have a dimmed memory of the feeling, the experience of happiness, of love, of concern, of caring, of awareness that we live in context. Yet, regardless of how far down any of us has gone, I have yet to meet anyone who has completely obliterated their living process or their link to the process of the universe. Our awareness of that connectedness offers us the opportunity to be more than we believe we can be. That connectedness opens us to the nobility of spirit that is our birthright.

TRUE BUT NOT HONEST

Negativism erupts when we don't take care of ourselves.

I know that I am only a victim by my own choice.

Jimmy

At dinner last night I was commenting on how I can't fool myself into believing any longer that things outside myself can bring me a sense of well-being.

Anonymous

Sometimes we try to get away with something that is true but not honest. Often, we use the "truth" to avoid something we don't want to deal with that would be much harder to face than whatever we are putting out as the truth. Here is an example of true but not honest:

Joan had a good job with a lot of freedom, and basically, it was up to her when and how she got the job done although she had certain responsibilities. However, she had been getting some feedback from her boss and others that she did not seem to be functioning very well. Whenever her boss was gone on a trip, little or nothing was done. Things began to look suspicious when she did not want to sit down with some of her best friends and talk about what was going on with her. She said that she didn't feel safe with these people and felt too much shame around them. Her friends tended to be fairly clear, and they suspected that it was not really Joan who wasn't safe around them, it was whatever she was trying to hide.

When they met, Joan openly and freely shared that incest issues were coming up for her, and she also believed that she was a workaholic and could not do her work because of these two issues. She did *not* mention, however, that she was planning to quit her job and move to another city to be with a former lover with whom she'd had a tempestuous relationship at best. It was clear that what she was sharing was true, <u>and</u> it was not really honest as to what the real issues were that were behind her behavior. She was using her "truth" to cover up her dishonesty.

She *did* have incest issues coming up. She *did* feel shame around her friends. She *did* use work to gain acceptance. All were true—just not honest. She had built up the entire system to protect her dysfunctional sexual and relationship issues. She was focusing upon workaholism as her problem, <u>and</u> that was not the *real* obsession contributing to her current "craziness." She was *using* issues that were true to avoid the bedrock issue of relationship obsession. She had conned herself and those around her, while avoiding those who would be most likely to catch her or her con.

Her friends had only a gut reaction of "something's wrong here" to go by. When they confronted her, she would indignantly fall back on the "truth" of her statements, become righteous, and paralyzed by her shame. All this was a good setup not to do her work.

Much to her credit, Joan hung in there with her friends and broke through her true but dishonest layer. It was only then that she could face what she felt to be her basic problem. Her "true" statements, even including that she was a workaholic, were being used to protect her from being honest. When her friends asked her if she'd be willing *not* to move to the other city, her stomach clutched, and she immediately got sick, a good indicator as to what really was going on.

This is a good example of how we can use "true but not honest" to avoid facing ourselves and moving inside to do the work we need to do to become more whole.

BEING CLEAR

We have a personal responsibility to be clear in everything we do. If we are not clear, we need to sit with ourselves until clarity comes. Being clear may mean admitting that we are muddled. Admitting that we are muddled is a process of clarity about a content of unclarity. Whenever we have a process and a content issue going on, the process issue is always the more important of the two. For example, if someone says to you *"I'm not upset!"* pay attention to the way they say it, not *what* they are saying. Being alert to the process issues is just as true when we are dealing with ourselves as when we are dealing with others, perhaps even more so.

If we want to grow and become clear, it is important not to interact with persons who are not clear, and this includes ourselves! In fact, when persons are not clear, it is a waste of time to try to interact with them. When we are not clear, it is a waste of time to try to interact with ourselves or for us to attempt to interact with others. Imagine what the world would be like if everyone took the responsibility to be clear before they started to deal with others—a lot quieter for one thing!

Susan describes her experience of doing her work and Living in Process very clearly.

I've just gotten a raise and am in the process of getting a promotion here at work. What is happening is that the agency is growing, from grassroots to being established. As I mature, what I can offer to the agency has been expanding. So my supervisors want to respond to that, to my growth, by providing new opportunities. The process is interesting because I'm just beginning to see that I am capable. I used to think the *image* was capable and the image wasn't me.

I feel as though I've been walking around in awe of this new awareness for weeks. I guess I'm involved in the process of integration. I'm reminded of my father standing in the living room with his suit on, prepared to go out and spend the day being a businessman. I see him, smell him, as if he were right here. When he would go out for the day, he was no longer my father, he was . . . the insurance salesman. You know, I really missed him when he was no longer my father. I always wanted to grow up and be just like my father. I even write like him. I wish that he could have known that it was all right to be my father, to be himself while he was selling insurance, and while he was taking me for a walk. I wish he could have known what I know now.

I'm sitting here in the sunlight at work watching the traffic go by and I am so saddened by all the people who believed as I once did and as my father did before me, that who we are born to be is not enough. That has all just been a terrible mistake.

I want to go outside, or open my window, and shout to the world, "It's all a mistake." I wish the whole world could stop and feel things, see things differently. I guess that's the systems shift you've been referring to. A total shift in perception of what is *real*.

And I know it is a step-by-step process. I imagine all these people with little lightbulbs over their heads like in a cartoon. What a glow we would have if all of the lights went on at once.

Susan

All my life I've been looking for someone to tell me how awful I am and nobody will . . . not even my process.

Barbara

We have to be who we are before we can be someone different.

HELP

Often, a big factor in our ability to grow and change is our willingness to ask for help. Not asking for help when we need it can be a form of dishonesty.

Not asking for help is the same *quality of feeling level* as keeping secrets.

Yvonne

If we need help and we are not asking for it, this is a way of keeping secrets and being dishonest with ourselves and others.

Harry framed his dishonesty as what he did when he was trying to be a "good boy." He was almost seventy when he wrote this!

> A person who has decided to be a good boy is self-centered. He has no center in himself, so he is living out of the center of others. He has no boundaries. He is always needy. He does not believe in the affection that others give him. He acts in order to be accepted.
>
> *Harry*

Being a good boy is a form of dishonesty; it is a way of asking for the wrong kind of help. We're asking others to provide our center for us. No one can do that.

When I am self-centered, I am out of touch with myself.

Self-centeredness is actually a needy state of being out of touch with ourselves and looking outside ourselves for something—anything—to fill us up. When we are in touch with ourselves, we are "in" ourselves and connected with the All.

We have all kinds of help available to us on every level of our existence. Our most important help, of course, is within us. Our living process that connects us with the infinite is always there if we are willing to ask.

Being an Individual

PARADIGM SHIFT

As we learn to respect and live our process, we find ourselves making a complete shift in the way we experience the world and the way the world experiences us.

The way that each person Lives in Process and how this living unfolds between us and our Creator is unique to each person. No one can judge another person's process, and frequently we cannot even understand it. What does happen, however, is that as we become respectful of our own process, we become more respectful of other people's processes. This respect is a by-product of doing our own work.

We begin to see that we need not project the image of knowing everything and having it all together. We start to see that adulthood is a system shift—a paradigm shift. It means that we have the ability to respond. Adulthood is about being fully honest, being fully oneself. It is about ego integrity—or egoless integrity!

So the distinction between childhood and maturity has to do with life experience and growth and the continual development of the core, like the budding of a flower. All of the flower is there from the beginning.

Every person must follow her own process. No one else knows what is right for another.

There is no goal in living our process, except to live it. Our processes can change. Our lives can change as we participate in the process. Our only requirement is to trust the process and live in faith. Our responsibility is to live out what our Creator asks of us. To live our lives. Living our process demands a deep spiritual commitment of being one with one's life. Our primary relationship is with the Great Mystery, and our process is one with the Great Mystery. We are our process and we are more than our process.

Remember, depression and other feelings just *are*. They are there for a reason. If we can welcome them as possibilities for healing and learning, we will get the lesson. Whenever we fight a feeling or an awareness, it just gets bigger. Sometimes our inner process can get depressed if we don't listen to it.

As we learn to trust and live our process, we have a feeling of greater and greater responsibility for our lives. We *want* to take responsibility for our lives. We are eager and willing to accept the consequences of our behavior and our decisions because we know that we will grow from this acceptance. Growth is important to us. Living in Process implies taking responsibility for the self, and with this responsibility comes a freedom heretofore unimagined. New possibilities and vistas emerge.

Remember, all change starts with the self. As we live our processes we become open systems, and open systems generate open societies.

Living in Process shifts our perception. As Tina says:

Night before last I was watching a TV show on Shakespeare's *Hamlet*. Film clips of well-known actors showed their interpretations of the role, and directors were explaining their own perspectives on the play and the character of Hamlet. The program also had several examples of different interpretations of the play.

A 1960s-era version produced in San Francisco, called a "collage," used scenes from *Hamlet* in an impressionistic, experimental version. The producer and players were trying to find out if the original message and meanings would remain intact in a modernized avant-garde presentation.

Other efforts were discussed. Alec Guinness starred in a *Hamlet* based on Freud's psychotherapy model, *très chic* for the 1950s. Applying the Oedipus model to the motivations for the character's behavior, they were "explaining" the dynamics of *Hamlet* via the structure of psychotherapy. The director spoke of this work in hindsight as somewhat of an error—an overly analytical effort influenced by the strong personal interest in Freud exhibited by the actor and director.

Why is all this variance from the original *Hamlet* interesting? Is it possible that the play and character itself are recognizably so universal, so deep in human truth, that it can be played and received well within a multitude of perspectives? However, one director, his name unfortunately escapes me, felt that any type of specific interpretation diminished the play. He believed that the play would be best as originally structured, feeling that any variance would diminish the intended impact of the original play. Any effort to structure it from another perspective would serve to restrict the full potential of its available meanings. The application of another structure that biased the play would, in effect, lessen the watcher's ability to have all possibilities open for understanding or questioning.

I was very excited with this concept, and the words *Add nothing; take nothing away* occurred to me. Meaning that applying any system to another system would detract from the first, because it would be filtering the second system with the first, deluding and biasing, detracting from the truth in the original system. I believe everything is a system, and much more that the play *Hamlet* would be affected by this process. Inherent in this is, of course, the impossibility of ever being objective about that second system, or seeing that system as it really is.

However, just knowing that this process occurs has great importance. Adding things—projection, transference, lying to self unconsciously or to others consciously, affecting other systems for manipulative purposes—all are "adding things." *Add nothing* doesn't mean don't contribute. Listening may be enough. Comment and explanation, teaching and other self-serving activities may be add-ons that obliterate the original meaning. If I'm ready to present self and my reality, I may miss an opportunity for growth, as I grow primarily by listening and receiving. The concept of *less is more* would be applicable.

As far as the *take nothing away* part—do not detract from the process, self, or others. *Take nothing away* is also concerned with the insidious presence of destructive attitude—one-up and one-down activities, self-abuse, shaming self and others overtly or covertly in self-esteem wars, activations of scarcity models, general negativity, or denial and manipulation for self's sake. *Add nothing, take nothing away* is quite clear in principle, but may be difficult to balance considering the dysfunctional aspects of systems in today's society.

For the artist, there is a metaphor here. When drawing, there are two dimensions on the page and two types of space—positive space and negative space. Positive space is the object that I am drawing; negative space is everything else. Take a tree on the horizon: the tree represents the positive space and the sky the negative space. The negative space is frequently "not seen." (You may have seen the dual visual shapes that are used in psychological testing and the classic face-or-cup visual used to represent this concept in art training. The graphic object looks like two dark silhouette faces on profile facing each other, then if you blink, the object seen changes and looks like a white cup on a black background. Blinking can flip your visual perception between the two, but we cannot by the nature of our visual capabilities see the two together—unless you have very unusual pathology. Ha. One version of the two usually becomes the dominant or preferred visual.)

So, positive and negative space fit together exactly. We have a tendency to allow positive space to dominate our awareness. To draw, to become an artist, more needs to be seen, and the relationship between these two types of space becomes critical.

Lao-tzu said, "We are helped by what is not to use what is."

Without both what is and what is not, there is no structure, shape, or form, no distinction between one thing or another. What I have come to understand is that they are equally important, and although I prefer to have the illusion of one being dominant for my own comfort, it is not true. The reality of this concept comes when the two meet, in the line that shapes and defines the object. There is great power in becoming aware of this relationship, becoming able to see both shapes with their own intrinsic integrity, and holding both in balance. The single line dividing the shapes contains the boundary of both, in reality, dividing them not from each other, but supporting and shaping each in the same stroke. Here comes the significance of paradox in nature and spirit, of the myth of dualism. Yes, one. Yes, the other. Both are true. Can you hold both simultaneously? Can you see they are not whole without the other, and with both you have more than either combined? Back to *Add nothing, take nothing away.*

The understanding of the significance of the above associations in my process came from the eternal internal. I can relate this directly to my healing process. It is about balance and boundaries, freedom from enmeshment, freedom from judgment, and about knowing self and accepting other. About intimacy and relatedness, difference and growth.

In applying this new awareness to my relationship to other systems, people, for example, I have come to understand that it means I am not to add anything or take anything away from their process. I am not to add anything or take away anything to my process. To do this principle I need to decide what is the best action for a specific context or experience. In the checks and balances of my Living in Process recovery system, I keep this balance or I feel bad.

If I even get close to the mark, a slight movement toward health, I am rewarded with greater survival potential. I see the way clearer, am able to hear more, become more sensitive—sensitivity defined as the ability to *notice*. And notice means notice *only*; not do, not react, not engage. Just notice.

Tina

Our way of seeing shifts as we shift paradigms.

As we live our process we begin to evolve an efficiency in our living. We have a clearer idea of what is important and what isn't for us, and we more consistently choose that which is important. We spend less time going around in circles, backtracking, and jumping up and down in one place. We begin to move forward with grace and ease. We have less tolerance for foolish insanity and we are often joyous.

When we trust our own experience, we begin to see that "scientific truth" is not the absence of distortion; it is often systematized distortion. We begin to experience the difference between abstract "scientific truth" and our experiential truth.

As we shift paradigms we live in abundance, and life's little nitty-gritties ebb and flow, as do fun, joy, laughter, and humor. Our priorities become clearer as we become clearer. Discipline is not something imposed upon us by ourselves or others, rather it's something that we welcome as it flows from within us. When we live our process, discipline is never external and never unhappy. Discipline is freedom.

When we live our lives in process, it doesn't mean that everything is always easy. It's not.

Julie tearfully shared the pain that she experienced during one of her deep processes. She started into this process very slowly. We had an old woman elder with us who had come to spend some time with our group, and as she began to talk, Julie started to feel some things very deeply. She took herself to the mats and stretched out to let her deep process come. As she went deeper into her process, she became an old native woman and felt and experienced some of that woman's life—and it had been a very hard one. Julie was in the process for some time. When she came out, she was quite shaken.

She told us what she had experienced on a soul level, the *"pain about the knowing that what I do to myself hurts the universe."*

Julie will never be the same. She *knows* that the self-destructive behaviors in which she indulges do, without question, hurt the universe.

Now, Julie is a gentle person. Rarely does she do anything harmful directed at another person. She has remained, however, judgmental, self-abusive, and hard on herself. Through her deep process she is now gaining direct information that her willingness to be harmful to herself has repercussions beyond herself. These self-directed actions hurt the universe. In her deep process Julie experienced the oneness. She did not conceptualize the oneness. She knew it with her entire being. Julie will never be the same.

PARADIGM SHOCK

Dianne wrote and said, "Anne, please write about paradigm shock. I am experiencing it more and more." She went on to say that she has been doing her inner work and is dedicated to her deep-process work and is learning to live her life in process.

"I feel better about myself than I ever have," Dianne said. "I am happy most of the time even when things are difficult, and I have a serenity in my life. I am trying to be honest, stay on my side of the street, not operate out of fear and self-centeredness, and it's working. The problem is when I go to work, I experience 'paradigm shock.'"

She went on to say that being honest and staying on her side of the street is not exactly rewarded at work. She feels very vulnerable when she admits her wrongdoings and nobody else is admitting theirs. Yet, internally, she feels better than she ever has in her life.

We said earlier that one aspect of this work is a commitment to go all the way with our healing. Jesus warned us that as we follow a spiritual path it becomes narrower and steeper. What is often not expressed are the deep rewards of that path.

Living in Process is simple. It's not always easy.

My secretary, Pete, also shared a "paradigm shock" experience. He had been typing this book all day, and then in the evening we sat down to watch the news together. He experienced the huge discrepancy between the centeredness and peace he experienced from reading the book and the adrenaline and horror of the news as a paradigm shock. Yet, on the whole, his life is more serene and happier than it has ever been.

We need our places and times of sanctuary, and as we grow and heal, we bring our serenity and happiness into whatever situation we find ourselves. Remember, this work is about *living* life, not just passing through it or withdrawing from it.

SOLITUDE

We have talked about the necessity of alone time and its relationship to Living in Process. Yet, in discussing the individual and some important features for the individual as we learn to Live in Process, we need to revisit the importance of solitude.

We need times to gather ourselves, upon waking, from the far-flung parts of the universe.

Living in Process is not possible without alone time. We need time alone to get centered, get clear, go inside, and be with ourselves. Solitude and time alone give us the opportunities to be aware of the subtleties of our inner process. Our process is very caring of us and will get our attention one way or another when we have something available to work on, and if we have quiet time to tune in to ourselves, the "doors" may not have to be so drastic.

We also need solitude and time alone to see what we see and know what we know. We are constantly being bombarded with information, stimuli, and the world. Solitude offers us a time to be still and know. Alone time is different from prayer or meditation. Usually, both prayer and meditation have some inherent form (control). Solitude and alone time afford us the opportunity to wander—whether with our minds, beings, or bodies—and aimlessness has its purpose.

Years ago we had a big old "Sandy-like" dog named Bubber. I noticed that he would sit on our deck in the mountains and just look. I often wondered what he was doing; I assumed that he must be "doing" something—projecting human habits on him. One day, I took some time and went out on the deck and sat with him for several hours and just looked. That time with Bubber was one of the most important training experiences in my life. I learned how "just to sit" and how "just to look." I believe Thich Nhat Hanh calls it *The Miracle of Mindfulness*. These times are essential when we wish to live our life process. I am so grateful to have had such a wise master as Bubber to teach me this lesson.

> When sitting—just sit. When standing—just stand.
> Above all . . . don't wobble.
>
> *Zen Buddhist saying*
> (*from* The Gospel According to Zen)

Another aspect of time alone is giving ourselves the space we need to stay with our process. Beth says it better than I:

> Most important to me now, I feel that I am learning more
> about "staying with" and how important that is for me . . .

to give myself the space and acceptance to stay with my process and learn from the truth that comes from staying with. I have had a lot of energy around doing things "right," saying the "right" things, and judging myself harshly when I am not "clear." I am noticing that I am really hard on myself and cut myself off from what I know by getting rigid and perfectionistic and judgmental around how I should be if I were doing my healing "right." Then self-abuse and comparison get in there. When my self-abuse takes over, I feel like I lose my reality. I find that form-as-fix applies to how I "do" process sometimes and my need to be meeting some already determined standards. I see this as objectifying process, giving it a form, and then doing all this control and judgment around how I am doing or not doing it right. Staying with my process and what comes from that is teaching me about myself.

Beth

No one will give us solitude, alone time, and time to wait with except ourselves. The responsibility and the decisions are ours.

INTIMACY

This work is about getting and being intimate with yourself.

Intimacy with the self breaks the spell of techniques.

Few know much about intimacy with themselves, with others, with their environment, or with the All That Is. In order to live our process we have to become intimate with ourselves. Being with ourselves, trusting our process, and doing our deep-process work result in levels of self-intimacy rarely imagined. As we do our work and explore ourselves, we may not always like what we see and what we learn. That's all right. We're allowed that. Yet, in learning truly who we are, the good and the bad, the acceptable and the unacceptable, we come to the *what is* and that's what is important. It's only from *what is* that we're able to move to *what can be*. If we will not or cannot explore and accept the *what is*, we are doomed to be stuck. Paradoxically, it's only as we accept our truth, who we are, that we have the possibility of changing.

Intimacy with self in an externally focused society is not easy, yet, this is where we must start.

Often, we believe we are intimate when it is just our image, our facade—how we believe others want to see us or who we would like to be. This is not intimacy. This is dancing with a shadow. Yogananda said, "Good manners without sincerity are like a beautiful dead woman." Many of us are trying to be intimate with the beautiful dead woman in ourselves.

Our living process and our deep processes are our intimacy. Both take time. It is not surprising that we often feel an emptiness and a loneliness when we stop for a moment. Instead of rushing off for a fix to make our feelings go away, we could stop, sit with, go into, and experience the loneliness and see where it leads us.

Only as we become intimate with ourselves can we ever hope to be intimate with others. Many believe that we find out who we are in relationships. Not true! We must have a self to bring to the relationship in order to establish a relationship with someone else. If we are looking to the relationship to define us, we're simply using it as a quick fix and it is doomed to fail. Relationships aren't meant to tell us who we are. Relationships can add to who we are; they can never define who we are.

Being an Individual

Never compare someone else's outside with your inside.

Living in Process is the ultimate form of loving, for we are intimately connected with All That Is. Our concepts of intimacy have become screwed up. In the process of losing the experience of true intimacy, we have become progressively confused about what love is. We have approached intimacy through paths that are guaranteed to avoid intimacy, such as romance and sex.

Returning to our own living process and reconnecting with the process of the Great Mystery will remind us of what we've forgotten about love. Unfortunately, we have warped our concept of unconditional love into self-sacrificing martyrdom. Genuine unconditional loving has nothing to do with this distorted sham. Unconditional love involves every cell of our being returning to and being connected with the wholeness and the oneness of which we are all already a part. When this connection occurs, we move into spheres of loving that are unselfconscious and flowing like a never-ending celestial river. We cannot will this kind of loving. It is a by-product of doing our inner work. The solution is allowing our loving to flow. What we call sin is not something. It is the absence of something. It is the absence of love. We do not have badness in our DNA. We are just not able to tune into the goodness sometimes. We have shut off our awareness of love and goodness. Then, when we try to make changes, we focus on and try to analyze the problem. We have learned our mechanics so well. We need to admit the problem and then shift our focus to our goodness, to our loving, to our given connectedness with the Great Mystery.

When we are reconnected and have taken our place in the oneness of all process, when we are not experiencing the aloneness and alienation that our isolation and removal from our living process precipitates, death becomes another process of participation. Time is not what we perceive it to be. Space is not what we perceive it to be. Death is not what we perceive it to be. When we participate in our living process, our linear perceptions are dissolved or dissipated. As we begin to become aware of the unseen forces and processes in our lives, we start to realize that the unseen may be even more powerful than the seen. Ultimately, we realize that we do not know and cannot know all the ways we exist.

Chapter 9

RELATIONSHIPS

Life is relationship.

Our lives are shaped by those who love us and those who refuse to love us.

We have looked at the reality that we exist only in context, and that in order to have any relationships at all we must have intimacy with ourselves. Now, let us take one step back from our intimacy with ourselves and look at our primary relationship.

OUR PRIMARY RELATIONSHIP

Our primary relationship is with our living process, our spirituality, our God, our Higher Power, our Creator, the Great Mystery. Whatever we wish to call it and however we wish to conceptualize it, our primary relationship is with that in which we live and move and have our being. This relationship, this intimacy with what the philosopher and author of *The Courage to Be*, Paul Tillich, called "the ground of our being" is the defining process of our existence beyond our existence. This is the relationship that must be pulsating, flowing, moving, enfolding in order for all else to have meaning or even for all else to exist. If this relationship with God is alive and flowing, all else is alive. When we are living our process, we are one with this relationship.

Words are so inadequate to describe this relationship, this intimacy. Even using the word *relationship* to describe this process seems static. How do we describe an intimacy that is within us, outside of us, around us, and beyond us simultaneously? Scholars, theologians, poets, and sages have all tried.

Our oneness with God is at the same time defining, encompassing, and reality itself.

Probably one of the most important ways to grasp this relationship with the ground of our being is to look at what we have done with and to it in our relationships with spouses and family.

Whenever the term *primary relationship* is used, it usually refers to a spousal or a partnership relationship. The assumption is that our relationship with a spouse is primary and therefore all other relationships are secondary. In this model, our relationships with our children, our parents, our friends, our extended family, our spirituality, and our planet are all secondary. We have many frightening tales about people willing to make a relationship primary that resulted in destruction to their lives.

Recently we read about a teacher who had a child with her fourteen-year-old student. She was convicted of abuse and told that if she was caught with this young man again, she would be put in jail for seven years with no chance of parole. She was caught with him right after she was released on parole. She seemed to have no concern for herself, him, her husband, or her other children. She saw her primary relationship as the one she had with this young man. She was obsessed with this relationship.

A milder form of this is the modern marriage. Many modern marriages are built on a model of an exclusive, enmeshed relationship. Happiness is believed to be the togetherness of the pair, and all other relationships are seen as secondary, and a potential threat to the primary relationship. This concept of marriage has replaced the extended family and the tribal community systems, and resulted in isolated nuclear families that cannot possibly meet the needs of the individuals in them.

For years Trudy had felt that she needed to do her art. She was invited to spend some time with a well-known artist to get started. This artist had worked with other aspiring artists and had a good track record as a mentor.

A time was worked out and Trudy planned to spend ten days devoted to her art. Just before she left home, her husband decided that he would like to come along to have a vacation. He said he definitely would not intrude on Trudy's art. Trudy left it up to the artist to make the decision if he should come.

During the ten days Trudy felt she needed to keep her husband happy. Near the end of her time there, she reached a point where she needed to spend some concerted time on her artwork and use the opportunity to get feedback from the artist. Her husband, however, wanted to do some sight-seeing and take pictures. He did not want to go alone. He wanted her to accompany him.

She wanted to work on her art, and she wanted to keep peace with her husband. The artist suggested that Trudy really needed alone time to let the ideas bubble. Trudy's response was that she could go with her husband and give him what he needed, like holding hands, and yet not have to be truly present to him. What a tremendous sadness! They lived their marriage like a prison. They are both unhappy yet have the outward form of a good marriage. Their idea of a primary relationship is incarceration.

These may seem like extremes, yet we can see the quiet little ways these relationships have choked and suffocated those involved, how they have diverted each from her/his spiritual journey, clogging up their souls in the process.

If the meaning of life is to live it, and that implies moving along our spiritual journey, then our primary relationship is with our spirituality. All other relationships exist to augment and enhance that relationship.

Putting our spirituality or our living process first does not mean that we're not committed or irresponsible. Quite the contrary. When we live out of our spirituality, we consider our commitments very carefully. We do not rush in on impulse. We slowly and expectantly wait for clarity before making new commitments. When we enter a committed relationship, we do that only as it goes through the Creator, and we give that relationship honor and respect. Our primary relationship with our Higher Power demands that we live an intimate connection that requires honesty, respect, and honor. When our primary relationship is with our spirituality, we are responsible for and to the gifts of the relationships we have in our lives, and we are able to open ourselves to the sometimes frightening depth of intimacy that is available to us.

When our primary relationship is rooted in and living out of our spirituality, we do not let our spousal relationships or familial relationships dictate our lives. Our relationships with family and friends are opportunities for participation, not dictation. We must also remember that everyone's primary relationship is with their spirituality, and that an important aspect of intimate relationships is respecting, supporting, and facilitating, where possible, this spiritual journey.

Imagine a world where every child picks up in the womb that their prime responsibility in life is to grow and mature spiritually. Imagine that we were not conditioned in the womb to try to fill the void we feel with relationships and children. Imagine if we all accepted that our primary relationship is a relationship with God.

Imagine a world where there was not a pressure to be a couple and/or have children. In that world, people are not frantically rushing around believing that they should be trying to find a "cosmic mate." What would it be like if our focus was on our spiritual growth, and we entered into a relationship when we were truly ready for it, when our living process presented it to us, not when we "willed" it? Not when the other person willed it, or society willed it. Imagine a world where children were taught that they needed to nurture their spirituality, and only when they were clear and emotionally and spiritually ready, God *might* require of them that they become a couple. What if children were clearly taught that they were whole, with their Creator, in and of themselves? What if they grew up knowing that they need not use relationships to work out who they are, that relationships, when they have them, are just another avenue for knowing God? What if we lived in communities where "single" was respected? What if we lived in communities and societies where we had children only when we were ready and it was right, and children were treasured, loved, and nurtured by everyone? Imagining this world can give us a clearer perspective on the world we have created.

God has no grandchildren.

Everyone has her/his own unique relationship with a Higher Power. I cannot interfere with that relationship.

Living Our Process
in Human Relationships

When we live our process, we are not self-centered, and we are not defined by others. Others may not always like our respecting our process, <u>and</u> they will like it when we are respecting theirs.

I ran into a friend I hadn't seen for a long time and she looked marvelous. The last time I'd seen her she was depressed and angry and complaining about her husband and seemed to spend a lot of time in this state. I remarked on how well she looked, and said that I was pleased to see her so happy.

"Oh, I've just spent two weeks in a cottage by myself at the beach. It was absolutely marvelous," she exclaimed.

Knowing that she and her husband had plenty of money, and seeing the effect that being at the beach had on her, I said, "Why don't you get a cottage at the beach so you could go there whenever you want?"

"That's out of the question," she said. "My husband hates the beach. He likes the mountains. We have a place in the mountains. I am a married woman and one has to make compromises," she growled, returning to her angry, depressed state.

It's difficult to believe that this is what the Creator asks of us in this intimacy of relationships.

Too often, we have structured our relationships so they cannot meet the needs of those within them. Often, typical relationships that could be meaningful and growth-producing are busy with seven simultaneous relationships.

Relationships

THE SEVEN RELATIONSHIPS

I & 2. Each person has a relationship with their spirituality—their self. These two relationships are essential primary relationships and are necessary for any other relationships to occur.

3 & 4. These two relationships are each person's fantasy relationship with the other. In healthy relationships these relationships can be fun and playful and are usually shared: "I see you as my knight in armor." "You are poetry in motion." These fantasy relationships can enrich relationships when both individuals know that they are clearly fantasies and not real or important. It's only when one or both partners keep these fantasy relationships secret and/or project them onto the other that the relationship is in trouble. Honesty is critical. If the relationship cannot tolerate honesty, it's in trouble.

5 & 6. These are the mask relationships. Mask relationships are made up of my mask relating to your mask and are the hallmarks of dysfunctional relationships. Most relationships have some aspect of masked selves to them. Relationships, and hopefully intimacy and reality, can melt the masks fairly quickly and the relationships evolve. There are some marriages and other relationships that are built entirely on mask relationships, and one feels a progressive deadness in those relationships.

7. This is the real relationship that exists. This relationship may never be present in some lives, <u>and</u> it is always a blessing when it is. This relationship is the one that mirrors, reflects, and augments our primary relationship with our living process. When experienced with another human being, this relationship is very precious. This relationship is a process, not a "thing."

WAYS OF BEING
THAT FOSTER GOOD RELATIONSHIPS

There are certain ways of being and behaviors that are essential in good relationships. These suggestions offer some possibilities for us to experience living relationships.

1. We have good relationships when we are centered in ourselves, but never when we are self-centered.

2. Good relationships require honesty. It is most effective when we're being honest about what we want and need while staying on our side of the street. Honesty means owning our own behaviors and leaving it to the other person to find out and own their issues.

3. To be in Living in Process relationships we have to take the responsibility of doing our own deep-process work and not "puke our process" on others to distract ourselves when we have something coming up. We have no need to use others to avoid dealing with what is going on with ourselves.

4. In Living in Process relationships, we recognize that when we have a strong reaction to something our spouse or friend is saying or doing, it may have nothing to do with the situation at hand. It may very well be triggering an old deep process in us that is now ready to be worked out.

5. We need to remember that we exist separately from our relationships, and each person has to find her/his own way.

6. As we respect our own process and others' processes, we will begin to experience the many ways of letting go.

7. We need to remind ourselves that expectations are illusions of control and will become premeditated resentments.

8. We must let ourselves remember that love cannot be controlled. Love is only a gift. We have it only to give. We cannot force others to give love to us.

9. When we have feelings, we don't need to control them, and we don't want to dump them on others. We need to go into them and do our deep process work. No one ever died from feelings, _and_ many people have died from _not_ feeling them.

10. Remember, as we respect our process, we learn how to respect the processes of others.

11. We never need to set boundaries or work on "the relationship." When we work on the relationship, it means we're trying to control the relationship, which never works, as we're seeing the relationship as static. We only need to do our own work and the relationship will follow, if it is right for us.

12. When we are truly _in_ our relationships, we are _living the process_ of them. If we find ourselves looking around for something better, we have left.

13. We cannot treat a living relationship mechanically and still have a good relationship—"if I do this, then this," and so forth.

14. We are open to where our paths will lead even if that's in different directions.

15. No drama is good drama.

16. Compassion and caring are essential in relationships, any relationships.

17. When we see that we're not present in our body, and others are not present in their bodies, it's useless to try to carry on a conversation. Just to sit and listen passively is to contribute to the insanity. Being judgmental is never helpful at these times, nor is fighting back, or being wise. We need to check out with ourselves what we need, see what is going on inside us, if possible share that information—without judgment—and do what we need to do.

18. A "process pause" is essential before responding to any situation—especially if a situation is heated. Even when it's not, it's wise to stop, wait, get clear, and do our own work if necessary before responding.

19. It is dishonest and disrespectful to ourselves and others to try to connect with someone who is not truly present.

Relationships are processes. They move with time.

MAKING LOVE

Confusion and ignorance about sex abound. Our obsession with, concern about, and fear of sexual relationships have not done much to alleviate our confusion and ignorance.

Some believe that sex should be indulged in only for procreation. On the other end of the spectrum are those who believe that everything is sexual and sex should be indulged in at every possible opportunity. Like most dualisms, neither end feels right and probably is not right for any of us. Also, like most dualisms, there is no way to find a happy balance in the middle; staying in a dualism *anywhere* only keeps us stuck.

> Love your body.
>
> *Auntie Angeline Locey, Hawaiian Kapuna*

> The best thing for your body is making love with a righteous partner every day.
>
> *Auntie Margaret Machado,*
> *Hawaiian Kapuna and Kahuna*

We have distorted sex and tried to make it into a way of creating intimacy. This approach will result only in loneliness of the soul and will never achieve intimacy.

Lovemaking is possible only after the process of intimacy is well established. Making love is sacred. Lovemaking between two people who are intimate with the Creator, themselves, and intimate with each other is the way of the spiritual Creator. When we are truly compassionate, caring, and respectful of ourselves and the other person, our loving is one of the avenues we have that allows us to let go, get outside ourselves, and touch the Infinite.

Perhaps those who are obsessed with sex are seeking the spiritual, <u>and</u> they have forgotten the context.

> *The context of sex is sacred. It's only when we are connected with our spiritual process that we are ready to make love.*

I remember many years back, I became clear that there was something very confused with sexual relationships in this society. I was seeing and hearing about sex, <u>and</u> I was not seeing or hearing much about the sacredness of making love. Yet, I knew this sacredness to be the basis of any relationship. Something was wrong in my relationships and in those of others. I decided to step back and see what was needed for me to have the depth of intimate relationships I knew was possible (when in doubt, don't!). I knew it would support my spiritual growth.

First, I decided that I would not be sexual unless the situation was clear. This eliminated many possibilities. Then, I knew that I could not be sexual unless I was clear. This eliminated even more options. Then, I knew that I could not be sexual unless the other person was clear. This eliminated a large number of situations, and the combination of the three resulted in celibacy. That long period of celibacy offered me a good breathing space to explore and understand intimacy with myself. I learned so much.

When we are truly making love with another, that other is the beloved. When we are truly making love, there is the possibility of the spiritual process that is in each of us coming together in ways beyond our imagination. When this happens, it opens doors to greater depths of spirituality and spiritual connectedness than we could ever have dreamed. In pure lovemaking, we are caressing the God within the other. When both people are letting go and focusing upon the other, great depths of life and spirituality emerge. Down deep inside of us we know this kind of relating is possible, yet all too often the sacred memory is only a dim shadow, and we seek it in ways that will never get us there.

Techniques, whether ancient or modern, will never guide us to the kind of love that our species memory tells us is possible. We can move toward these possibilities only if our primary relationship is with our Creator, and our most intimate human relationship is grounded in our relationship with our spirituality and our living process. Far too often what we call loving is only the shadow of what is possible for us as beings in process.

Relationships

INTIMACY IN RELATIONSHIPS

We can make love in everything we do. Making love is not just limited to sex, and in our most intimate human relationships, sexual-spiritual lovemaking is very important.

> Intimacy is not something that happens between the
> sheets; it happens between the souls.
>
> *Cathy*

We have already discussed the importance of intimacy with the Great Mystery and with oneself, and that both of these are necessary before intimate relationships are possible. We simply cannot look to another to find out who we are.

Intimacy between two people is like a combination of three infinity signs that build as time and shared moments grow.

First, each person must have a vertical infinity sign within herself or himself.

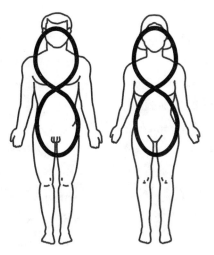

Each of these signs is the relationship with the self and the relationship with God, our spirituality within ourselves.

When these two are established, we are ready to reach beyond our-selves. We then have three infinity signs operating.

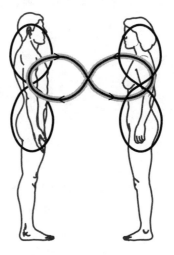

When you send me love, you send it from your heart. This loving energy enters into me through my solar plexus, moves up my body, and I take some out for myself, and I gather more loving energy inside myself, as it moves toward my heart. When it reaches my heart, I send it back to your so-lar plexus.

It moves up your body and you take out all or some of what I have sent and you add more. Then, it comes out through your heart and comes back to me. As we are both filled with love, it becomes possible to send it on.

The possibilities are limitless.

There are also numerous possibilities for blockage. I may not feel good about myself, so I won't let the love energy in. Or I may feel that I don't deserve it, so I take none out. Or I may feel that I have nothing to offer, so I add nothing. I may feel angry, so I do not send any to you. There are many ways to block the infinity of love, and when we do, we lose.

I remember once I had a friend and this energy often flowed be-tween us. Sometimes, however, I felt that my spot just above my navel reached out to his spot above his navel, <u>and</u> nothing reached back to clasp my hand. At those times, I experienced such a feeling of emptiness; it felt as if I were reaching into a void. I had myself, <u>and</u> my quest for connectedness found nothing.

Intimacy is a process. Intimacy is not static.

Intimacy cannot be held on to or reproduced. We must approach each moment fresh. For example, doing the same thing over and over sexually will probably not result in the same feeling.

Intimacy is not confined to linear time and space, or any time and space. Our infinity signs can span time and space. Allowing the other to leave when they need to is another aspect of intimacy.

Intimacy is magical, not of this world, not of this plane. We have no real language for intimacy. Truly, intimacy is inexpressible. It is feelable.

There are different kinds of intimacy. Intimacy with God, ourselves, our spouses, our children, our friends, our coworkers, our animals, our cars, our homes, and with the earth.

Intimacy is a complete leap of faith. It can also be fun and playful. In intimacy we can be fools, <u>and</u> it is best not to be foolish with it.

Intimacy is silence together, and endless sharing.

Everything is relationship and we are in relationship with everything. Whenever we forget that we are the animals and we are in relationship with them, we feel the right to destroy them. The same is true with our relationship with our cars, our houses, with all of nature, and with the universe. Everything is in relationship, and the more intimate and respectful these relationships are, the better we all function.

Chapter 10

THE FAMILY

*Our wealth is our children and our elders. Why don't we put our
money where our wealth is?*

Parenting is a sacred trust.

STYLES AND FASHIONS IN PARENTING

Parenting, like Paris fashions, seems to move through modes and trends.
The one aspect that most of the fashions have in common is that they seem
to come from the head and rarely from the heart. Often, the latest fad is a reaction to the previous ones, setting up a series of dualisms and never moving
into a new paradigm.

I have lived long enough to see many parenting fads come and go.
Few, if any, produced healthy, well-adjusted children who are ready to take
responsibility for their lives and live them fully. We all have done the best we
can as parents. Most of us really want to do a good job, <u>and</u> current parenting
theories have tended to focus on what we did wrong rather than helping us to
move out of the paradigm in which these theories themselves are embedded.

266

The Family

Looking over some of the fads and trends in recent history may help give us some perspective on where we are now, because vestiges of all these approaches are still active today.

AUTHORITATIVE PARENTING

Most of our grandparents in Western culture were raised by authoritarian parents. The parents—usually the father, directly or indirectly—decided how the parenting should be carried out, and the rules were strictly adhered to under all circumstances. There was an assumption that parents knew best and knew what they were doing. Often, they were parenting exactly the way they had been parented.

There was usually a tacit agreement that children were inherently bad—the old original-sin theory—and this evil had to be exorcised from them. This was done either through beatings or punishments that could be quite severe, or by controls that were so strict, children never had an opportunity to exercise their "evil" nature. Parenting in authoritarian style consisted of manipulation and control, mostly control. There often was love in authoritarian parenting, <u>and</u> it was always subjugated to control.

In extreme cases of authoritarian parenting, children were beaten and tortured to rid them of evil. Some people even assumed that children were better off dead than left to their inherent "evil" natures. Authoritarian parenting has produced generations of individuals who are rigid, controlling, detached from their bodies, living in their heads, out of touch with any feelings and intuitions, terrified of intimacy, and constantly struggling with their "human" aspects of love, caring, tenderness, and being.

LAISSEZ-FAIRE PARENTING

As a reaction to authoritarian parenting, an approach to child rearing developed that could best be described as laissez-faire parenting. This approach was based on the belief that children were basically good, inherently knew what they needed, and did best when parents left them alone. It appears that some of the adherents of this style of parenting just didn't want to parent and found a theory to support what they wanted to do, although this was certainly not true for all.

Much of this approach was based upon the psychological belief that most problems in the psyches of individuals were caused by their parents, and the best approach that parents could take was to keep their hands off. This style of parenting was accompanied by a general "mistrust of parents" by professionals, which led to an underlying belief that it would be best if this most important of human functions were left to the professionals. Parents became afraid of their children, and so concerned that they would do something wrong that they basically stayed isolated from their children.

Children who had laissez-faire parenting grew up angry, bewildered, insecure, and self-centered, basically having to figure out for themselves some way of coping with life, with little or no guidance from their parents. Adults who were raised during this era often have no concept of intimacy or context. They feel adrift in a sea of bewildering confusion, and fear and anger underlie almost everything they do.

Many of these parents loved their children. They relied much too much on the "experts," and often did not take the responsibility to do what they knew deep inside was right. Also, many of the parents of this era had been raised by authoritarian parents, and much of what they did as parents was in reaction to how their parents had raised them. They knew what they didn't want. They just did not know much about what they did want.

SCIENTIFIC PARENTING

The unsuccessfulness of this dualism in parenting set the stage for the evolution of a spate of approaches based upon the belief that there was a correct way to parent that could be scientifically developed and tested—that it was possible to do it "right." We all want to be good parents, and many in the latter part of the twentieth century have put their faith in the God of the twentieth century, science. We reap what we sow, and mechanistic science applied to child rearing has not resulted in a functional society.

Please note here that there are two ways to be controlled by the type of parenting each of us had. The first is to do our parenting exactly as we had been parented, assuming that our parents were right and we're right. This approach is also based upon the assumption that if it was good enough for us, it's good enough for our kids—*if* these parents reflect upon the issue at all. However, much of parenting like our parents parented is done unconsciously with no reflection at all.

The other side of this coin is to do the exact opposite of the way we were parented, as far as we are capable, although when scrutinized carefully from a distance there are more similarities than differences. This is reactive parenting.

Either approach is controlled by our unresolved issues with our parents. Many individuals coming out of this unresolved dualism have adopted various "scientific approaches" to parenting, which have become popular in the latter part of the twentieth century. There are basically five of these parenting styles with much overlapping.

Benevolent Dictator

After having studied much of the literature on parenting and the current pertinent psychological theories on personality and child rearing, the benevolent dictator decides that he/she (usually she) knows absolutely what is best for her child, and with singularity of focus sets out to raise the perfect child.

Of course, raising the perfect child often involves seeing the child as an object to be controlled and manipulated. This approach also involves the image of the parent as the perfect parent. Unfortunately, this image is often more important to the parent than the child is.

The benevolent dictator will take advice and counsel only from the experts. However, frequently the experts have not actually raised children or are very young themselves. The *theories*—the emphasis is on theory—used in this kind of parenting have developed out of mechanistic science, and ultimately the belief is that the child is neither good nor bad but an object to be molded and manipulated.

The illusion of objectivity is very important in this type of child rearing. The ideal situation is for the parent to objectively remove the self from the self and to remove the self from the child and not be emotionally involved with the child. The ultimate "goal" in this kind of parenting is to set up a laboratory situation where all variables are carefully controlled and manipulated for the good of the child. This reliance on the myth of objectivity results in the parents becoming suspicious of themselves and their own motives as well as the child's. There is frequently, on the part of the parent, a fear of being manipulated by the child.

The scientific form of parenting gives rise to frequent analyses of the situation to interpret what is really going on, and what is the "correct" course of action. (See Chapter 5 on the dangers of interpretation.) This approach results in a "disembodied" approach to child rearing, where most of the activity is in the head and where one is constantly analyzing the right thing to do.

According to the theories underlying this style, love can and *should* be given in the right way, at the right time, and under the proper conditions. Spontaneity is suspect unless prescribed by the theory. One can easily see the relationship of the benevolent dictator to the authoritarian parenting style, although they may look very different on the surface. This style of parenting is difficult for both the parents and the child. As with any mechanistic approach, it attempts to static a process and manipulate and control it.

Also, this approach requires that parents must always be on their toes and thinking. This activity is not only exhausting, it demands a removal from the self and from the context. The milk of love and compassion get squeezed out in this process.

This approach results in hurt, angry, resistant children and empty, exhausted parents. No one is getting their needs met, and unconscious resentments often build up in the process. Unfortunately, both parents and children in this setup are left wanting something from the other that they can never get.

Mechanistic parenting stops feelings.

Self-Centered Parenting

Self-centered parenting fits under the rubric of scientific parenting, although this may not be obvious at first glance.

Self-centered parents have children to meet their own needs, whatever those needs may be. With the knowledge of birth control—which some cultures have had for over forty thousand years!—most of us in Western culture have a choice about having children. With the crisis of overpopulation throughout the world, there is more and more need to give careful consideration to having and raising children. Sometimes, in our self-centeredness we believe that it is our *right* to have children, and no one dares question this belief, least of all ourselves. We want the "experience" of being pregnant, birthing, and having children. Or, we may feel that we have a need and a right to carry on our genetic lineage regardless of what we or the planet needs.

It's our unalienable right! We do not see that we live in context and can live only in context. We want what we want. We have the *right* to have children *of our own*, not realizing, perhaps, that in a system of oneness all children are ours!

We may also want to have children to fill our emptiness in some way. We may not feel right about ourselves, and we think having a child will prove that we are really all right. We may have a dead marriage and hope that having a child together will mend it. Or we may not know what to do with ourselves, or have some serious deep-process work coming up and believe that a child can properly distract us. We may just want attention, or we may be honestly convinced that having a child is the right thing to do. There are more self-centered reasons for having a child than there are dandelion crowns blowing in the summer breeze.

A child cannot fill up an empty parent any more than a relationship can. We may feel better for a while. Ultimately this ploy will never work.

I am not my children.

Empty-Vessel Parenting

Another variation of scientific parenting is empty-vessel parenting. This form of parenting is another form of mechanistic parenting, although on the surface it looks anything but.

Empty-vessel parenting is based upon the belief that it is the responsibility of the parent to "fill up" the child in the formative years, and that the child will then function happily and adequately for the rest of its life. Usually, there is an unspoken assumption that the child knows exactly what it needs—going back to a variation of the laissez-faire method—and it's the role of the parent to meet every need of the child for the first five or six years of its life. Then the child will have a proper foundation for life. In *theory* meeting the child's needs is important. In practice, this *theory* often works out in bizarre ways.

Years ago, I knew a man who was basically a bachelor and a loner. He became involved with a woman who had several young children and who espoused this form of child rearing. Interestingly enough, I have found that this method of child rearing is often linked with women who somehow believe that their role is to produce children— lots of them—as a kind of earth mother. They often have one child right after another. At the time my friend met this woman, she had two of her own children, and was very eager to start producing children with him. All in all, they had five or six children before they stopped and were eventually divorced.

When the children were babies, her belief was that as parents they should be in constant attendance and give the children everything they wanted and needed. When the babies cried at night, she believed that someone should get up with them. And if they wanted to stay up and play or just stay awake, someone (usually him) should stay up with them. Like many husbands who are in marriages with a scientific child-rearing approach, he believed his wife to be an authority (she'd read all the books), and he tried to follow her dictates. Unfortunately, he had some physical problems, and getting up at night and staying up long hours was physically impossible for him. He almost became homicidal toward her and the children in the process.

The empty-vessel type of child rearing is very labor-intensive. Ideally, in this approach, all the time and attention of the parents, especially the mother, should be devoted to parenting. During the first five years of each child's life, the parent should be completely devoted to the child.

In some families, this focus on the child is carried to such an extreme that the child's schedule completely determines that of the parents. This means that no one but the parents can care for the child or that the child cannot even be in another room away from the parents. Grandparents, friends, and family can be with the child only *in the parents' presence*, and there is no such thing as a baby-sitter.

One theoretical base for this kind of parenting is Jean Liedloff's *The Continuum Concept*. The writer observed that native Indian children in

South America seemed to be happy, well-adjusted children. He then observed how parenting was done. For example, the children were carried all the time by one person or another, the jungle floor offering all kinds of unsafe dangers for babies and young children, and were always looked after by someone. They did not leave the "protection" of constant adult attention until they were ready to go out on their own and initiated the separation themselves.

Many women have resonated with the *ideas* and *theories* in this book and have tried to apply it mechanistically to their own situation. Unfortunately, as the old African proverb states, "It takes a whole village to raise a child," and modern mothers in this culture are not a whole village. Often, they are isolated in individual homes with their children with little or no help at all. The stress of this parenting approach is intense on the child, and even more so on the mother.

Again, the child is treated like a machine in very subtle ways. The parent has a theory about good child rearing, and it *will* be carried out regardless of the toll on those doing it. Parents often become angry and overwhelmed. I have met with many people attempting to parent this way who have reached such a point of desperation that they were on the verge of physical and mental collapse and literally wanted to kill their children or themselves.

The children, too, were resentful and frustrated. They never had a moment alone to go inside and be with themselves, and they had this exhausted, angry parent who would not leave them alone. Also, since they were so isolated, there were no significant others to whom they could turn. Many children raised this way are angry and insecure, and as they grow up they feel confused and guilty. How could they be having these feelings when their parents had sacrificed everything for them?

*It's impossible to fill up someone else. When we feel empty and
exhausted ourselves, it is idiocy to think we have anything to give.*

The Family

The Little King/Queen Approach

The little king/queen approach bears much similarity to the approaches already described under mechanistic-scientific parenting. However, it is significant enough to deserve its own category.

This approach to parenting sets up the entire house and the lives of the parents to revolve around the child as the other scientific methods tend to do but with a different twist. In this approach, the child is all that matters. Neither parent—or anyone else for that matter—should have any needs whatsoever and the child is worshipped. Whatever the children want they get. There are no boundaries or limitations set on anything and they get and can do whatever they want when they want it. Frequently, these children sleep in their mother's bed for many years and are allowed to structure the family as they see fit. They are not taught to take responsibility for anything, even their sleep.

Again, this is an exhausting form of parenting and is very hard on the relationship of the parents. Few marriages survive any form of mechanistic parenting.

I knew one little boy raised like this. Whenever he was sleepy, like many infants and toddlers, he would fight sleep. In order for him to get his rest, his parents would either walk endless hours with him in his carriage during the day, or take him out driving in the evening until he fell asleep. He never learned to take responsibility for his sleep or himself.

When I visited his family years later, his parents, some other guests, and I were watching a special television program we had looked forward to seeing. He was about ten years old at the time. We were all engrossed in the program when he burst into the room and said, "Where's my bathing suit? I want to go swimming." (They had a pool

275

and he was a good swimmer.) He was standing in the doorway with his hands on his hips.

Immediately, both of his parents jumped up—his father was over sixty by this time—and started rushing around trying to find his bathing suit while he continued to stand in the doorway with his hands on his hips, glaring. The rest of us sat there astonished. I was saddened to see that his patterns of early childhood not only had not changed, they had worsened and intensified with age. As I sat there, I had the thought flash through my mind that these people were raising the next little Hitler.

This little boy had shown some endearing qualities as a young child and he was very intelligent. By the time he had reached ten years, he'd become a totally self-centered tyrant. His keen intelligence was being used to sneak around, intimidate, and dominate. He appeared to instantly dislike anyone who saw through his con. His parents had developed a pattern of cutting off anyone who had any candid comments to make about their parenting or their son and thus were becoming progressively isolated. Their marriage had long ceased to exist, and they lived a deadly and deadening coexistence that centered around their son. They have since separated.

Frequently, in this mode of parenting, the parents will have only one child or children very far apart. The energy needed for this type of parenting is just too much to imagine having others, and often this type of parenting is so destructive to the marriage relationship that no other children are conceived.

Children raised like this have no concept of context except as it exists to meet their needs. They have no idea that others, especially their parents, may have needs, and if they do perceive needs on the part of others, they see them as an irritation and hindrance to their getting what they want.

Ironically, these children are almost always angry and full of hate. Children who have no boundaries inwardly seem to resent the power they have. They also lack the security that emerges when one is assured of a context and being an integral part of that context.

In contrast, Helena Norberg-Hodge, in her book *Ancient Futures*, observes just the opposite in the children of Ladakh. She observed that the children of Ladakh seemed to be especially happy and secure. She also observed that these children seemed to have little or no concept of the individual or self as we have in Western culture. Her observations convinced her that the security they exhibited was related to their absolute knowing that they belonged to a larger community and had a place in it.

Parents who raise little kings and queens are afraid of their children and are therefore disrespectful of them. While they appear to be overparenting, they are actually abusing their children. They are not emotionally present to them. They, too, are parenting from their heads and not their hearts.

Children who are parented this way learn to use "love" and affection to manipulate and control. Down deep they seem to have disdain for their parents. The parents' illusion of a "happy little family" may be the cover on a powder keg with a very short fuse. Often in these families, one or both parents have a great investment in looking good as a parent, children may simply be an unhappy side effect of this wish.

Perfect-Parent Parenting

There are two other variations on the themes of scientific parenting. First is that of the perfect parent.

In this scenario, children do not exist in and of their own right. They exist to fulfill the image of either the perfect family or the perfect parent. Often, in these families the adults don't even want to be bothered with parenting. They simply abdicate the parenting responsibilities to others—

usually hired, not extended families unfortunately for the child. They themselves spend the minimal amount of time possible with the child.

On the other end of the dualism from those who want only to look perfect as a family are those who are hoping to find their identity in parenting and spend all their time with the children.

In both of these types of families, the children exist to fulfill the identity needs of the parents. These children are often extensions of the ego of the parents and are not seen to exist in and of their own right. Also, perfect-parent families are often very obsessed with materialism—either pro or con. They either have every kind of technique and gadget in the world as a prenatal and postnatal "learning tool," or they believe the good parent should not be involved with materialism and avoid "things." Both are materialistic obsessions.

Perfect-parent parents, like other mechanistic parents, are always completely versed in all of the latest parenting techniques and are very willing to try them all on their children. They parent out of their heads and truly believe their own armory of techniques makes them safe as parents. They are frequently emotionally, psychologically, and spiritually absent. Under the guise of doing all the right things, they are often very self-centered and self-seeking, and would be angry and horrified if anyone ever suggested such a thing to them.

Their image of themselves is that they're doing everything they can for their children and that they are deeply concerned about their welfare. They see themselves as devoting their lives to their children, and this may just be the problem. These parents mean well, as all parents do. They have just not done their own work. They have had children to find out who they are, rather than waiting to find out who they are and then seeing if they want to have children. These parents, too, are often afraid of their children and feel guilty toward them because at some level they know something is wrong.

The Family

Any parent who parents scientifically believes in form as a fix. In a very mechanistic approach to life, these parents have staked their own and their children's lives on techniques and believe that ultimately techniques will save them. They try desperately to separate their heads from their hearts and bodies and will admit feelings into their sphere only when properly controlled and expressed in the proper way. Consequently, these parents "blow" every once in a while, or one feels the explosion waiting just under the surface. Children are especially sensitive to these just-below-the-surface feelings and walk on eggs, or take the rage in themselves, or try to precipitate it and get it over with.

Perhaps because of the great value placed on perfection, these are usually tense, unhappy households. No one is getting her or his needs met, and the theory and technique are being followed to the letter of the law. Everyone feels guilty. Children raised scientifically do not learn to take responsibility for their lives and to live fully.

The pictures I have painted of these mechanistic approaches in parenting styles are rather stark. This is not to say that parents who have adopted these approaches do not love their children. Most of them do. They have put their trust in the best scientific knowledge of their time to try to do a good job of parenting, and ofttimes they have not necessarily focused on wanting to raise happy children. Rather, they often have wanted to do the right thing and their trust in the scientific approach is misplaced.

One of the most important issues to understand here is that these parents have not done their work, and they have put their trust in a mechanistic scientific system that cannot possibly meet the needs of spiritual human beings who are in process. Regardless of what the theory is, whether it makes sense or not, or whether it has worked in other settings (like in the jungle of South America), it is still approaching parenting as a technique, not as a process.

Living in Process

In our culture, parenting consists of trying to kill (the spirit of) our children to help them fit into a dead society.

PROCESS PARENTING

We are a process. Our children are a process. All living is a process.

BEFORE WE HAVE CHILDREN

If we were Living in Process—respecting our process, and respecting the process of others, and living in the context of oneness and wholeness, basing our lives on spirituality—there probably would not be as many children on this overcrowded planet as we have now.

We have the responsibility to take the time and energy to do our own personal work before we consider having children. There is probably no one born into this material world who does not have work to do. That's why we're here. If we respect that the meaning of life is to live it, and if our parents are living and respecting their process, we have a recognition that the process of our life is very important, and we approach it with consciousness and awareness. Since most of us have not had process parenting and have not been raised in a process way, we may have to be the generation that breaks the chain that binds us and paves the way for a new way of living.

As we do our healing work, our deep-process work, and learn to Live in Process, the veils of confusion will lift from our beings and we will be clearer and clearer about what we need to do in this life. If we follow the "when in doubt, don't" proverb, our childbearing years may pass before we are clear. If so, we can honor this and use our newfound wisdom to help nurture other children who need it.

For the children who are already here, and those who come along, we can develop some more respectful ways of parenting them.

The Family

CHOOSING PARENTS AND FAMILIES

In their deep-process work some people have very clearly become aware that they have chosen their parents. They have discovered that on a very deep soul level they came in to their life situation because they would learn what they needed to learn there. They no longer can be victims and must focus on their learnings. I will never forget when I first heard this concept; I felt such relief. I had made many mistakes as a parent, always trying to do the best I knew how, <u>and</u> sometimes, I fear, it wasn't good enough.

When I heard the possibility that my children had chosen me for what I had to offer—good and bad—the guilt lifted. At that point, I had been doing the Living in Process work for some time, and I knew very clearly that the only thing I could really do in this life that mattered was to be myself and all else would emerge from that.

I felt joyful when I heard several people report that their deep process had led them to the conclusion that they had chosen their parents because it was with them and in that situation that they had the opportunity to learn what they needed to learn. I had never been able to be a *Brady Bunch* mother, and I had inherently lived to be myself to the best of my ability. What a joy to think that my children needed *me* to bounce off of, and not some intellectualized mother.

Martha says this very well:

> I want to say in celebration that this is the first major life
> decision that I have allowed my whole being to participate
> in. Comparatively, past decisions seem to have been made
> (or not made) from numb, ambivalent, or agonizing
> places. In making these decisions, I usually ignored the
> needs and desires of significant portions of myself. Now,
> for the first time, I have chosen a direction for my life that
> my whole being responds to with joy and enthusiasm.

I have always felt drawn to be in the position of helper/therapist. I have fought it, resented it, and felt drained by it. I have always known, however, that this life direction has come from a need deep within. Previous attempts to explore this issue have only taken me back to the awareness that I was assigned to this role in my family of origin. The knowledge that I was performing this role as a very young child has only made me more angry and resentful.

However, since I have begun to do my own process work, I have had a very profound awakening to the idea that I may have been born into my particular family for the precise reason of learning how to become a helper/therapist. The implications of this awareness seem to be far-reaching and full of richness. They also delve into areas that I do not fully comprehend. At the same time, this awareness has given me a greater sense of integration and inner peace than I have ever experienced. I know now that I have a strong and loving spirit that has survived many devastating experiences. During that time, I learned a great deal about pain and the healing process. I feel almost as if it is my obligation, and I know that it is my deepest longing, to share what I have learned about this process.

Being a helper/therapist no longer feels like a role I am blindly acting out, but feels like an integral part of me, and I am beginning to do it with a measure of joy. I also know that I still have many unresolved feelings and issues surrounding the circumstances that I grew up in. I feel strongly that this training will help me deal with these and carry out my mission from a position of clarity and wisdom.

The Family

Doing my process has taken me on a path of knowing that I cannot turn back from, and is greatly impacting the way I want to approach my professional work.

In my current position as a school social worker, I have operated at a competent level and have helped many people grow and begin to realize their potential. I feel, however, that it has been within the parameters of a fairly controlling model of change, and within a system that is entrenched in mechanistic science ideology.

I am now fully realizing that control, as a therapeutic model, does not totally heal people of their psychological and spiritual dis-ease. I am now more aware of how some of the traditional techniques that I employ with clients may only be helping them fit in better to a system that is very threatened by wellness and health.

My experience with Living in Process work, on the other hand, is that it touches the core of a being and then allows the external dimensions to take on their natural, proper, and meaningful form. In Living in Process work, wholeness and integration are allowed to happen, thus counteracting the trends toward alienation and incompleteness that even the best traditional therapeutic models seem to reinforce.

Martha

Over the years I have seen time and time again that children love honesty. They often tend to be quite honest, especially if they have honest parents, and they respond to honesty. Honesty in adults creates a safe environment. This means being honest with children, with ourselves, and helping them to be honest with each other and with themselves.

Living in Process

Children come here to this world knowing only honesty, and we teach them confusion and dishonesty.

If children choose to get born to us because we have what they need to learn the lessons in this life, then their best chance is for us to do our work, and to interact as openly and honestly as we can with them, to simply be who we are.

CONTEXT AND NEEDS

Kids learn about respect when parents own their own needs.

No parent is always able to be there for a child. Zombies and robots can always be available. People cannot. Human beings need rest, alone time, quiet time, time with other adults, exercise, outside interests, recreation, a life. Only when we have a life of our own can we truly share it with another being.

It is the responsibility of the parent to show the child that it lives in context. This teaching is much easier when it is done in community, and the lesson needs to be taught even in the isolated nuclear family. When children see that parents have needs, that their needs are expressed (honesty), and that parents have a right to get these needs met, they feel relieved even at a very young age. They know that they're not going to be expected to meet the needs of their parents, and they also recognize that it is acceptable for them to have needs and to get them met. These are megaimportant lessons that can only be taught experientially as parents do their own work. Another learning in this aspect of process parenting is that it is possible for children—even at a very young age—to recognize that other people besides their immediate family are capable of meeting their needs. This extends their connections and their possibilities, and gives them even greater feelings of security.

In my first visit with Koori (Aboriginal) elders in Australia, one of the first comments they made to me was about child rearing.

The Family

"Why do you white people have only two parents for a child?" they asked.

I replied that some children did not even have two parents.

"We think it is very primitive for a child to have only two parents," they said. "Our children have their mother who birthed them, and all her sisters are mothers. Their birth father and all his brothers are fathers, and everyone else is aunties and uncles or grandparents. How can a child or the parents get what they need with only two parents? It's very primitive," they said as they shook their heads in sorrow.

As I sat there I realized that their entire family structure and community structure was organized around meeting the spiritual needs of the individuals and the community. I had lived only in cultures that were organized around economics. I had often wondered what it would be like to live in a culture that focused upon the spiritual needs of the individuals and the society, and made these spiritual needs the basis of the society.

In the Koori culture, everything is spiritual. The culture is not divided into the secular and the spiritual. Life is a spiritual process and living it is spiritual. In line with this spiritual process, at some point it may be necessary to go on walkabout or journey to a particular sacred site for spiritual purposes. If the mother or the father needs to make that journey right after the birth of a child, that child will not be deprived. That child has many mothers and fathers.

We do not own our children. They are a gift of the Creator, and we have the joy and responsibility to support their process for a while and share our process with them.

The nuclear family cannot possibly meet the needs of its members.

Living in Process

These words were spoken to me several years ago as I sat with a group of elders. The implications were so far-reaching that I needed to sit with them for some while. During this time of sitting with these words, there were national elections in both the United States and Germany. In both countries politicians were putting a major emphasis on the "family." I found it fascinating that this emphasis seemed to be "spontaneously" happening in both major Western countries, and I was very curious about the emphasis. Certainly no one could assail the family and get away with it politically, and yet, why such an intense focus?

If the old elder was right and the nuclear family could not meet the needs of its members, I wondered whether by making the nuclear family the basic building block of our society, we had ended up with a dysfunctional society because the basic unit was itself dysfunctional. For some time before this thought, I had been aware that "dysfunctional family" had become a diagnostic buzzword, especially when diagnosing children, and also adults. "He/she came from a dysfunctional family" had become a major diagnostic criterion for problems of all types. Concurrent with this information, I was hearing from more and more people that their families "looked good on the surface" and were "really sick." I looked at statistics and concluded that the dysfunctional family was the norm for Western society. It was the building block on which we were staking our culture, and it seemed to me that just as the nuclear family failed to meet the needs of its members, so did our culture.

About this time I started spending more time with native people and reading more of their stories and history. I discovered that one of the tactics of the Western colonizing nations was to break down native communities and try to force the people whose land they had invaded into nuclear families. For example, here in the United States, when Indians were put on reservations, they were told to isolate their nuclear family, and to try to feed and support them on a very small piece of ground. Even when they were starving, they were not allowed to organize a hunt in the community to gather food the way they knew would work. They were forced into nuclear families and given meager, nonedible handouts. This scenario has been repeated the world over. There was an attempt to break down community with an emphasis on the nuclear family.

I was talking to a Maori woman leader about the nuclear family not being able to meet the needs of its members, and she said that she agreed with that observation completely. She then talked about her extended family and how important it was.

"My son is very keen on team sports," she said. "He plays most sports and is very involved in them. The only athletic sport my husband likes is trekking. He loves to trek in the mountains, but my son has no interest in trekking at all. If my son had only his father to turn to, he would probably be in trouble. Luckily, he has his uncles. His uncles are all into team sports and are good at them. He spends most of his time with his uncles and is much more like them than he is like his father.

"Then there is my sister's daughter. She and my sister just don't get along at all. I have pretty much raised her. It's worked out well for all of us."

I told her I had the image of a great big tribal family flowing and changing and meeting the needs of its members.

"It's true," she said. "I know our nuclear family could not have met the needs of its members."

Communities have many options for love and support and interactions.

Part of the role of the parent is to do our work so we can get our egos out of the way and be able to focus on the needs of our children.

Living in Process

I was very touched by Sally, a mother I met a few years ago. I had met her daughter long before I met her, and her daughter and I had formed a very warm, close bond. I thought she was beautiful inside and out, and in an unusual moment of weakness—I usually don't meddle in his relationships—told my son that he should meet her, as she was very special.

His response was, "Well, Mom, I have a girlfriend right now, but if she's as great as you say she is, I sure would like to meet her." He then decided to go right out to the West Coast and "check her out." They have been best friends ever since, and the three of us are a family within two families.

When I first met her mother, I was a little nervous. Would she be jealous of the relationship we had that was so mother-daughter-like? I felt very open toward her mother, <u>and</u> I did not know what I would be getting back. When we met, she seemed genuinely open and friendly. She was eager to know about me, and was excited about the things I had done and was doing. I liked her very much, and this liking seemed genuinely mutual. I told her that I'd been somewhat anxious about what her response to me would be. I said that I just loved her daughter and felt very close to her.

"I'm so glad," she said. "When my daughter was born, I took one look at her and could see that she was very powerful. I was a bit afraid of her, as I knew I wasn't that powerful. I was concerned and wanted her to get what she needed. Throughout her life she has been able to find powerful women as surrogate mothers when she needed them. I've been so grateful, and I'm grateful to you for being there for her and loving her."

I was so touched. I immediately felt love, compassion, and respect for this woman. She was a good parent and a very wise woman.

Our responsibility as a parent is to see that our children's deepest needs get met. We don't have to meet them all ourselves.

Some parents are concerned about maintaining their image as an adult who knows and can do everything. Persons who are Living in Process would take these feelings to the mats and see what these feelings are about as they worked through them. They would not impose them on their children.

Children are often the unhappy recipients of our unprocessed feelings, and they have an innate feeling of injustice about this dumping. Children often come to the Living in Process intensives and training sessions, and we are impressed how easily they integrate to Living in Process work and seem already to know it.

One woman related that after her six-year-old had been to one training group, when she would try to dump her process on him, he would say, "You're dumping on me. You're not supposed to do that. You better go to the mats and then talk to me."

She reported that he was absolutely right!

As parents, we have the responsibility to help our children learn that they live in context, and that none of us is isolated and alone. Children who know that they belong to a larger world feel more secure.

Ironically, even if their every need and whim have been met from birth, when children do not see themselves in context, they will be fearful and lonely. There has been so much "scientific focus" on gangs and teenage peer groups, yet I see them as expressions of our children's obvious need for community.

Learning about living in context is better when learned experientially. We can tell our children that they live in context, but if they don't experience it, how will they know? We're experiencing a worldwide environmental crisis right now. As a race we seem to have forgotten that we all live in context. We cannot save nature unless we know we *are* nature. Some children have never even seen dirt. They live in a world of concrete and asphalt. How could they possibly know that the earth is a living being teeming with life? Deep-process work has provided the doors for some of them to reconnect with their cosmic oneness and experience context. Their parents failed them in this area of their spiritual education, and their process has provided another avenue for experiential learning. They are lucky.

ELDERS

An important aspect of living in context and contextual education is learning from our elders and spending time with our elders. Elders carry the wisdom of the ages. They remember knowing someone, who knew someone, who knew someone . . . when the world was different. Elders have the perspective that can come only with age. In many cultures, it is the elders who do the child rearing, leaving those of the parents' age to deal with the material world. It is very difficult to try to do both, and elders can bring needed relief to parents. By their very existence elders bring children an awareness of perspective and context. Those who accept their role as elders can bring to a child time and patience that the parents don't have. They know how important our children are and can teach the proverbs, the myths, and the legends of the family and the culture. They have time for the wisdom of the ages.

Unfortunately, in this day and age, many of our elders have not been process parented themselves, and they may be hurt, angry, and confused, not knowing how to do their own work. They may not be ready to be elders to our children. Yet, they still have something important to offer to our children and need to be integral to their lives.

DOING OUR OWN WORK

Children pick up Living in Process very easily because they already know it and are near to it.

The most important thing we can do to be good parents is to do our own work. Children do not need perfect parents. *Children need parents who are living their own process and respecting the processes of others and who model this while respecting the processes of their children.*

Children are not afraid of deep-process work regardless of how loud it gets. They seem to know it. I think of the sounds that people make while in their deep process as the sounds of birthing themselves.

Often what we perceive as tantrums or fits of anger are children doing their deep-process work. If we can just sit with them, wait, and not interfere, they will come out the other side with what they need. And if we are not clear enough to sit with them, then maybe someone else will be.

Years ago, when I was a psychotherapist, I decided that it was inappropriate to have my office in a business building, partly because this work is not a "business," and partly because people often were not free to do their deep work in that setting. So I moved my office to my home. My living room became my waiting room.

One day I was working with a couple. I had been working with each of them individually and occasionally saw them together. He was a big, muscular forest ranger, and she was a petite secretary. During their joint session, she had some deep-process work come up and said that she would feel better if he waited outside the therapy room. They were quite enmeshed as a couple. He went out and watched television with my son, who was fourteen at the time. He and my son had become friends over the years.

As he sat there, his wife's noises became quite loud, and he became quite agitated.

"Doesn't that bother you?" he asked my son.

"What?" my son asked back, glancing up from his TV show.

"All that screaming and yelling and hitting the pillows," he said, even more agitated.

My son looked at him in puzzlement. "Naw, that's just the sound of healing," he said, and went back to his TV.

Children understand and respond to deep process at a very deep level.

In Europe, we have a little four-year-old boy who started his Living in Process training when he was in the womb. Throughout his mother's pregnancy, she and his father were both in the training group, and he started coming to the groups as soon as he was born. He's a Living in Process kid.

He has many good friends in the training group, who are in a Living in Process group with his parents and live near his home.

One day, when he was about two and a half or three years old, he'd been out playing in the yard with some of the other children and adults who were there. At that time, there were quite a few people on the mats doing their deep-process work, as well as the group going on, so the room was busy and congested.

He burst into the room and said, "Where's Jenny?" (a young woman who is one of his good friends).

"She's on the mats," his mother said.

He stood, looked around, spied her, grabbed a box of tissues, and went and sat with her process!

He knew what you do when you sit with another's deep process!

When children see us do our deep work, they feel free to do their own.

When children grow up doing their deep-process work and having it respected, they have some important tools for dealing with reality.

Just last month a two-and-a-half-year-old who was at the training with her mother and who is very articulate became very upset about something.

"Do you want to go to the mats?" her mother asked very respectfully.

She nodded, and off they went, with her mother sitting with her and handing her the tissues. She came back clearer and happier and had not "puked her feelings" on her mother.

Process parents can show that feelings are all right to have and very important, and that it is not all right to hold them in or dump them on someone else. They can demonstrate that there is an option of healing and seeing what is behind the feelings and working them through if they do their own work.

Process parents can also demonstrate that they respect themselves enough not to let others dump their feelings on them, by offering the child the option of going to the mats. When children see parents make mistakes—like getting mad and dumping on others—then do their work and then come back, take responsibility for their anger, and make amends, children learn that mistakes are okay if you take responsibility for them and do your work. Children don't want perfect parents. They need parents who model the process of being human and the process of living. They want parents who will participate in these processes with them.

Children like honesty. They know that their parents are not perfect, and neither are they. They need skills to participate in their lives and learn and grow from the processes of their lives. Good parenting starts with doing our own work and respecting the processes of others. When children see parents do their own deep-process work, heal, make amends, and be honest, they learn these behaviors. However, they learn a different set of behaviors when they see parents hide and repress their feelings, be dishonest about who they are, be disrespectful of themselves and others, be externally referent, and look outside themselves for their meaning, their spirituality, and their identity. These children learn to look outside themselves for cues about how they should behave and who they should be, which means they're giving away their power. Fear dictates behavior when we're cut off from our living process, our spirituality.

We are so eager to teach children about math, science, business, capitalism, materialism, and free enterprise, <u>and</u> we seem to have less concern about values, spirituality, connectedness, and reality. <u>And</u>, it is difficult, if not impossible, to teach what we don't know.

The following story, I believe, gives a good example of the process of parenting with children:

First of all we have some good news: our baby, a little girl called Annilea, was born on March 10. We are all very glad that she takes part in our life now. At the same time it is a change for each one of us. Our family situation is different now and it will probably take some time until we find our rhythm again. Annilea was born at home and this was a really good experience for me. I had a lot of support, Christel took care of Sebastian, I had two midwives (one of them is my sponsor), Jenny was here (Lois's daughter), and, of course, Gerd. For me it was a very nice and supportive atmosphere. And I experienced the birthing [as] very different [from] birthing Sebastian. With Sebastian I didn't have (or use) as much support, and at that time I just was in a different place. I felt a victim of my pain for a long time during the birthing process. And this made the pain even worse. With Annilea I didn't feel a victim anymore, and I really could experience how I changed through Living in Process work. I could allow myself to express any feelings I had (anger, pain . . .) and this was a relief. And, I really could participate in this birthing process.

Yes, I am grateful for this work. Also for Sebastian— we could see the fruits of this work. He was used to our screaming or making all kinds of different noises from the mats. And he seemed to take care of himself very well. Every now and then he had a look into the room where I was, and sometimes he stayed for a while. When he had enough, he went to Christel again, and he seemed to enjoy the time with Christel. Only, when the baby was here, he wanted to hold her and be there. I am very glad and grateful that everything went so well.

Brigitte

We can respect children as a process and respect their process. We can live and practice what we preach. We can let go of ownership, the illusion of control, molding and using our children to validate our own choices.

We need to participate in our own life process as fully as possible and accept the privilege of participating in the processes of our children as guests.

TRAINING OUR PARENTS

Process parenting goes in two directions. It is the responsibility of parents to nurture and teach their children, and it is the responsibility of children to teach and nurture their parents.

Over the years, I have been aware that there are many unruly, untrained parents running around out there. These are parents who treat their grown children without respect and believe they are still "their children" to be dominated and controlled.

As a psychotherapist, I used to listen to endless hours of some of my clients saying, in true victim fashion, "My parents didn't do this. . . . They did this or that to me. . . . My parents didn't love me. . . ." Now I know that the issue is not what your parents did or did not do. The issue is, what do *you* need to do to heal from whatever they did or did not do? We can blame parents, unfortunately, with little or no healing results. Or we can do our work with whatever life has dealt us, knowing that we have the capacity to heal from anything. It's as simple as that.

Yet, there is something about not taking the responsibility to train your parents that is important here. Admittedly, some of us had quite unruly parents, and they may have been quite a handful for us as children. Yet, we still have some continued responsibility as adults.

The Family

I know a man who decided that he needed to have no contact with his family while he focused on working through some of his healing and spiritual issues. He needed time for himself, and he called his family to say this and to ask them to respect his wishes. As time went by, given no information from him, his family was left to their own imaginations (always dangerous). Instead of doing their own deep-process work and dealing with their feelings as they came up, they fed off each other until they were in a frenzied state. They were sure that he was being mind-controlled and in some sort of cult.

In this dramatic state, they called his wife and made a veiled threat to come and kidnap "their son." He was thirty-seven years old! This is surely a case of untrained parents who showed no respect for their son or his process.

His wife stepped back and said that these issues were his to deal with, and that if his parents wanted to kidnap him, he would have to deal with it. This was not her issue, and she would not come after him. Untrained parents often live on drama.

As a parent, I'm aware that my children started training me as soon as they were born. They let me know very quickly what they needed and what they did not need, and it was my responsibility to see the larger picture and protect and nurture their process. For example, when my first child, my daughter, started eating solid foods, I wanted slowly to introduce a variety of foods. She was a good eater and feeding her was fun. However, I will never forget the beet incident. She had always eagerly tried new foods, and the whole process felt like an adventure for both of us. Then came the beets! I love the color, the taste, the texture of beets. I just love beets, so I just assumed she would, too. I gave her a spoonful of beets, and she looked shocked. She then proceeded to spray them all over me. I looked shocked. I tested the temperature to make sure they were neither too hot nor too cold—just like the other foods. I tried one more spoonful—just to be sure—and got sprayed again. That was the end of beets for us. Her communication was clear and direct. If she wanted to try beets again, as far as I was concerned, it would be when she chose to do so on her own at the family table.

I have also noticed that some of the training that my children have done with me continues today. As babies—they are now thirty-seven and thirty-one years old, respectively—they liked to keep me moving when I held them. I would often stand and sway from side to side holding them when they cried, and they would quiet right down. To this day, when I hear a baby crying, I will start swaying from side to side. They took their parent training very seriously.

A few years before my father died, I had an experience with him that, I believe, is a good example of a trained parent. And I also want to say here that I was blessed with trainable parents.

Some time ago, I bought a piece of property. It was more than I'd ever paid for anything, and I'd gone out on a limb to buy it as a leap of faith. I'd taken a ten-year mortgage on it and was about halfway through paying it off when one of the "energy crises" hit and there was fear of an economic depression.

My father had lived through the Depression in the 1930s and like many people of his era had a tremendous fear of such economic depressions. Unbeknownst to me, he'd been worrying over my "losing my land." After a period of "stewing" he called me and asked if I'd be willing to come up to see him (an hour's drive), that he needed to talk with me. I was eager to see him and hear what he wanted, and went up the next evening.

He started out very respectfully. He told me that he really trusted me and that he knew I was competent and responsible. He also told me he didn't want to pry into my affairs, nor did he want me to think that he didn't trust me. I couldn't imagine what he was building up to and told him that I knew all this. He then said that he had been thinking about my land and the possible depression, and he was afraid that I would lose it—owning his own feelings of fear. He wondered if I had taken any precautions.

I was deeply touched that he was so concerned and was honored by the way he was treating me with such respect, and I told him so. I then told him that I would be happy to share with him what measures I had taken to protect myself. We then rolled up our sleeves and went over all the details together.

When we were finished, he said he felt relieved and was very proud of me. And I felt respected and loved. I told him that I was relieved, too. It was good to have gone over all my thinking again, and I appreciated his concern and wisdom. We hugged and chatted about other things, ending with a lovely meal. He was not an unruly parent. I was not an unruly daughter. We each owned our own feelings and respected our own process and that of the other.

Parents, like children, will get away with whatever they can if they are not taught to respect another's process. Sometimes, the children have a lifetime job ahead of them.

Of course, what we learn in parenting and in being parented can be modeled in all our relationships.

Living in Process

Living in Process teaches children that they have everything needed within themselves in relation to their living process (spirituality) to live their life. This internal depth of knowing is the greatest gift we can give them. We will not be able to teach it unless we know it and can live it ourselves.

Chapter 11

COMMUNITY

The awareness of and participation in community becomes increasingly important as we learn to Live in Process. As I explored earlier, the more we become who we are, do our healing work, and live our spirituality, the more we come to know that we live in context and can truly live only if we are in context. In the 1950s and 1960s, there was a song that took John Donne's famous phrase "No Man Is an Island," and epitomized this reality. The sentiments of that song are true today and very important as we tend to isolate.

Communities exist whether we participate in them or not. The reality is they're there. Most of us have several communities of which we are a member that are often overlapping. We have our living communities, our social communities, our work-organizational communities, and our spiritual communities. Some may have the same memberships and some may be made up of persons not active in any other aspect of our lives. They are still communities.

Benjamin told me about when he worked at a major metropolitan newspaper as an editorial assistant. He had the task of working in the sports department editing box scores and answering phone calls. He said he had no concept personally and wasn't aware of anybody else having the concept that they were a community—that they had any responsibility or connection to anything other than their particular job function and task at hand.

The employees came to work, did their specific job, but never questioned the overall function or community of the newspaper. Benjamin said they were unaware that they were part of anything bigger than their specific job. He said he never considered taking responsibility for the opinions of the newspaper, or for the fact that they were using so many trees to produce the newspaper, or for the overall well-being of the workers.

He believed that such questions were "not his responsibility." All of the employees he was aware of accepted the illusion that they were not part of the bigger community. They did their work and when it came to issues larger than their specific job or their specific department, they took no responsibility whatsoever. He was a member of the community of the newspaper staff but never saw himself participating in anything other than his own compartmentalized job.

Modern societies have experienced an alarming breakdown in communities. As I mentioned earlier, when colonizers have invaded a country, in addition to killing off the native people through disease and violence, they have always focused on breaking down community. The most effective way to destroy a culture is to destroy the language, the spirituality, and the community, all supported by the introduction of alcohol and drugs. This pattern of destruction has been used and is continually used throughout the world.

One of the major breakdowns that we are experiencing in modern society is that there is no mediating process between the nuclear family and the society. If we accept the fact that the nuclear family cannot possibly meet the needs of its members, we can then more clearly see the importance of community and nurturing healthy communities. If the nuclear family is dysfunctional, which is statistically true, this means that we are using a dysfunctional building block with no functional intervening processes or structures to create a society. Given this reality, we can see why we have not produced a very functional society. We need to take the issue of community seriously.

In the last few years, I have noticed a growing interest in and deepening awareness that we need to build functional communities. Unfortunately, many of the attempts have been exactly that, to structure and build communities. This approach is based upon the same assumptions that the mechanical method employed to "fix" people. In this approach we see the old assumption of "form as a fix" being applied to the "problem." We diagnose the problem assuming that a mechanistic adjustment will solve it. Just like in individuals, relationships, and families, the solution is not mechanical. The solution is a process. What happens when we take our new paradigm, our path of living, our path of the soul into our communities?

All of the basic truths described in Chapter 4 apply to communities as well as individuals. As discussed in Chapter 7, individuals are the true building blocks of all the process spheres extending all the way to the infinite knowing. Furthermore, we exist individually as well as in wholeness. We truly cannot change anyone or anything other than ourselves. So, as we change ourselves, those changes reverberate through all of the spheres of our existence. When we practice honesty with ourselves and with our family and in our relationships, that honesty will begin to show up in our communities.

Living in Process

Communities are not built, they emerge.

As we get more in touch with ourselves and our spirituality we begin to know deep in our beings that we are part of larger and larger wholes. We begin to see that we must practice the same basic truths on a community level that we practice on an individual level.

LIVING COMMUNITY

We all have living communities and we live in communities.

A few years ago Tracy went on what her family and friends all laughingly and lovingly call her "power mower kick." Her neighbors felt the need to put an ornamental iron fence between their property and hers after a new survey of their land added about five feet to their yard. The line between the two houses had been determined by a row of lilac bushes that had sufficed for a hundred years and was now seen as inadequate and inaccurate. Of course, if the fence is on the line, this means that half of the concrete footings for a fence she didn't even like were in her yard. She had never liked fences. Anyway, two of the footings stuck up and were always covered with grass. The college student who lived with her always mowed the lawn, and when the second power mower she owned was destroyed by running into yet another concrete footing, she began to consider the importance of power mowers. Shortly thereafter, the power mower became her symbol of the community crisis in our society.

Everybody in her neighborhood owned a power mower, as well as wheelbarrows, weed whackers, and gardening tools. She used hers once every one or two weeks for about an hour; so did everyone else in the neighborhood. "Why does everybody need to own power mowers?" she wondered. "What sense it would make to have one power mower for the neighborhood," she thought. "We could all use less natural resources and put the financial savings into something important. We would have many more interactions as a neighborhood because we would have to interact over the power mower," she reasoned. "We would have many more opportunities to practice our basic truths for living such as staying on our own side of the street, being honest, letting go of control, living in context, just to mention a few. All of this would be possible if we shared a mower," she concluded. The power mower became her symbol for problems we can solve when we shift our perspective.

Clearly, we would not need to make so much money if we didn't have to buy power mowers. The community gains could far outweigh the individual limitations. We wouldn't have to worry so much about jobs and the economy if we shared resources.

What does it mean to live in community? Living with the people we know means knowing the people we live with. Knowing and being known are two of our greatest needs and a pair of the greatest terrors of our society. We need to be known. We want to be known. Communities offer us the possibility of knowing and being known on a larger scale. We have the capacity to be intimate with those who live around us. We may not like or agree with all the people in our living community, yet we can learn to love and respect them by honoring our differences.

I have often said that if we distill the issues of the planet down to its very essence, that essence is: *Can open systems survive supporting the right of closed systems to exist, when the very essence of a closed system is to be in control and destroy every-thing unlike itself?*

Our living communities allow us to practice living as an open-system person. Open systems are basically process systems. They welcome change, eschew control, and respect differences. As people learn to live their process, they become more open and vulnerable while growing stronger at the same time. When we live our process, we see differences as an opportunity for growth and welcome them. When we learn to live our process, our concept of the sameness that binds us expands from relationships to families to communities and beyond because we begin to experience oneness on levels never previously available to us. As we live our spirituality, our world expands.

When we begin to truly live in community, we find that our opportunities to participate and to be of service expand exponentially.

Two years ago, there was a bid to put a large shopping center in our neighborhood. The village where we live was carefully planned years ago designating only two expandable areas as commercial. The remaining land was to stay residential. This proposed center was squarely in a residential area. I went to a community meeting and realized that almost all the community that was represented was against it. However, the developers insisted that the elders supported it.

When I heard about it, I was immediately opposed to it. Yet, I was cautious because I have always respected the opinions of the elders. There are many elders living in my neighborhood, and I decided to go to every house and listen to what they had to say. I found myself in the middle of a misinformation campaign. It appeared that they were told that a very small shopping center with a bank was to be built. The facts were that it was to be a very large shopping center, bigger than any nearby. And it might or might not include a bank. All the seniors said that a bank was what interested them. They preferred it to be located near the post office since we don't have home mail delivery. The area near the post office is one of the two commercial zones.

As it turned out, none of the elders supported the shopping center. In fact, they were very much against it since many of them take their walks along the road where the increased traffic of over 150 additional vehicles would spill onto it daily. Many elders signed the petition opposing the proposal. Some were afraid to speak out, and they told me that it was dangerous to speak out against economics, expansion, and "development" where the bottom line was money.

They were right. I was soon threatened with a lawsuit from one of the developers involved in a seemingly unrelated matter. It was clear that the suit was untenable, <u>and</u> I was forced to hire a lawyer and spend even more money to defend myself.

Closed systems often use litigation or threats of litigation to maintain their illusion of control.

Today, the shopping center is on hold.

Over the years, I have seen and experienced how the system militates against community and often punishes us for trying to build or maintain communities.

In the early nineties, a group of us bought an old hot springs hotel in Montana as a center to conduct Living in Process work. We wanted to have a place where there could be an open-ended living community, where people could come to live, heal, and do their work. We wanted a place without professionals and with a natural healing environment. The Boulder Hot Springs was the perfect location.

The partners decided that they wanted to set up a legal and financial structure based on trust and the principles of Living in Process. We invited a well-known accountant and lawyer to meet with us. After three days of conference, they were both impressed and also in tears.

"The legal, tax, and monetary systems militate against trust, honesty, and community. It is impossible, legally, to do what you want. We will do what we can, <u>and</u> the options are very restricted within the limits available to us," our accountant and lawyer both agreed.

We are still at the old hot springs. We have a strong living community there; the place has become a great resource to the larger community. Some of the original owners have moved on, and those left are more and more active in a growing global community.

Is it any wonder that we are in crisis at the level of community? We are being trained and legislated not to trust one another, to put money first, and to isolate and try to dominate and control our own little worlds.

Living in Process offers another, more open-ended system.

We need living communities to support us as individuals, parents, and human beings. Living communities and our participation in them emerge when we truly live our process.

SOCIAL COMMUNITIES

Where do we play? Who do we play with? Who are the people we choose to relax with? All of these areas offer the possibility for community.

How do we play these days? I immediately think of movies, the theater, cocktail parties, spectator sports, and television. None of these things is exactly conducive to building community, although some permit light interaction.

Community sharing on a social level has become almost extinct in large cities except for the above activities, yet, how many people rush to community fairs when they occur!

One amazing experience happened while I was traveling out of the country when I accepted an invitation to spend the night in the lovely home of a professional acquaintance.

I liked this person. Since our time together had been quite hectic, I assumed this occasion would permit time to chat and visit.

We arrived just before dinnertime, and I knew my host wanted time with his wife and child, so I chose to retire to my room and rest.

I looked forward to dinner together and a long, casual talk. When I came to the table, the man and his daughter had just sat down and were eating. By the time his wife arrived, I was just getting seated. As I was settling in, the man and his daughter finished eating and left the table. The wife also ate her meal and departed, and I was still finishing up. I was stunned by their behavior. This dinner was certainly not what I would call social.

I have noticed that I slow down more when I am in touch with myself and that rushing keeps one detached from process.

For some of us, our social community has become the delicatessen owner, dress shop keeper, pharmacist, local pub bartender, florist, receptionist, cashier, and waitress at our favorite restaurant. Formerly, I would have included the local book and record store. However, they have become so big that we are virtually unknown as customers in most of these establishments. Coffee shops can give the illusion of community while allowing us to escape from intimacy quite nicely. People who do too much always try to combine social activities with getting other tasks done. Farmers markets, garage sales, and dinners offer more interaction.

What happens to social life when we Live in Process? Quite simply, it evolves.

As I became clearer with myself, I made a decision to spend time only with people who delight in my company and in whose company I delight. I continue to be amazed with how many people this includes.

I can be around other people, of course, <u>and</u> when I really want to play, I like to be around people who are open, honest, take responsibility for themselves, and are fun. I love to play; I do it often in many forms. I love to have people in my life who will play with me.

WORK

No discussion of Living in Process would be complete without an exploration of work and how we can expand our personal experiences, knowledge, and wisdom to our work.

> *Living in Process is not isolated in the individual. We have the possibility of Living in Process in every aspect of our lives.*

> In the Western world, I have learned to live with the unimportant and to leave the important behind.
>
> *Anonymous*

> *The practical should always be in the service of the important.*

Community

Some of us make a distinction between our work and our vocation, believing that work is the way we earn a living and our vocation is our life's work. When one Lives in Process, splitting ourselves into segments makes little or no sense. A process is a process. Processes cannot be divided into pieces.

When we are Living in Process, we do the work that unfolds before us as our life progresses, and we get what we need to live a life of spiritual abundance. Material wealth or any specific goals or agendas are irrelevant. Living in Process means that we live a life of faith and trust that we will get what we need. And, we need to take responsibility for our material welfare and not be ruled by it.

Trusting our process doesn't mean that we sit around and wait for something to happen. No, quite the contrary. When we Live in Process, we often work very hard. We must do our footwork and participate in our life. Since Living in Process is a life of participation, we welcome the opportunity to participate in and live our life, and this means that we do our personal work and we contribute.

A friend of mine who is an Indian medicine man put it very well. "When I was drinking, everything I did was for myself and that didn't work too well. After I sobered up, I realized who my boss is. My boss is the big guy upstairs. And since I realized that, I just do what He wants and things go real good."

Many of us with inner knowing about the nature of our work have possessed this wisdom from the time we were very small. In fact, some of us knew what our work was even before we had language to describe it.

Unfortunately, most of us do not receive the kind of education that teaches us the language of the internal, or the language of the Creator. It's sad when our training at home and at school has taught us to stifle, shut off, and tune out the whisperings of our soul.

It is very difficult to listen to that which we cannot hear!

Our intuitions, knowings, sensings are all very necessary in finding our work. Each of us has a unique work; we just need to find it.

MATERIALISM

Materialism is one of the biggest obstacles to finding our work in life. When we live in a society that believes that the only reality is external and whatever can be experienced must be done through the senses, then our work becomes focused solely on the material. We look to the material world to meet all our needs, and the more empty we become, the more desperately we turn to whatever we've been taught will make us feel better. Maybe this is what Jesus meant when he said that it would be more difficult for a rich man to get into heaven than it would be for a camel to pass through the eye of a needle. We have serious confusion about the roles of money and poverty in our culture.

One of the most pervasive addictions in our society is the process addiction to money. Interestingly, the addiction is not really to money itself. That would be simpler. The basic addiction seems to be to the process of accumulating money. No matter how much we have, it's never enough. One of our cultural mainstays that seems to have an absolute obsession with money is our religious institutions. The dualism of wealth-poverty is a source of continued obsession and controversy in Western religion. Churches talk about being churches of the poor while amassing huge fortunes. Those who work for the church seem to be caught in the dualism of disdaining money and being obsessed with it. In Western culture there is some inviolable belief that God likes big buildings.

Money can never meet our needs. It can give us some comforts, and having comforts is gratifying to the ego. Yet, as a process, comfort is completely without spirituality. In fact, money seems to function as a spiritual black hole for many people, sucking off their spirituality.

At one point, I believed that money was neither good nor bad. It was what people did with it that mattered. Then, I read Jerry Mander's book, *In the Absence of the Sacred*. He suggests that many people have the same attitude about technology that I once had about money, and that many believe technology is neither good nor bad. It's what people do with it that matters. He then goes on to point out that technology itself is harmful. Take the manufacturing of a computer chip, for example. This industrial process creates toxic waste that is polluting and destroying the environment. His thesis made a great impact on me.

Some time later, I had the opportunity to test the same thesis out on the subject of money. My corporation was embezzled by my office manager and my secretary, forcing me to spend a year and a half working with money issues almost daily to try to get taxes, books, records, and bills straightened out. I believe I dealt with it all in a healthy Living in Process way. I felt good that I did not fall into the victim-perpetrator dualism and that I handled the situation in a way that was in keeping with my spirituality. The office manager will have to deal with her own spirituality.

At the end of this period, however, I began to realize that after dealing with money issues on an almost daily basis for so long, I felt more spiritually depleted than I had ever been in my entire life!

I want to add here that I was taking very good care of myself during this time. I was resting and eating well, exercising, nurturing my spiritual life, and doing my inner work. Yet I still felt depleted. After this experience, I concluded that money itself was invented by humans, not by the Creator, and possessed no intrinsic spiritual value.

This, of course, is just my perception. Others may differ with me, and I accept that. I only share this as my experience with money. I feel that we must look at materialism and money when we talk about work because they are so inextricably bound together in our culture.

There is no other place where the slave mentality is more obvious than in relation to money, and work loses its intrinsic worth when it is tied to money. We must separate money and work if we are to understand the meaning of work.

Living in Process

THE JOY OF WORK

I have often said that I never really trust someone who doesn't know how to work. There is something about a person who knows how to pitch in and get her hands dirty that can be trusted. I've known people who believe that their goal in life is to make enough money so they never have to do anything for themselves. I don't trust them. It is as if their inability to deal with their material world leaves them groundless, floating out of touch with their spirituality.

People who work together pray together.

Good work is a prayer. When people work well together, they feel bonded and grounded. Westerners seem to be able to use routine work as a meditation when it is approached in a prayerful way.

When we are doing "right" work in tune with our spirituality and ourselves, we are one with all things. Our right work will find us if we risk Living in Process and do our deep-process work. When we live our process, our work is integrated into our life. We don't go to work and have a life. We don't have a worklife and fall exhausted in a heap. We have a life that includes work. Our work contributes to our life and our life contributes to our work.

I have noticed that it is in relation to their fears about work that many people want to back off and run from their pursuing of their spiritual quest to Live in Process.

There are several major obstacles that appear as people do their work, where I've observed a general exodus and people running from their commitment to be willing to pursue their healing as far as they need to go.

When individuals first come into this work, most have been living in the old paradigm for many years. Many have a well-developed technocratic, materialistic, mechanistic personality (TMMP) and they are dualistic and controlling. For some, the easiness, openness, and honesty of the Living in Process groups is quite threatening. For others, they feel like they have come home. Still others are hoping for a quick workshop fix where they will feel better for a while and not really have to change. Those who stay soon realize that they have the opportunity to really change. For some, this growth and change at the personal level seems insurmountable and they disappear. For those who persevere, the next level holds even more terror. They begin to see the possibility that they can no longer tolerate nonintimate, death-producing, unhappy relationships, and this awareness scares them to death. Still reverting to old thinking patterns easily, they flip into a dualism that they either must stay in the relationship the way it is or be alone and be a bag person forever. Dualistic thinking is almost always linked with negativity. In their fear, there is no real faith that they can change, their partner can change, their relationship can change, or that they'll be all right if the relationship disintegrates. The terror of facing and healing their dysfunctional relationships is so intense for some that they arrest their growth and return to what has felt safe, even if it's destructive.

For those who survive these first two obstacles, their lives continue to open up and deepen. Then they face the next obstacle, which makes the other two pale into insignificance in comparison: *work*.

As people learn to live their process, they become uncomfortable with trying to manipulate people and things. Often the level of dishonesty that is accepted as commonplace at a corporate level becomes intolerable. For some, as they come to feel connected with others, all life, and the planet, they actually begin to think in terms of the next seven generations. They find themselves developing a new morality about the planet, nature, other peoples, and their place in it all.

If the panic about their facing themselves and their relationships seemed big, it is nothing compared with what they are experiencing about their work. In our culture, much of our identity comes from who we are and what we do. Loss of identity—as they've known it—seems a very real possibility. Again, there is the temptation to bolt and return to old behaviors.

Unfortunately, or fortunately, there is no turning back after they have tasted a path of being fully alive and there is no place to run.

A big part of Living in Process is learning to live a life of faith. People who have reached this level in their healing often have had enough experiential learning that they have experienced trusting the process. They may not be able to see how all the pieces will fall in place, _and_ they are beginning to know that they will if they do their own work of putting one foot in front of the other until solutions become clear.

Some leave their jobs, finding their workplaces to be too toxic to tolerate. Usually, these people set up their own entrepreneurial corporations or workplaces where they can support themselves and practice their truths of living.

Others stay where they are and try to influence their organizations to grow and change. They hire consultants with new visions like Margot Cairnes of New York and Sydney in an effort to change the climate of the workplace. Both those who stay and those who leave can become the models of the future.

One old Koori man said to me, "You know what's the matter with you people? You work. Work is your main problem." This statement has been very rich in levels of truth for me.

ORGANIZATIONS

Organizations are very important in contemporary society. They are the critical infrastructure that holds the dysfunctional individual-family and the dysfunctional society-planet together. Many multinational corporations, while seeing themselves in crisis, are searching for creative solutions as they move into the new millennium. They have the vision to see that the old structures, procedures, and assumptions will not work as we become a planetary community. They have no road maps for the future. What we do with our organizations is essential to the future of all life on this planet.

Most work is carried out in organizations. I spent many years doing organizational consulting, and finally became so discouraged that I stopped. I could not find any organizations that wanted to go to the necessary lengths in the quest to become healthy places that support healthy people. In fact, as individuals do their own inner work and become healthier and healthier, they discover that they're no longer able to fit in sick organizations. Usually, the organizations fire these people, or they leave to start their own businesses or live more simply. Hence, organizations are often actively eliminating the healthiest people they have, people who would be able to move the organization to new levels of functioning, while entrenching those who continue to support the dysfunction of the organizations. Organizations also have TMMPs.

Organizations often hire consultants—frequently for huge fees!—when they want to give the appearance of change, while at the same time not threatening the homeostasis of the organization. These processes seem unhealthy for all involved. I knew that they were unhealthy for me, and my prayers suggested I turn my energies in other directions.

Organizations are key in overall global change, with some taking up the challenge to be innovative.

Can organizations be spiritual? A good question. Do they want to be? Another good question.

Being spiritual means doing and respecting one's processes and others' processes, and recognizing and participating in the oneness of all things, which ultimately means not destroying and exploiting the planet. This is a great challenge for most organizations. This is also true when it means that the individuals in that organization need to walk their own spiritual path and respect the path of others.

Yet, I have seen individuals healing through Living in Process, when my professional training told me that this could never happen. What wonders could be possible in organizations?

In recent years, I've been working with a few organizations that are making great strides toward new ways of functioning. I feel grateful to have had these experiences.

Earlier I imagined what it would be like if every home was designed with a deep-process room. I have carried the image further and imagined each corporate office with a similar room, complete with mats, near the boardroom. When board members felt angry, confused, or uncomfortable (of course, they would have to be aware of these feelings), or when the board reached an impasse or sensed something was wrong, they would hit the mats. Imagine, if you can, board members stretched out and doing their deep-process work until they felt clear and were ready to make decisions congruent with their spirituality.

Along with boardrooms, we could make deep-processing rooms available to all workers. What a different society we would have if we had a room open to anyone wishing to do their deep-process work or supporting that of others.

It is possible for a society to be organized around the spiritual needs of the individuals and the culture and not around money and economics.

SPIRITUAL COMMUNITIES

Before I leave the topic of communities, I want to say a word about the spiritual communities in which we are involved. For some people, these are the most confusing communities of all. We expect designated spiritual communities to be concerned with the spiritual and to support our spiritual living. This support is often not forthcoming.

The technocratic, materialistic, mechanistic culture has deeply influenced religion and spirituality organizationally and institutionally. The type of institutions spawned by this worldview have developed some of the characteristics seen in individuals with TMMP. A number of religious institutions have become greedy, materialistic, supportive of or detached from concerns about the destruction of the environment. This stance indicates a dualistic approach in their thinking (we-them), a sort of style that is controlling, dishonest. In many respects, these cornerstones of society appear more concerned with perpetuating themselves than fostering and supporting spirituality. Often, they have lost the awareness of oneness, and instead create and exploit divisiveness.

Yet, being spiritual beings, we all have spiritual needs and many of us look longingly to organized religion to meet these needs. We sense something is there, yet sometimes whatever it is, it is difficult to find.

Perhaps the biggest mistake we and organized religion make is in attempting to separate spirituality from the rest of our lives and to place it in the hands of religious institutions. Historically, it was the Christian Church that at the time fostered this split with the rise of mechanistic science and materialism. The Church supported the secular belief in and adherence to mechanistic science while maintaining the realm of the spiritual for itself. This split gave the organized church tremendous power in Western culture.

For most of us personally, it has been devastating to separate our spirituality from ourselves. When we relegate our spirituality to a time and a place, we lose our awareness that we are a spiritual process. Our spirituality can't be divided from our daily life. Everything we do is spiritual. Whether we know it or like it, it is.

When we splinter off our spirituality from the rest of our being, we fragment our process, become disempowered, and disconnected from the oneness with the Great Mystery. We do not need intermediaries to connect with our God. We are connected. That connection is our birthright.

Many churches and organized religions try to help foster this connection. Some succeed, some don't. Also, many forms of organized religion try to foster spiritual community. Some succeed, some don't. Those who do succeed are those who are able to leave their dualistic thinking and move beyond the we-they dualism. Any community that establishes its being over and against something else is not a true community.

The very essence of a closed system is to be in control and to destroy everything unlike itself. Can open systems survive if they support the right of closed systems to exist?

A very wise American Indian elder once said to me, "We don't care *how* a person prays. What we care about is that he *does* pray. The Great Mystery can hear all kinds of prayers. Whenever a person prays I can stand beside her/him."

Open systems are almost nonexistent in organized religion. Yet, there is hope that as individuals learn to Live in Process and become open systems themselves they will be able to bring a positive influence to their spiritual organizations.

As we learn to Live in Process we see that none of us has the whole picture. We have something to learn from all spirituality because we are all spiritual beings.

However, since each person's process is her/his own, none of us will come out in the same place at the same time as we try to Live in Process. As we attempt to learn to live our process, we do become more open.

Chapter 12

S O C I E T Y   A N D

N A T I O N S

❧

As our boundaries expand, our process interacts more with the sphere of the society.

Societies and nations are created by individuals. Sometimes we give our power away to others and let them assume the responsibility of building and molding the society. When we do this, we *feel* disempowered on a larger scale. We cannot control the society. We can participate in it. All too often we give our power away to people who are not clear, who have compartmentalized their spirituality and do not have the best interests of all the members of that society at heart.

CONTROL AND PUNISHMENT

Daniel Quinn, in his significant book *My Ishmael*, explores the fact that our current TMM society has existed for an almost minuscule point in time if we look at the history of human beings on this planet. He points out that it has not developed a very functional way of operating. I was fascinated with Quinn's focus on the "thou shalts" and the "thou shalt nots" as one of the major issues in a dysfunctional society. His perception is that in tribal community-based societies there was no major focus on the "thou shalts." In community-based societies, the assumption was that it's in the nature of human beings to err and that the focus was on returning to balance—not control and punishment. In a "thou shalt" society, the focus is to maintain the society through a series of controls and punishments. Quinn's opinion is that control and punishment are not and have never been effective, and by existing they have moved us away from the restoration of societal balance. Control and punishment also set up an effective dualism of good and evil and result in our splitting ourselves from ourselves. When we see our mistakes as evil and not something giving us the opportunity to learn, this attitude starts a snowball effect of self-hate that is very difficult to overcome. On a societal level, the control-punishment approach and the self-loathing have devastating results. In *When Society Becomes an Addict*, I observed that any society that is built on the illusion of control is an addictive one that will consequently develop TMMPs.

When Elizabeth's son was little, he had a best friend who after twenty-five years is still his best friend.

As the boys were growing up, Mary, the mother of her son's best friend, would arbitrarily decide that they couldn't play together, which was traumatic for both children. After this separation from each other had happened a few times, Elizabeth could see how painful it was for her son. She asked to sit down with Mary to see what the problem was.

Elizabeth asked if her son had done something wrong or if there was some problem with his behavior.

"No," Mary said. "He's always well behaved."

"Do you dislike my son?" Elizabeth asked.

"No," she replied. "We all like him very much."

"Then, what's the problem?" Elizabeth asked.

"We feel he doesn't get punished enough," she said.

Elizabeth was stunned. She had been raising her son in a process way and Mary's accusation was true. He was rarely, if ever, punished. He didn't need to be punished. A look, a word, or a discussion were usually more than enough. He was a very sensitive kid and keenly in touch with his feelings.

"Do you think he needs to be punished?" Elizabeth asked.

"Yes, we do. We believe children need punishment," she fired back.

Mary's son has grown up to be a good man, doing the right thing. Yet, he is not very happy and certainly not in touch with his process. He has, however, become a good cog in a TMMP society.

Elizabeth's son, on the other hand, is happy, self-assured, enjoying his life, and enjoyable. He does not fit into a TMM nine-to-five job and has chosen creative work where he is his own person.

In Samoan society, when people become ill, and they go to a healer, the healer does not just focus on the individual. The healer assumes that the normal state for the human being is health and that if the person is ill, there must be something in the internal or external environment that is causing the illness. The healer looks at the person, his family, his village, and the larger society to see where the problem is and how balance can be restored.

In our TMM society, there is a growing awareness that a very high percentage of medical problems are caused by prolonged and acute use of addictions. The effects of overeating, alcohol, nicotine, sugar, fat, caffeine, overworking, sex, and addictive acting out account for a large percentage of our medical *industry*. If we dealt with our individual and societal addictions and took responsibility for our lives, that number could be greatly reduced.

If we add pollution, contaminated water, toxic waste, and carcinogenic foods to the illnesses caused by addictions, we can clearly see that the level of disease that we have in a TMM society is caused by that society. We have created a society that is not conducive to our health and we accept it as reality. The realities we have created are not reality. They are the realities of our life at this moment, <u>and</u> they can be changed. If we step outside our current reality, we gain a larger perspective. When we make even a small step outside our current TMM reality, we can see the wisdom of the Samoan healer. Unless we are willing to look at illness on a societal and even global level, we will not be able to care for our individuals. Societies are one of our contexts.

Doing our deep-process work and learning to live our spiritual process results in our being more available to broaden our perspective.

As stated earlier, any society based on the illusion of control is a TMM society—one that supports and requires addictive behaviors. A society based on control cannot further the spiritual development of its members. In fact, true connection with the Creator comes out of the unexpected, not the regulated.

> Last night, I heard on the news that obesity is a growing problem with the American public. In fact, the commentator stated that obesity has reached epidemic proportions and that there was a growing belief that the *government might need to step in to regulate the problem.*

We have created a culture where the purpose of the government is to regulate and control with the underlying belief that the ultimate control is the threat of punishment. Can you imagine what a society would look like if its mandate was not regulation and control? Societies still exist on this planet whose primary purpose is to facilitate living at one with ourselves, at one with each other, at one with nature, and at one with the All That Is. We have much to learn from these societies if we will only listen.

ILLUSIONARY SOCIETY

The society in which we live is an illusionary society. It has been built by isolating our spiritual reality and using disembodied mental concepts. Our thinking has become our reality and often is not grounded in our experience of reality. Frequently, we live out of our disembodied, nonexperienced interpretations of our world. We casually accept "experts" who pass along disembodied information that fabricates causality—"This is because of this," and "This means that." We never stop to check out for ourselves what is real for us and if what the experts are saying rings true. Often such interpretations are logical and rational. They just don't make any sense. When we come to realizations in our deep process, they are on a soul level and free us from the virtual reality around us.

We have created a TMM society based upon the illusion of control, imagined dualisms, the illusion of perfection, dishonesty, and distorted thinking ungrounded in our true oneness and connectedness with the All. Is it any wonder that economics and money (both abstractions) have become our Gods?

When we Live in Process, we move beyond our illusions and have the opportunity to become aware of and deal with our reality.

ECONOMICS AND MONEY

Any society that is based on economics and money will not be able to meet the needs of its people.

In our current society, many of us are becoming aware that political and even what pass as moral decisions are based upon economics and money.

The bottom line is money. Money is sacred. We have slowly come to understand that our political leaders are businessmen, and their success is based upon how well we are doing economically as a nation and how effective they are at keeping big business happy. Political leaders who try to lead by spiritual or moral mandates are laughed at—for example Jimmy Carter or Al Gore when he first took office. We have, indeed, split our day-to-day functioning further and further from our spirituality.

As I stated earlier, money is basically amoral, and it can't and never will feed our soul. It's a man-made commodity that seems to have the ability to separate us from our soul.

International financial consultant Bernard Lietaer, in his forthcoming book tentatively titled *The Future of Money: Beyond Greed and Scarcity*, discusses the formation and functioning of our current monetary system. In his experience with monetary systems, which is vast, the current monetary system is based upon scarcity and greed and is dependent upon poverty.

He uses a simple story, which I will paraphrase, to illustrate this fact.

Lietaer asks us to imagine a remote village where everything is done by barter. Their life is not centered around work and making money. They live a good life and have a great deal of leisure time. Remember what the old Koori man said about work in the last chapter!

Then, a stranger arrives. He says, "I have a simpler way. I can make life easier for you. Why don't we try an experiment?"

He then takes a cowhide and cuts a hundred round circles out of it, ten for each family in the village. He then shows the people how they can use the circles to stand for a chicken, or a house, or a job needing to be done, and this "currency" will make life simpler and easier.

The villagers are thrilled with the concept and agree to the experiment. The stranger says that he will come back in a year, and at that time he wants eleven circles from each family. This, of course, means that one family will have to lose all its circles for the others to have eleven.

Of course, this experiment completely changes the climate of the village. The families begin to work harder, because they feel they must. Competition starts, mistrust develops, community breaks down as they realize that in order to meet their obligations one family must have nothing. Money becomes the focus of their life. Their quality of life deteriorates.

This story, of course, is an allegory. Yet, it is an accurate picture of the way the current monetary system works and the assumptions behind it.

Money is integral to materialism and money supports progressive materialism.

SOCIETAL COLONIZATION

Basically, the "great" years of land colonization and the great empires are behind us as a civilization, though not completely. We have entered an era of ideological, societal colonization.

Arthur lives in a sailboat in the South Pacific. For many years, he has spent his time sailing around the smaller islands of the Pacific, living with the peoples on these islands and enjoying their life with them.

About six years ago, he was living on one of these

islands, and while he was there, the community got television. His painful observation was that the islanders' culture was destroyed in less than two weeks.

We've moved into an era of societal colonization, which is deemed good for the economy. The question is whether it is better for the planet and the individuals on the planet. The cultures of this planet are becoming endangered species as the TMM culture exercises its societal colonialism. Those who take a broader perspective of the needs of the planet as a whole see that endangered species and plants are important to the balance and survival of the planet. We are dysfunctional here. We exhibit almost all the characteristics of ancient Greece and Rome before they collapsed as societies. How can we believe that our dysfunction should be shared?

The TMM culture is like a line of termites looking for something to devour, which may just be the very air we breathe.

BEYOND THE TMM SOCIETY

We need visionary leaders who are spiritually functional.

The beauty of living in process and doing our deep-process work is that we do not have to confront everything at once. We do not even have to deal with issues on a timetable that has been artificially constructed. When we Live in Process, we only have to put one step in front of the other and do the next "right" thing for our process. Life, with its opportunities, obstacles, and possibilities will unfold only as we are able and ready to deal with them.

If someone had said to me years ago that I would be up to my eyeballs in the issues of society, the planet, and the universe when I was just tentatively working through my own personal issues, I would have thrown up my hands in complete overwhelm and disappeared. The beauty of learning to Live in Process is that we learn to trust our process. If the invitation to sit down with the old Aboriginal elders had come twenty years earlier, I might have accepted it, although I would not have been at a place in my own personal process where I could get the full meaning of what they were saying. Or, more accurately, what I would have learned would have been in keeping with what I could have heard then. When I went and sat with the elders, I was able to hear and respond to the issues on a societal, global, universal level.

Some of you may have no interests in the societal implications of Living in Process. That's all right. These chapters will be here if you ever do, and reading them before you're there may help stretch your vision. Who knows?

LIVING IN PROCESS SOCIETY

What would a Living in Process society look like? I actually don't know. I do, however, have some ideas. I have seen possibilities as I spent time with native elders throughout the world. I am very clear that we need all of the wisdom available to us to evolve into a world society that is good for all peoples, the planet, and the universe and that is spiritually participatory. We see glimpses of wisdom from various corners of the planet. No one group has it all and we need all the pieces we can get, ancient and modern. I am clear on one thing. Whatever evolves for a functional future will be a society that knows and respects process and lives in a process way. Process is the basis of all life and living.

Sometimes I think I could more easily describe the new paradigm, the new way of being in and participating in the world, in terms of what it isn't rather than in terms of what it will be or can be. When I am tempted to do that, I can only shake my head sadly and see that I still have my feet mired in negativity and dualism.

I would like to share some of what I have experienced on a societal level that I like and treasure. I will use some of my experiences in Hawaii as an example.

I live part of the time in Hawaii, and I have come to respect and treasure the Hawaiian culture. In the Hawaiian culture, the spirit of *aloha* is vital. I mentioned earlier that most Hawaiians believe that they are here on this planet to impart the *aloha*—the living breath of God—to all those with whom they come in contact and to the planet. The Hawaiians accept a monetary culture <u>and</u> it's not the core of their culture. I find this comforting.

My experience with the Hawaiians and most native peoples is that they know that we are family, and if anyone is amenable, they welcome them as *ohana*. I am family with several Hawaiian clans. Luaus, holidays, and special occasions are times to get together with food, music, and visiting. There is always music and dance. Spirituality is in the living. No one has much money and what we have is shared. My *ohana* needs lots of flowers for the graves for Memorial Day. I have lots of flowers in my yard so I drop off tons of flowers for them. They call to say that they have caught some fish, would I like some? The neighbor has just given us some fish his son caught and grapefruit from his yard. We have just told him that he can garden the vacant lot we own next to his house. None of us have recently gone to a store because we have abundance.

Let me quickly say that I know that not everyone can have this experience. This is the experience that my process has led me to and it fits me well. Other people have other processes, other needs, and other lives. I trust their process will be wise with them.

I like to live in Hawaii partially because I find the *'aina* (land), the culture, the nature, the weather, and the people supportive of learning to live my process. When I first came here from the mainland, I expected to be here and not change the way I did things (TMMP). I expected that I could plan my days. I would plan when I would go to the beach. Wednesday would be a good day. I believed that I could work on Monday and Tuesday and reward myself with a five-minute trip to the beach. When I first started living there, I would stick to my discipline on Monday and Tuesday even if they were bright sunny days. On Wednesday when I finished my work, it would be pouring rain. We can't control people, places, or things. I would be angry and upset with the weather and become resentful of Hawaii. Slowly, I began to see the locals headed for the beach when the weather was nice and worked inside when it was raining. What a concept! They were living *with* the process of the *'aina* and the weather. I had carried with me the belief that if I didn't structure and discipline myself, I wouldn't get anything done. The reality has been that the more I trust my process, the more productive I am.

Living in Hawaii has forced me to tune in to what I need and want and not what I *think* is good and right for me. I work better when I take a walk on the beach. I work better when the smell of gardenia fills my room. In respecting my own process, I respect others' process, the process of the *'aina*, the bigger process.

For me, the Hawaiian culture has been an important teacher in my learning to live my process. I find my spirituality operationally integrated with my life and decisions.

Living in Process

What would a society look like that Lives in Process?

Those of us who have learned to Live in Process must evolve to find out.

Can there be societies that Live in Process?

Yes, they have and do exist on this planet.

Can there be societies that Live in Process that differ?

Of course, when we Live in Process, we evolve differently, we respect and welcome differences, and we are open systems.

Can open systems exist in a world that is fast becoming a closed (TMM) system?

They have to! This is our challenge. Can we meet it before the TMM societies make the planet uninhabitable, thus taking away our choice?

As more of us are one with the Creator, new options will emerge.

Chapter 13

THE PLANET

For many of us, the planet has become our backyard. We've begun to recognize that the planet is not a ball floating in space that's made up of unrelated nation-pieces. The planet is a whole. It's an ecosystem. It's a process.

We've touched upon the sphere of the planet and how individuals, families, communities, and societies influence and are influenced by the planet. Now let us delve deeper into that reality.

Some say that the planet is shrinking because of faster and cheaper air travel. Larger numbers of people are able to explore the farthest reaches of this planet that we call Earth. Others say that it is because of electronic technology that the planet is shrinking. Radio, television, the Internet, and computers have brought the world to our doorstep. Still others believe that the environmental crisis, and planetary issues of contamination, pollution, and the destruction of the world ecosystems are the real problems. Others would argue that the international monetary system, multinationals, and the world economy are the primary forces at work here.

Clearly, all these forces and influences have played a part. When we are able to consider larger spheres of process and take an eagle-eyed view of the planet, it doesn't really matter what the causes are. We need to find solutions. The TMMP believes that understanding the why will dictate the how. So far, that approach has never worked with living organisms and Planet Earth is a living organism.

We need to treat it as such and respond to it as such.

All of the forces mentioned above are inherent in and part of the planetary shrinking process. We need to explore those forces and see their influences from a larger perspective. Although the processes themselves individually and cooperatively may be pushing us to the brink of destruction, such forces may be positive in the long term. Perhaps that very process of being pushed to the brink is what is needed to shift our worldviews, to move us deeper into our spiritual connectedness, and to participate in increasingly larger wholes.

For example, in my many years of working with addicts, I was continually amazed by the power of the disease of addiction. A familiar saying in the Twelve-Step program is that the disease of addiction is cunning, baffling, powerful, and patient. I have seen people with twenty years of sobriety go out and drink again. I have seen people with everything going for them destroy their lives with addiction. However, one thing that has continually impressed me is that most addicts who take recovery seriously are those who have been brought to their knees and have no place else to go than sobriety. They are like the individuals in Chapter 2 who had to experience a serious illness or accident to make a shift in worldview, before embracing the reality that life is a process to be lived and that process is our reality.

Perhaps we as human beings on this planet are being brought to our knees with the implications of the TMM personality and society. Perhaps we have pushed the planet just about as far as we can. It is time that we remove our blinders about our interdependent global reality and the destruction we are perpetuating on the entire planet.

Now Reuben Kelly's words ring even truer.

It's not that science is bad. You had just not evolved enough spiritually where you could develop a science and technology that was spiritually based. You developed science and technology out of a spiritual void. Therefore, it is not a science or technology that can heal you or the planet.

Reuben Kelly, Koori Elder, Australia

Perhaps the choice of spiritually ungrounded science and technology will destroy the planet. We have the opportunity to reverse the effects of the choices we have made.

TECHNOLOGY, MONEY, AND MATERIALISM

There are times when we have an experience that changes us at a soul level—and our lives are never quite the same after that.

I had one of these experiences of pure awareness and knowing one time when I was driving in northern Italy, not far from the Austrian border. I love this part of Italy, as these two countries are places where I am so happy. I especially like the part of the terrain where the two nations come together. The highway ascends into a big, beautiful valley. A fast-moving river plunges down through the green valley, and the gentle rolling hills breasting the river are covered with vineyards and old villas. Behind these hills, the snow-covered granite mountains pierce the sky. The drive is breathtaking and reminds us that we are mere human beings.

On one of my trips through this valley, I decided to

explore a side road that led to what looked on the map to be a beautiful lake surrounded by mountains. It was just before twilight. Since I was in no rush, I had decided to give myself the gift of staying in this place I enjoyed so much.

Coming around a sharp curve in the narrow mountain road, I spotted the lake. I heard the noise and saw the destruction. This end of the lake was dirty and ugly. Big trucks and heavy machinery with bright lights were working late into the evening in this area, busily destroying the mountain.

I was so filled with intense emotion that I turned the car around as soon as I could and beat a fast retreat. There was no way I could spend my last night in Italy there! I later learned that they were mining some metal or mineral at that site. Mining had destroyed the mountain in the process.

At that point in my life, I had been doing the Living in Process work for some time and had reached a point of clarity and honesty where my denial system was not working as well as it once had. Over the last few years, I had several deep processes about the actual physical pain I experience when I see the destruction of the earth. By trusting my process, doing my work, and getting stronger, I had come to a place in my growth where I was ready to "see what I see and know what I know." I had reached a place where I trusted that I could confront and handle whatever was coming up for me in my deep process. I trusted that regardless of how big or painful it was, I was ready for the learning. I rented a hotel room on the other side of the mountain from the mine, stretched out on the bed, and let my deep process come. My tears, rage, and deep sobs were absorbed by the thick down pillow in my little attic hotel room.

When at last my deep process subsided, I was aware of connections I had never made before. I felt a clarity rarely experienced.

I could *see* and *feel* the connection between the myth of objectivity, mechanistic science, and materialism. I could *see* this connection. I knew this connection. My world had shifted.

I knew that mechanistic science believed that the highest level of functioning was to be objective and that to be objective, we must divorce ourselves from ourselves. This means that all our information has to come in externally through our senses, because it has to be repeatable and verifiable by others to be valid. Therefore, what is valued and valuable is that which is external to us. Our feelings, our intuitions, our knowings, and our spirituality do not lend themselves to this repeatability, external validation, or measurability, and therefore are not only not valuable, they don't exist.

We have set up a situation where the most important aspects of our lives do not exist. The unimportant elements of our lives have become reality. Our virtual reality is all that exists for the TMM society. If the material is all that is, then that is where our heart is—in that technology and the materialism that supports technology. No wonder we have come to believe that things will be our salvation. We do not question the premise behind this belief system or the belief system itself. We question ourselves and why we are not satisfied, while seeking more things. A scientific worldview based upon the myth of objectivity and materialism will never meet our needs. It will only create more materialism.

When we isolate spirituality from our everyday lives, we open ourselves to distortions and misconceptions of reality. My deep process had revealed to me the utter fallacy of the scientific method in understanding and living with our world. It had shown me how and why we can justify the destruction we are doing.

The technology that the TMM society has developed requires this kind of destruction. The technology that the TMM society has developed makes this kind of destruction possible.

As we discussed earlier, every colonial power that has invaded a civilization has introduced a monetary system. What are the alternatives to a monetary system? Some people, like Bernard Lietaer, are beginning to explore options.

If we are to have a planetary consciousness, we have to deal with technology, money, materialism, and population.

At this point in our process, we may not even be able to imagine what a technology that is spiritually based would look like. I know I can't.

I do know that if I and others practice the basic truths for Living in Process and continue to do our deep-process work, options will emerge that will be spiritually based. We will not be able to envision the truths we need until we are ready. We can become ready only by doing our deep-process work and taking one step at a time to live our process.

We live so little of our potential.

The Planet

THE ENVIRONMENT

With the advent of Rachel Carson's *Silent Spring*, the TMM society was introduced to a popular book that raised a concern for the environment and began to bring environmental issues to the foreground. Many native cultures have been built on environmental concerns and living with nature. Falsely, they have been dismissed as primitive and earth worshippers. Yet, their spirituality is often very complex and sophisticated, holistic, and integrated in their living.

Today, our concern for the environment has reached a level of global awareness. In spite of our global technological sophistication, I have found that a massive, global denial about the planetary environment is pervasive around the world. Most people, if you quiz them, will admit that their particular area is polluted. In fact, I cannot list the number of places I have been where the residents proudly state that their area is the most polluted place in the world. I have found that most citizens of this world are not world citizens. I have also found that the concern for the environment is one of the major issues that seem to be uniting people on a global basis.

THE CHRISTIAN CHURCH AND THE ENVIRONMENT

Organized Christianity has been a strong antienvironmental force in the history of the TMM culture. The Judeo-Christian tradition has taken very seriously the belief that nature and the earth exist to be subdued and razed by man. Western theology has been in the forefront of separating humans from nature and making humans superior to nature. Nature is then at human disposal to be exploited at will. In this belief system, the earth has been equated with the feminine. Institutions rooted in such beliefs tend to be notoriously sexist.

In recent years, I've questioned whether Christianity, as we know it, and environmental concerns are not completely antithetical to one another. Two major Catholic voices, Matthew Fox and Paul Collins, an Australian priest, have raised the same concerns. Fox has attempted to point out how the Catholic Church has historically stressed environmental concerns as part of its tradition, and yet has failed to maintain that concern in modern times. Needless to say, Fox was silenced by the Church and pressured to leave. Because of his beliefs, Paul Collins is being accused of heresy. Of course, these are not the only issues these two men have raised, and I do find it curious that both have such strong environmental concerns embedded in their other concerns.

Perhaps the real heresy is that both men have begun to shift their perspective and worldview away from the old TMM society. Both have tried very hard, I believe, to keep environmental concerns within the Christian tradition.

Paul Collins basically says that we need nature for a full experience of the infinite and that if we destroy nature, we will have irreparably destroyed our avenue to the infinite. Collins paraphrases Martin Heidegger, the German existentialist philosopher, when he says that "we have focused so much on technology and its particular applications and we have become so involved with it that we have lost our sense of the reality of the world that lies behind it." Collins goes on to say, "Our concentration on technology is so complete that we can no longer recognize or get in touch with real being-in-the world."

Collins cites Heidegger's belief that the "ecological crisis that has resulted from technology is metaphysical rather than ethical." In Collins's exploration of the ecological issue, he comes to the conclusion that the environmental crisis is basically a theological issue. I differ with him on this. Theology is thinking about God. We have done enough disembodied thinking.

We need to reconnect our spirituality with all of life, live our process, and let ourselves connect with that process in us that is the Great

Mystery. When we experience and know that which is our oneness with the All, dealing with the environment becomes dealing with ourselves.

I find nothing in the teachings of Jesus that says that it is all right to destroy the world we have been given. In fact, I find reverence for all creation. Jesus spoke to the concerns of his time in order to touch and activate the divine in all people. If he were to preach today, I am sure that his parables and stories would include the environment.

BIG BUSINESS AND THE ENVIRONMENT

Very simply put, most businesses that are not service organizations are dependent upon exploiting and destroying the environment. Manufacturing, refining, and building businesses depend upon using up nonrenewable resources. Often, when we human beings have had the choice to develop resources that are renewable, we have chosen to exploit the earth. We seem to have forgotten that the earth literally feeds and clothes us in addition to giving us a place to live, water to drink, and air to breathe.

Money and jobs are the bottom line. If an issue comes down to economics and/or the environment, we have created a TMM society where the bottom line is always the economy. I believe that we make these antienvironmental decisions at great sacrifice to our soul and our oneness with the Creator. As we learn to do our deep-process work and learn to live our process in a more complete manner, we are more connected with the All That Is, and our decisions change. Deep in our souls we know that we *are* the environment. At least, this has been my experience.

As we get clearer in our Living in Process work, we discover that our decisions can no longer be made with disembodied heads. They must be made with our being.

When the elder said that we had not reached a level of spiritual development where we were ready to develop a technology that was spiritually based, I heard his words and knew they were important. Yet, I had no way of imagining what he meant. Now that I work with people throughout the world who are learning to live their process, I have begun to understand the meaning of his words. Clearly, we are moving into a time of planetary change.

In Chapter I, I mentioned how I arrived at a place in my own life where I felt the need to listen to native elders for my own healing. They give me much more than I had ever hoped. They give me an eagle-eyed view and a planetary and spiritual perspective. I want to share more of that perspective with you.

LIVING IN PROCESS
AND NATIVE WISDOM

Our myths and legends told us that we needed to preserve the old knowledge and keep it hidden so it would not be taken away or destroyed. We were told that a time would come when our knowledge and wisdom would be needed to save the planet, and that time is now. Now we must speak and share the wisdom of our ancestors.

Elders from Hopi, Lakota, Cherokee, Mohican, Papago, Maori,
Hawaiian, Samoan, Australian Aboriginal, Canadian Indian,
Inuit, Athabaskan . . . native elders the world over

Living in Process is ancient wisdom for modern times. As individuals have simply and sincerely sought to grow and heal, they have also sought to walk the simple path of the soul, discovering these profound truths within themselves and connecting with ancient knowledge the world over.

We knew this is the wealthiest part of the continent because here the Great Spirit lives. We knew that the White Man will search for the things that look good to him, that he will use many good ideas in order to obtain his heart's desire, and we knew that if he had strayed from the Great Spirit, he would use *any* means to get what he wants. These things we were warned to watch, and we today know that those prophecies were true because we can see how many new and selfish ideas and plans are being put before us. We know that if we accept these things, we will lose our land and give up our very lives.

Dan Katchongva, Hopi

There is so much to learn and we have the opportunity to learn it. *Yet, we will learn nothing if we continue to keep trying to destroy everything we don't understand.* The truth within us and the truth without are the same.

There are many truths. The Great Mystery would not give us only one way of spirituality. We are all trying to find our way back to our oneness, our wholeness, our living process. We will never be able to learn if we think we have nothing to learn or feel superior to those with the wisdom.

We must learn to listen to our elders. We must learn to listen to the earth. We must learn to listen to the trees, the animals, the rocks. We are the youngest ones here. We have much to learn.

The following are some excerpts from an interview with a native Australian woman, Mary Graham, that appeared in Community Aid Abroad's *HoriZon* magazine. In it, she shares her truth with us. I found her observations very pertinent to what we are discussing.

For us, when the whites arrived in this country, it meant the end of living and the beginning of surviving. It was— and still is—a disaster for us, and it is only now that we are slowly getting to grips with this enormous trauma. But we didn't lose our culture. There are two sides to culture: the outer one, like eating, dressing, dance, etc.; and the inner one, our way of thinking, feeling, behaving. The inner side is still as solid as granite. The fact that Aborigines keep on insisting that they are Aborigines is exactly what is annoying to so many whites.

Only by caring for the land—by doing it, not only thinking about it—is our humanity reconfirmed. By looking after the land we learn to look after each other. This, for us, is the meaning of life; this is what forms our collective spiritual goal.

In Aboriginal culture, the group—not the individual—is central.

Aboriginal people do not ideologize conflict or life itself.

Even achieving something in life doesn't exist for us. We're not on the way to somewhere; heaven and hell don't exist either. That's why we don't need leaders or hierarchies in the Western way. The nearest thing to a "hierarchy" is the hierarchy of knowledge. For us the question, "Why do we exist?" is already answered. That's all that counts.

We have been observing Europeans for the last two centuries. They carry an enormous weight on their shoulders. They're full of ideals, full of plans, and always want to achieve more. They continually carry an enormous shopping list: they have to be all kinds of things, they should be law-abiding, and if they're religious, they have to believe in a certain God in a certain way, etc. . . . They work with blueprints about how society ought to be and how things ought to be achieved. They are continuously trying to match an ideal. This seems to put an enormous pressure on people and their relationships. We say there is nothing ideal about people. We're "poor fellows," we're very vulnerable. We're neither good nor bad. To be as human as possible—that's already more than enough!

Creating relationships is central. You can only grow peace; you cannot "make" it.

For me, two kinds of games exist in the world: the finite and the infinite games. Chess, war, court procedures, democracy—these are finite games. They lead, all the time, to winners and losers. The infinite game is not concerned with winning or losing; you just play and can continue eternally. Within the infinite game you can play finite games, but not the other way around.

Caring for the land is the infinite game. But we also play finite games and we also play the finite games of white people; we step in for a while and then we step out again. It is not permitted to declare one of those games an ideology or an "ism" because that would be seen as a sign of immaturity. You cannot take finite games too seriously. Only the infinite game has real meaning.

It seems to us that Western culture declares these finite games to be "reality." It takes ideologies, "isms," incredibly seriously. The whites in this country are waiting till we start taking their games seriously, but they'll be waiting a long time. We play the infinite game in the first place.

Mary Graham

Living in Process is the infinite game.

For Mary Graham, white people are equated with a TMM society because that has been her experience. As we develop a global view, we see that the TMM society is not confined to only one culture or race. The TMM assumptions are a planetary issue affecting all people. We each have our own particular experience of these assumptions, and each of us has our piece of truth to add. Some, however, are so enmeshed in the TMM society that they are incapable of stepping outside of it and having a clear perspective on it. All too often, persons enmeshed in a society or worldview come to see it as reality. They have lost the ability to step outside it and view it.

We need the perspective of people like Mary Graham to help us see what we can't see or don't want to see, recognizing that her perceptions are from her perspective, nothing more, nothing less.

We have the opportunity to be taught by those who have the wisdom to teach us a new old way. As we do our deep-process work, heal, and attempt to Live in Process, we seem to be discovering truths that reach beyond our individual selves and yet are connected to All That Is.

The following is a powerful story that was shared with me by a Cherokee woman and was given to her by the ancestors.

> I was angry. "Why," I asked the grandmothers, "did you deny your heritage—our heritage? How could you adopt the ways of the white man, the conqueror, and embrace the ways of people who disrespect the Earth Mother? How could you conceal from future generations their own identity and conceal even from your children that you and they were Cherokee? How could you do these things? How could you?" I felt betrayed by my own ancestors.
>
> The smile was gentle and wise, but the voice was firm. It reverberated with strength. Power. "Standing Feather, you have much to learn. You will study the medicine of the Corn Mother and you will understand. We chose our path out of knowledge—the true and lasting knowledge of who and what we are as a people, the teachings of the

Great Mystery and the Earth Mother, and the wisdom of the Selu. Do not be quick to judge. You do not know the whole truth, do not understand our purposes."

I trembled, but the fire still burned. I had to know. "How could you?" I saw missed opportunities—traditions forgotten, precious wisdom lost, and a world badly in need of knowledge that was no more, would never be again. Tears stung my eyes.

Laughter, and gentle chiding. "Standing Feather, you are as a child. Your tears are for nothing, the foolish whining of an infant who only considers herself and lacks the wisdom required for understanding. Stop this nonsense and be about your true mission. You walk your path for a purpose. Do not waste your tears. Our heritage is alive and well. It grows stronger with each sun. Help our people, do not cry for them. Respect our ways, do not see them as diminished or lost. Honor our wisdom. Use your heritage with pride. Everything we had—everything you think we denied—all you believe is lost—is whole and strong, and living in your world. It waits for you now. You only have to claim it."

I saw no way this could be. So much was gone, so much forgotten, so much swept away because it was denied. Lost. Surely they didn't understand.

"But, Grandmother, for so many years I did not even know of my heritage. I didn't hear the stories, didn't learn of the healing, didn't know the beauty of the Great Mystery. I admired our people from a distance, not knowing I was one of them. My heart broke for their sorrow and for what was lost . . ."

"Have you learned nothing? You felt a kinship with the

people you watched from a distance, even without understanding it. You carry our ways and our wisdom within
you. They are as complete as your spirit and as available as
your heart, yet you cry for them. You require the most elementary instruction. Put out your hand. Touch what you
seek. It is all there, waiting for you. It has always been
there."

"But you said you were Black Dutch, born in a foreign
land. You denied . . ."

"The most elementary instruction. What hangs on the
wall in your home? What rests on the table, on the hearth?
What sits beside the door?"

"Grandmother, I don't understand."

"Answer."

"There are pictures of my children and grandchildren, a
chain carved from a single length of cedar, ears of dried
Indian corn, a painting of the hills and trees in winter, a
staff with prayer ties, a raw crystal from the Earth, a
length of finger-woven leather strips, a quilt and a rug
made by some of you, a vase of pheasant feathers, a
wood carving of Chief Dragging Canoe, a handwoven
basket . . ."

"We chose our path deliberately. Times were hard. Our
people, our ways, were in danger of annihilation. We were
hunted like the deer. There was no place we could go that
was safe. Our land and our possessions were stripped from
us. Homes burned, people killed. Many died. Our children
were taken away to boarding schools and forbidden to
speak our language. Sometimes we never saw them again.
There were prohibitions against our ceremonies. Our very

beliefs were outlawed. The spirit of our people was dying. We had to find a way to preserve these things."

There was a pause and I felt the eyes upon me, burning through to my soul.

"We turned for help to Grandmother Corn, and she taught us how to survive. We studied her teachings. We practiced her ways. One tiny kernel of corn carries everything that is needed to nourish our people physically and spiritually for all time, with enough left over to provide the same for an entire world. Within that one kernel, one seed, there is food, fuel, material to build homes, ceremonies, teaching, nourishment for the spirit, wisdom—the greater part of what is needed for a people to survive. The way of the seed is the way Grandmother Corn survives, has survived for thousands, perhaps millions, of seasons. The grain of corn, the single seed, carries the heart and the spirit of the mother. When it is planted in the sweet Earth, it rests, then when the time is right, it comes forth. It grows. First the sprout, then the blade, then the cornstalk and the ears. It is the mother reborn, with her heart and spirit intact. We knew then that we must do as Grandmother Corn. We took all that was important to us and drew it deep within our spirit. It could not be seen by the outside world, just as the spirit of Grandmother Corn is not apparent in the seed. What appears to be is not always what is. We kept the seeds hidden and protected, knowing that when the time was right, they would come forth and produce fruit. We trusted the ways of the Creator, the Earth Mother, and Grandmother Corn. Our seed, our spirit, would live dormant but intact in future generations.

When conditions were right, our people's ways would live again. Nothing would be lost. It was the only way we could survive.

"The white man didn't understand the way of the seed. He didn't know how the Earth Mother can encourage the seed to bring forth the mature plant and the ears of corn. He believed that he could force us to speak his language, wear his clothes, follow his beliefs, and our ways would die. The white man would devour our people, make them part of himself, and we would be no more. We allowed him to believe that, and his own belief defeated his purpose. We wore the clothes, spoke the language, and appeared to follow his beliefs. We raised our children in his ways, not telling them of their heritage. But we had placed our spirit and all that was important to us in our seed. Children, grandchildren, and great-grandchildren carried it, unknown but safe. The white man could not take it from us. Nothing could destroy it. We looked into the swirling mists of the future, and we saw our Nation rise again from the many seeds we had planted. We saw the ceremonies and the traditions once again. We heard the stories, found the wisdom passed from generation to generation. We saw our baskets woven by other hands, our clothing covering other bodies, our songs sung by other voices. But they were us and we were them. We lived again, and all that was important to us flourished. It is the way of the corn.

"The white man is not the conqueror. He never was. He was defeated long ago, participated in his own defeat. The white man has always lived in the outside world, always cherished his material things—money, houses, status.

That is why his ways can't endure. Those things never mattered to us. We long ago learned the lesson of the corn. We carry with us what is important: Our spirit. And our spirit will never die, never be diminished. Our blood rushes through your body, our heart beats in your chest, and our thoughts fill your mind. You are our seed. You are Cherokee. Whatever else you are or may be, you are still of our people. You carry our spirit and the hope of our Nation. Honor us. Allow us to live again through you. Bring forth our traditions, our stories, and ceremonies, our knowledge and beliefs and wisdom. They will serve you well. Never forget the teaching of Grandmother Corn. And know that through the centuries, when men and women travel far from Mother Earth, when they do things that you can't even dream of now, they—your children, your grandchildren—will carry with them the seed they planted. And the seed of Grandmother Corn. They will grow corn in many places. And the Cherokee Nation will flourish, will survive to be reborn again and again in the hearts and minds, the spirits, of its children."

Standing Feather

Standing Feather's story is my story. It is all our stories. All of us came from tribal stock. We can create a world as yet unimagined, a world undreamed, yet dimly felt. We are like the corn. Mysteriously hidden within each of us are the seeds that can germinate into a new society, a new planet. Like the corn, we have hidden deep within our living process a wisdom that reaches back to all knowledge and beyond to all possibilities. Our very existence is potential. Potential is always that which is, as yet, unexpressed. We have the wisdom of the ancestors reaching back to the mighty power of all creation . . . within us.

Could it be that instead of being absorbed into the TMM culture and becoming "detached" that something quite different is happening? Could it be that, by being on this earth and eating the food and drinking the water that has been nourished by the blood and bones of the ancestors, we have their wisdom in our DNA and can call upon it when we need it? Could it be that by intermarriage the native people have not become "absorbed" but have infiltrated all our beings, that our growing mixtures of races and knowledge have created a soil where the wisdom of the ancestors is there, ready to come forth to save the planet? This is a very good possibility.

Our potential for healing and wholeness are great. We can travel the path of the spirit. Our deep processes can return us to the wisdom of our ancestors and our direct connection with the Great Mystery.

When we take the view of the eagle, perhaps we can see that we are the planet and we also understand that the knowledge that we have hidden in our DNA is exactly what is needed to move us into a new vision.

Every native person knows that each piece of the puzzle is important. If all of creation is alive and important, each place (the 'aina) and civilization contributes necessary pieces. When we know this, we realize that each culture and civilization is, indeed, like an endangered species needed to create balance and wholeness on the planet.

Living in Process takes time. It takes patience. It takes courage. It takes trust. And, it allows us to access the wisdom and the wholeness within us.

The center of the universe is everywhere.

Black Elk

Chapter 14

THE UNIVERSE
AND BEYOND

O
ne night, as I was standing quietly, looking up at the stars, I *knew* oneness. I experienced infinity. I was one with the infinite oneness.

We do not make these experiences happen. They are part of our in-
heritance as spiritual beings.

Brian Swimme in his wonderful book, *The Hidden Heart of the Cosmos,*
says, "The really surprising thing is that the news of the birthplace of the
universe was always here. I mean that for as long as there have been humans
on Earth there has always been this news of the universe's birthplace shower-
ing us day and night. This must be a central facet of human existence: to
have the truth right in front of us and yet be unable to see it or recognize it."

We have in and around us the story of the birth of the universe. Indeed, the birth of the universe is *our* birth story. According to Swimme, the
particles of light—photons—that carry the message of the birthplace of
the universe—our birthplace—surround us constantly and bathe us in the
information of our vastness.

Our DNA reaches much further back than our ancestors. We are of
the stars. We share all of creation with all of creation.

Living in Process

As we shed the cloaks of unawareness that generations of not-seeing have laid over us, as we, through our deep processes, plunge into our infinite unknown, we begin to experience the vastness beyond ourselves as ourselves. Our beings begin to convey the courage to know the void—not as emptiness—as an unknown filled with the fullness of creation.

The stars and the galaxies take us into themselves in created oneness, and we move deep within ourselves to all connectedness. There is no other. There is only oneness. And, yet, we are unique. Nothing like our individual selves has ever existed before or will again. And we are a part of the whole. We are a necessary piece of the puzzle that exists whether we recognize it or not.

As we move into the depths of our deep process and learn to live our process, we come to experience our connectedness at a cellular level. We do not think or theorize about it. We know and experience this vastness that is ourselves of the All.

At times, we may wonder if our beings can tolerate the vastness of this experience of the oneness of the All. Can our cells remember the birth of the expanding universe as our eonic birth and survive the intensity? Yes, only if we do our emerging deep processes. When we live our life as a process and slowly and confidently step into our deep processes as they become available to us, we are always ready for what comes next.

To know the birth of the universe and ourselves in it may engender fear, yet, the knowledge is already hidden deep within the cells of our being. Fear may push us to strive to keep our worlds small and controllable. Yet, each of us has the wisdom of the universe within us.

As we open ourselves to the universe within, and beyond, one of the treasures concealed there is unconditional love. Unconditional love has little to do with what we know as human love. In fact, for us to try to define or know unconditional love in terms of what we know as human love may get us off the track. Unconditional love cannot be described. It can only be experienced as we open ourselves beyond what we believed possible.

The Universe and Beyond

I do not wish to denigrate human love. It is wonderful. The ability to love is a gift and the ability to receive it is a gift. We do not create love. Nor can we make it happen. Love is an energy that is dependent upon process. Neither can we experience spirituality outside the context of process. When I am completely one with the process, I feel that I am one with the universe and connect with my participation in the All.

At one point, I experienced a very small taste of the power of unconditional love. In those moments, I was enfolded by a love so powerful I knew infinity. The experience with the Great Mystery was so intense that I feared I would explode. I questioned whether the human body could tolerate such intense loving. Yet, I did not want to leave it. <u>And</u>, I had and I survived. And I knew that this level of unconditional love was always available to me whenever I had the courage and the openness to plunge into it.

I was clear that had this experience happened to me five years or even one year earlier, I would not have been able to tolerate it. When it came, I was ready and it was magnificent!

As we learn to live our process, we develop the trust to know that we will experience what we need when we need it. We do not have to control or create it. We need only put one foot in front of the other and participate as fully as we can in what is in front of us, trusting that life will unfold as it should. If we are participating fully, that will keep us busy.

I have always been curious about the universe within and without and its oneness. I know some native shamans that wander around it at will. Sometimes, they take me with them. The real ones I know require no chemicals or techniques to get there. The universe, I believe, stands ready to welcome me. I am the reluctant one.

As for beyond the universe, I, on occasion, have known the Great Mystery beyond the universe. The part of the Great Mystery I know personally is wonderful. I welcome those into my life who share other perspectives and experiences of the Great Mystery. And I trust that as we are open to one another, we will all experience and know more.

Living in Process

I am open to my friends the animals, the trees, the plants, the water, the rocks, and the earth, air, sun, and moon to teach me what they know. My living process is helping me to be a much better student and my deep process is the door to the universe and beyond.

There are basic truths shared by the older spiritualities the world over which are augmented and confirmed by the truths hidden deep within ourselves.

In Summary

For some years now, I have been encouraging others to participate in a practice that has always been part of my life. I often stop and know and express gratitude with a discipline of being specific and clear.

I would like to suggest that each of you might want to make a short gratitude list daily . . . maybe only three items in each category.

What are you grateful for—
In yourself?
In your relationships?
In your family?
In your community?
In your society?
With the planet?
With the universe?
Beyond the universe?

Also, what are you grateful for—
From the earth?
From the air?
From the sun?
From the water?
From your ancestors?

Perhaps this will give you a new perspective. It has me.

I have attempted to share with you a spiritual, healing path that I have been walking with others as it has evolved over the last forty years. It is not a quick fix, or a path of adjustment. I, and others, have experienced it as a way of profound healing, inner peace, and participation in the oneness that is our birthright.

If you resonate with what you have read, I invite you to participate. If not, I wish you well on the paths you have chosen and thank you for exploring this book and these realities.

APPENDIX

I want to add a word about the training groups referred to throughout the book. Groups of people throughout the world are learning to live their process, meeting a minimum of three weeks a year and usually once a month as peer groups. The majority of this work is done right in their communities. These groups come together to learn more about Living in Process while lending support to one another. We have ongoing training groups in the United States, Europe, New Zealand, and Australia. We have been invited to set up groups in two African nations, Ireland, England, and China.

The following is a newsletter I wrote in 1996 about the training.

Today, I was aware that this, basically, is an ordinary day. What a gift an ordinary day is. When we haven't been having them, we sometimes forget and we forget to celebrate them. I celebrate the ordinariness of today.

This, in part, is what the training is about—ordinariness. The ordinariness of living our lives—whatever that may be. We celebrate the ordinariness of freedom, all kinds of freedom. The freedom to be ourselves. The freedom to live our process. The freedom to be one with all creation. The freedom to take responsibility for our lives, our decisions, and our behaviors. This freedom also means shedding the victim role, while avoiding the perpetrator role as well. Freedom also means reclaiming our personal power as we take responsibility for ourselves. The training teaches us a lot about freedom and reclaiming it.

The training is also about healing. We participate in our own healing and, as we do that, contribute to the waves of healing on the planet. Our healing reverberates out into the world. Our healing affects others—just as our dysfunction affects others—often those we love the most. There is no way that we can hold on to our healing tightly just for ourselves.

This work is about spirituality, not religion or cults. This work is about seeking and finding our own spirituality—and as we do so, coming to respect others' spirituality.

This work is about paradigm shift—moving into new-old ways of being. Deep inside of us we understand that the process of living has been buried under overlays of virtual reality. We need to cut through those overlays to find reality. Sometimes this process almost feels like pulling off masks that have been fixed to us with superglue.

This work is about community. We have the opportunity to learn about and participate in intimacy with ourselves, with others, with communities, with societies, and with the planet. We have to start with ourselves, and we need not stay only with ourselves.

Probably, most of all, this work is about the by-product of all the above—love and loving. If we focus upon love or loving and try to do it or be it, we will fail. If we do our work and support others doing it, love is a guaranteed by-product. Love is always, I believe, a by-product. We can't force it. We can't make it happen. <u>And</u>, it will always be there if we do our work and get out of the way.

The training is also about participation—participation in the moment. Spirituality is nothing but participation, being fully present to the moment and participating in it. The moment is, after all, all we have. We have learned to take ourselves outside the moment and watch it or analyze it. We have learned to leave the moment and go to the past or to the future. Staying and participating is a great puzzle to many of us at first, and the training is about both.

The training is about honesty. It is about being honest to ourselves, others, and our Higher Power. We have un-learned honesty and we need to relearn it. The training is a good place to do this. In my experience, one does not just "become honest" or "return to honesty" overnight. We have layers of dishonesty and it takes time for us to become aware of them. The training offers a safe atmosphere for these explorations.

So, that's what the training is all about—all of the above—and lots more.

I rejoice with those with whom I can walk this path.

For more information about Living in Process seminars, workshops, and trainings, please contact:

Wilson Schaef Associates
P.O. Box 1068
Boulder, MT 59632-1068
406-225-9180 fax
E-mail: bobbiwsa@gte.net

ANNE WILSON SCHAEF, PH.D., has gained an international reputation for her work in feminist theory, psychology, and recovery. In the early eighties, she gave up her work as a traditional psychotherapist and began journeying around the world to meet with indigenous spiritual leaders who have shared their wisdom with her and recognized and honored her as a spiritual teacher and healer. Today she devotes her time to leading Living in Process extended residential trainings and writing. The center for Living in Process is in Boulder, Montana.